Palgrave Studies in Alternative Education

Series Editors
Helen Lees
Independent Researcher
London, UK

Michael Reiss
UCL Institute of Education
London, UK

This series emerges out of a recent global rise of interest in and actual educational practices done with voice, choice, freedoms and interpersonal thoughtfulness. From subversion to introversion, including alternative settings of the state to alternative pathways of the private, the series embraces a diverse range of voices.

Common to books in the series is a vision of education already in existence and knowledge of education possible here and now. Theoretical ideas with potential to be enacted or influential in lived practice are also a part of what we offer with the books.

This series repositions what we deem as valuable educationally by accepting the power of many different forces such as silence, love, joy, despair, confusion, curiosity, failure, attachments as all potentially viable, interesting, useful elements in educational stories. Nothing is rejected if it has history or record as being of worth to people educationally, nor does this series doubt or distrust compelling ideas of difference as relevant.

We wish to allow mainstream and marginal practices to meet here without prejudice as Other but also with a view to ensuring platforms for the Other to find community and understanding with others.

The following are the primary aims of the series:

- To publish new work on education with a distinctive voice.
- To enable alternative education to find a mainstream profile.
- To publish research that draws with interdisciplinary expertise on pertinent materials for interpersonal change or adjustments of approach towards greater voice.
- To show education as without borders or boundaries placed on what is possible to think and do.

If you would like to submit a proposal or discuss a project in more detail please contact: Rebecca Wyde rebecca.wyde@palgrave.com. The series will include both monographs and edited collections and Palgrave Pivot formats.

More information about this series at
https://link.springer.com/bookseries/15489

Roger Cutting • Rowena Passy
Editors

Contemporary Approaches to Outdoor Learning

Animals, the Environment and New Methods

palgrave
macmillan

Editors
Roger Cutting
Institute of Education
University of Plymouth
Plymouth, UK

Rowena Passy
Institute of Education
University of Plymouth
Plymouth, UK

Palgrave Studies in Alternative Education
ISBN 978-3-030-85094-4   ISBN 978-3-030-85095-1   (eBook)
https://doi.org/10.1007/978-3-030-85095-1

This Palgrave Macmillan imprint is published by the registered company Springer Nature Switzerland AG.
The registered company address is: Gewerbestrasse 11, 6330 Cham, Switzerland

This volume is dedicated to Dr Melanie Parker, our friend and colleague who was a great champion for alternative education. She was taken too early, before her work was done.

Acknowledgement

We thank all who have been involved in the writing and production of this book, particularly given the difficult circumstances that we all continue to face during this global pandemic.

CONTENTS

Part I   The Contribution to Outdoor Learning from
         Non-human Animals   1

Introduction   3
Rowena Passy and Roger Cutting

**Paws for Thought: Reflections on the First Four Years of
Lakeside Care Farm**   7
Dean Sherwin

**Fear, Fiction and Facts: Animals in Outdoor Learning
Environments**   23
Fiona Cooke

**Learning About the World to Save the World: How Learning
from Animals May Provide a Means of Promoting
Environmental Awareness**   39
Roger Cutting

**Animals as Catalysts for Learning, Personal Growth and
Enlightenment**   55
Ben Hart

'All They Need to Know Is Tigers Are Awesome': The Place of Animal Pedagogies in Twenty-First-Century Schools   69
Rowena Passy, Katherine Gulliver, and Beth Gompertz

'When you have this intimacy with it, you do want to protect its environment.' The Role of Emotions on a Zoo Visit in Engaging Visitors in Wildlife Conservation   83
Susan Warren

Part II   New Frontiers: Contemporary Research into Outdoor Learning   99

'A Sea of Men': Supporting Men as Fathers Through Outdoor Learning Experiences   101
Ian Blackwell

The Scenic Route to Academic Attainment via Emotional Wellbeing Outdoors   117
Mel McCree

The Freedom to Have Fun, Play, Make Friends, and Be a Child: Findings from an Ethnographic Research Study of Learning Outside in Alternative Provision   131
Kelly Davis

All Aboard for Ocean Literacy: Marine Outdoor Environmental Learning in the South West of England   147
Alun Morgan and John Hepburn

Uncomfortable Learning and Ethical Tensions: Animal Butchery and Environmental Education   169
Lewis Winks

Outdoor Learning and Student Teacher Identity   187
Orla Kelly

Ecological Identity Work   201
Rosamonde Birch

**Gone Rogue: Re-wilding Education in Alternative
Outdoor Learning Environments**   215
Tonia Gray and Peter Bailey

**Philosophy Walks: Thinking on Our Feet, from Outdoor
Learning to a Philosophy of Education**   235
Graeme Tiffany

Conclusion: Love in a Time of Pandemics   251
Roger Cutting and Rowena Passy

Index   257

Notes on Contributors

Peter Bailey is an Independent Scholar and Retired Secondary School Principal, Ambassador for Public School Education NSW, Casual Outdoor Education Lecturer, University of Sydney, NSW Australia. After a long career in Education, Peter noticed the change from experience learning and relationship development between teacher and student to a risk-averse, norm-testing culture.

Rosamonde Birch has a background in Secondary Citizenship and Learning for Sustainability Education, with experience of lecturing at the University of Plymouth where she recently completed her MA researching hope, futures thinking and philosophical inquiry with young people. Rosamonde is now starting her PhD at the University of Dundee focusing on the philosophy of becoming and learning for future survival.

Ian Blackwell has worked in the learning outside the classroom sector for 25 years and was Project Manager for the Natural Connections Demonstration Project at Plymouth University. Ian is Forest School Programme Manager at Duchy College, Cornwall, and a Visiting Lecturer at Plymouth Marjon University (UK) where he teaches on outdoor learning and ESD modules. He is also the founder of Dangerous Dads CIC, a social enterprise that supports father figures and their children.

Fiona Cooke has worked with animal welfare organisations for over 20 years and regularly lectures in Higher Education settings. Fiona currently leads the European research team at The Donkey Sanctuary.

Roger Cutting was an Associate Professor in Education at the University of Plymouth. He has over 40 publications in peer-reviewed journals focusing on Education for Sustainability. He latterly became the Education Lead for the international charity The Donkey Sanctuary. He has subsequently retired but retains a Visiting Research Fellow role at the University of Plymouth

Kelly Davis is a lecturer of Science Education and Programme Lead for PGCE Early Years and PGCE Primary Teaching at the University of Plymouth. Her recent PhD research focused on learning outside with children excluded from mainstream schooling, attending alternative education centres.

Beth Gompertz has recently retired as Director of the Plymouth Institute of Education and has a background as a Primary School Teacher, Primary Science CPD coordinator and in lecturing and programme leading in PGCE and Undergraduate Initial Teacher Education in two universities. Her research has always had a participatory flavour and has focused on children and young people as researchers into their own education.

Tonia Gray is a Senior Researcher in the Centre for Educational Research, Western Sydney University, Australia. For many decades, her scholarship and practice have continued to build knowledge about human-nature connection in educational settings, health and wellbeing, leadership and gender equity, and curriculum development.

Katherine Gulliver is currently a lecturer and PhD student at Plymouth Institute of Education, University of Plymouth. Her PhD focuses on participatory research methods with young children, special educational needs and/disabilities and inclusion. Katherine has worked on a wide range of education and community research projects including animal welfare and conservation, sustainability, and voluntary woodland management.

Ben Hart has worked globally as an equine trainer, enhancing the communication between animals and humans. He is a much in demand conference speaker and has written a number of books on equine behaviour and training.

John Hepburn has played number of roles since leaving the Royal Navy in 2003, including Ocean Discoverability Project Manager, Secretary of Maritime Plymouth and a Sea Champion for the Marine Conservation Society.

Orla Kelly has a background in science and science education and the majority of her work at Dublin City University is in primary initial teacher education. Orla's current goal is to reconnect children with nature in their local places as a starting point for environmental stewardship.

Mel McCree is a Senior Lecturer in Education at Bath Spa University. She is a renowned academic scholar of forest school and outdoor play, with a focus on eco-social justice.

Alun Morgan has been involved in education for over 30 years as a teacher, Teacher Advisor, Teacher Educator, Lecturer, and Researcher focusing on Environmental and Sustainability Education, Outdoor Learning and Ocean Literacy.

Rowena Passy is a Senior Research Fellow in the Plymouth Institute of Education, University of Plymouth. She has a career-long interest and experience in different types of outdoor learning, and was Evaluation Manager of the Natural Connections Demonstration Project 2012–2016, the largest outdoor learning project in the UK at that time.

Dean Sherwin now works for Wiltshire Wildlife Trust in a variety of Learning in the Natural Environment (LiNE) roles with children, young people and adults with individual needs, and took over the management of Lakeside Care Farm in July 2017.

Graeme Tiffany Tiffany's career spans outdoor education and youth and community work, particularly in the street. He now works on an independent basis, as a trainer, lecturer and researcher. Graeme is a pioneer of Community Philosophy, of which Philosophy Walks are a part.

Susan Warren has 30 years' experience of working for local and national organisations in the fields of nature conservation, sustainability, and community engagement. She has a passion for connecting people with nature and for reframing and reimaging our relationships with non-human others. Her recent doctoral research has exposed the potential of fostering a relational engagement between people and animals in nurturing environmentally aware and active citizens.

Lewis Winks is a UK based outdoor and environmental educator and a researcher specializing in nature connection and transformative learning. He is a director at On The Hill, a land-based learning organisation which provides experiential residentials for all ages.

LIST OF FIGURES

'When you have this intimacy with it, you do want to protect its environment.' The Role of Emotions on a Zoo Visit in Engaging Visitors in Wildlife Conservation

Fig. 1   Emotional responses to animals at the zoo and the key factors
         influencing these   88

All Aboard for Ocean Literacy: Marine Outdoor Environmental Learning in the South West of England

Fig. 1   Using the 'Cornubia Guide to Plymouth Sound and Estuaries'   153
Fig. 2   On board rope work—hoisting the sails   154
Fig. 3   Settlement Plate populated with samples from pontoon   155
Fig. 4   The 'Do-it-Yourself' baited recoverable underwater video array,
         designed and assembled by John   156
Fig. 5   Crab attracted to BRUV—in situ natural behaviour on sea floor
         streamed to on board TV screen   157
Fig. 6   John using microscope technology to share samples in
         Cornubia's saloon   158
Fig. 7   On board activity sheet   159
Fig. 8   Collaborative plankton sampling on board Pegasus   159
Figs. 9
and 10   Evaluation survey sheet, pages 1 and 2   161

.

List of Tables

**All Aboard for Ocean Literacy: Marine Outdoor
Environmental Learning in the South West of England**

Table 1   Outcomes—Averages of levels of knowledge and satisfaction   163

Table 2   Children's narrative responses   163

Table 3   Adult (staff or carer) narrative responses   164

PART I

The Contribution to Outdoor Learning from Non-human Animals

Introduction

Rowena Passy and Roger Cutting

At the time of writing, in which the UK has vaccinated over half of its population just as the pandemic is wreaking a terrible trail of fear and destruction through India, it is important to reflect on the searing inequalities that Covid-19 has brought to our attention. Inequities between rich and poor countries, between rich and poor citizens within these countries, and between vaccinated and non-vaccinated have encouraged us—or at least those of us who are willing—to have a long, hard look at the ways in which humans abuse both each other and the more-than-human world, and to think of ways in which we can contribute to a kinder, more equitable, more sustainable way of life.

One insidious inequity that is at the core of this book is the overemphasis in Western nations on cognitive development that goes hand-in-glove with over-reliance on high-stakes testing. An education system that involves competition for places based on simplistic metrics of evaluation almost inevitably leads to a perceived sense of failure and isolation. For some, formal education systems offer little by the way of aspiration and at worst promote a sense of exclusion from learning; alternative strategies

R. Passy (✉) • R. Cutting
Institute of Education, University of Plymouth, Plymouth, UK
e-mail: r.passy@plymouth.ac.uk; roger.cutting@plymouth.ac.uk

© The Author(s), under exclusive license to Springer Nature Switzerland AG 2022
R. Cutting, R. Passy (eds.), *Contemporary Approaches to Outdoor Learning*, Palgrave Studies in Alternative Education,
https://doi.org/10.1007/978-3-030-85095-1_1

involve breaking down both the institutional and structural confines of formal education. Much work has already been done in the area of outdoor and experiential learning to provide such alternatives, with the result that taking children outdoors during school time is becoming an accepted practice rather than something regarded as risky or time-wasting. This is a cause for celebration; children in many different nations have a greater number of opportunities to engage with the natural world, to enjoy different ways of learning and to become familiar with the sensory experiences of being outside (e.g. Humberstone et al., 2016; Passy et al., 2019). The danger is that outdoor learning becomes a repetitive, going-through-the-motions exercise that lacks the wonder, awe and broader understanding that can be provoked by engaging with natural phenomena.

This volume aims to provide the reader with new approaches to alternative provision outside. The different chapters look at specific case-study examples drawn from across the UK and Australia in which the outdoors is primarily seen as the context rather than the subject of learning. Here the learning aims to be effective in areas such as behaviour change, social and emotional development, and confidence-building; too often it seems to be repairing damage inculcated by the formal education sector. Some chapters are written directly from the practitioner's perspective and are pathfinder pieces for those other educationalists who may wish to follow their lead. Some are rigorous research-based pieces of work that have critically evaluated the comparative successes and failures relating to the aims of such alternative approaches. Others are chapters that are expositions around the theoretical contexts of alternative pedagogies outside formal education. They were largely completed in late 2020, when none of us knew how the pandemic would develop; whether it would require short-term or a long-term adjustments to everyday living, or whether it would make fundamental changes to the ways in which different societies are organised. This means that few authors have addressed the issue of Covid-19 directly; the aim here has been to avoid the prospect of the chapters becoming time-limited simply by invoking the pandemic while we continue to be uncertain of its emerging nature and consequences.

The book is divided into two parts. The first consists of six chapters that focus on the ways in which we can learn from animals, either by being with them and/or learning about them in different environments. Dean Sherwin's chapter on the role of care farms as alternative provision and Susan Warren's on visiting Paignton Zoo demonstrate how learning with animals can provide opportunities for reflection on self and others.

Chapters from Fiona Cooke, Ben Hart and Rowena Passy, Katherine Gulliver and Beth Gompertz—on the impact of early learning about animals, animals as catalysts for personal growth and the potential of animal pedagogies respectively—offer more theoretical approaches based on empirical research and/or personal experience. Roger Cutting's chapter explores animal-based literature for all ages, arguing that this often provokes feelings of compassion that can, in turn, be linked to wider environmental concerns.

The second part comprises nine chapters that offer cutting edge views and research into outdoor learning. Ian Blackwell's exploration of the role of dads' groups in encouraging caring father-child relationships, Lewis Winks' discussion of the pedagogy of discomfort via butchery, and Tonia Gray and Peter Bailey's advocacy of 're-wilding education' in Australia demonstrate potentially transformative alternative approaches to learning. Orla Kelly and Rosamonde Birch discuss alternative outdoor learning approaches with university students; Mel McCree and Kelly Davis focus on disadvantaged and excluded children to show the contribution that learning outdoors can make to building relationships. Alun Morgan and John Hepburn write about teaching ocean literacy to children with disabilities, and Graeme Tiffany discusses how his 'Philosophy Walks' offer a radical approach to the development of democratic communities. Together they show the authors' commitment to exploring alternative approaches to outdoor learning that make a difference.

References

Humberstone, B., Prince, H., & Henderson, K. (2016). *Routledge international handbook of outdoor studies.* Routledge.

Passy, R., Bentsen, P., Gray, T., & Ho, S. (2019). Integrating outdoor learning into the curriculum: An exploration in four nations. *Curriculum Perspectives, 39,* 73–78.

Paws for Thought: Reflections on the First Four Years of Lakeside Care Farm

Dean Sherwin

'Peaceful' is the word most used by students, teachers and carers in describing the atmosphere at Wiltshire Wildlife Trust's Lakeside Care Farm. Often, the only sounds we can hear are the rustle of the trees, the calling of mallard and the occasional splash of a surfacing trout. Nestled next to Mallard Lake, a Site of Special Scientific Interest (SSSI), on Lower Moor nature reserve, Lakeside has become recognised as a thriving and effective setting that offers children, young people and adults with individual needs the opportunity for therapeutic and meaningful nature-based learning and work-based experiences in animal care, horticulture, nature conservation, farming and Forest School activities. Social Farms & Gardens, a UK wide charity supporting communities to farm, garden and grow together, of which we are an approved member and whose Code of Practice we follow, defines care farming as 'the therapeutic use of farming practices'.

D. Sherwin (✉)
Wiltshire Wildlife Trust, Devizes, UK
e-mail: DeanS@wiltshirewildlife.org

Lakeside Care Farm opened in November 2016 in direct response to the need for nature-based individualised learning for children, young people and adults with additional needs that had been identified within Wiltshire, Swindon and South Gloucestershire. This chapter outlines why a Wildlife Trust has set up a Care Farm, as well as a discussion of its ethos of providing a calm, productive and emotionally and physically safe setting that meets individual needs. The main focus, however, will be our modus operandi and reflections on the time we have been open, both of which will hopefully be of benefit to those considering starting similar initiatives.

RATIONALE

Wiltshire Wildlife Trust (WWT) is one of forty-six individual Wildlife Trusts, each of which is an independent charity. All share a common vision of people being close to nature, with land and surrounding seas being rich in wildlife. Each Wildlife Trust is a member of the Royal Society of Wildlife Trusts, a registered charity in its own right and whose role is to ensure a strong voice for wildlife at the national level and to lead the development of the vision.

A strategic aim of WWT is to help people connect with nature and live more sustainably by:

- Enabling people to engage with nature to improve their health and wellbeing
- Encouraging, supporting and providing outdoor learning
- Supporting people wishing to reduce their ecological and carbon footprints.

To this end, WWT has been working in education in its broadest sense since its beginnings in 1962. Most recently, and following a successful adult wellbeing programme based on the therapeutic effects of work on nature reserves, in April 2012 a specific 'Youth Wellbeing' programme started, funded by NHS Wiltshire Public Health, and supplemented by directly charging secondary schools to engage their students in conservation work on WWT's reserves as part of Alternative Provision programmes. The success of this led to a positive bid to the Blagrave Trust for a three year (2013–2016) funded longitudinal study led by Plymouth University of one group of primary school pupils undertaking Forest School activities in a local WWT wood (McCree et al., 2018).

In 2012, Lakeside House, a private property in the middle of Lower Moor nature reserve, was put up for sale. A case for acquiring Lakeside House was prepared by Gary Mantle (WWT's Chief Executive Officer [CEO]) in order to gain the support of WWT's Trustees and to approach The Underwood Trust as a potential funder. The purchase included a house, garden and adjacent approximately 3-acre field of low wildlife value. In an act of great generosity and faith, The Underwood Trust agreed to fund the acquisition.

As part of the review of options emerged a proposal to establish a Care Farm at Lakeside.

A feasibility study quickly identified the need for such a provision and showed how it would be entirely consistent with the Trust's aims and objectives. A business plan was approved in February 2016 by WWT's Trustee Full Council. The Care Farm buildings were completed in October 2016, with the first students starting in November 2016. I was appointed in July 2017 and came with experience of successfully developing, leading and delivering WWT's youth engagement project, youth wellbeing pro-gramme, longitudinal study and Alternative Provision programme.

Central to the establishment of the Lakeside Care Farm has been the WWT's CEO's firm belief in the value of using nature to improve mental health and wellbeing and the important role of Wildlife Trusts.

ETHOS AND UNDERPINNING VALUES

Our underlying ethos is one of providing a setting in which our students feel emotionally and physically safe. This feeling of safety is paramount in ensuring student anxieties are reduced, as anxiety is at the root of many of the challenges our students face. This anxiety reduction may take a matter of minutes or can take several months, depending on the background and prior experiences and challenges that individual students have faced. Alongside our aim of reducing anxieties, it is vital that students feel valued and feel worthwhile as individuals. We provide a 'stabilising' setting for children and young people who may have had, for whatever reason, tumul-tuous lives. Once anxieties have stabilised we are able to appropriately challenge students to try new things, try different ways, learn to cope with challenges and to see that to 'fail' is actually to 'not yet succeed' or to 'suc-ceed in a way that wasn't originally intended'.

Our students all struggle in traditional school settings, and attending Lakeside is a way for them to see that they can be successful. Whilst schools focus on literacy, numeracy and 'knowing', we focus on 'operacy' (de Bono, 1992). Operacy is the ability to do things; it is the skill of 'doing'. Students learn how to problem-solve, methodically plan and complete tasks, and express their creativity, all of which allow them to succeed and will help in the transition to independent living and adulthood. Lakeside is a wholly experiential setting and our students learn about themselves, others and the world by experiencing their own reactions, those of others and the natural world in which they are working. We very much focus on 'process not outcome', which sits neatly alongside learning by doing. Sometimes there are no set outcomes to what we are doing, and if there are and we don't meet them, then that is an ideal opportunity to discuss coping strategies and to build the capacity to learn by making mistakes.

In a school setting, learning is often reactive, in that students respond to work that is put in front of them. There is nothing inherently wrong with this and it is an important skill to master, but for students who experience low self-esteem, and who do not want to be seen 'failing', this can often lead to barriers being raised and anxieties increasing. At Lakeside we encourage a proactive way of learning which is implemented in conjunction with building operacy skills. By students discovering their own problems, achievable challenges and barriers in activities such as wanting to build a plank bridge across the pond to Newt Island, essential life skills and independent living skills are being honed on an individual basis.

As a former Geography teacher, I am well aware that prescriptive curricula mean that as soon as one topic area has been completed, the next one is begun in order that the full curriculum can be covered. There is little time for 'control and mastery', the repeated covering and practising of an area of learning. If a student at Lakeside wishes to undertake the same activity week in week out, then that is fine. We are there to make them feel at ease, to reduce anxieties and to build self-esteem. At some point, we will challenge them appropriately and stretch their comfort bubble.

Wind extinguishes a candle and energizes fire.

This quote from *Antifragile* (Taleb, 2012) highlights and, in a way, verifies aspects of the Care Farm ethos and approach. Since opening, we have been aiming to increase our students' antifragility. Antifragility is a step beyond resilience, the latter being able to withstand a stressor, the former being that students are able to develop and grow as a consequence of an external stressor. We want to develop 'fires' not 'candles'. It is also apparent that we build in Taleb's (ibid.) 'optionality' at Lakeside, namely having many choices and options from which to work throughout the day. It is part of our daily process to have several options ready in the pipeline should Plans A, B, C... not be working. It makes us antifragile. Finally, we appear to be naturally following Taleb's (ibid.) 'via negativa' concept, by which we have subtractive intervention, i.e. stripping away unnecessary levels of engagement and sensory stimulation, at least initially, and going 'back to basics'. We are letting children be children. We try not to 'jump in' when they are anxious, but step back to give them emotional and physical space to resolve their anxieties themselves. The ability to self-soothe is a vital life skill. Once students are less anxious and heightened, and thus feel physically and emotionally safe or safer, we can then work with them on solution-focused intervention strategies.

We are often asked how we manage students whose behaviour in class can lead to fixed term and permanent exclusions. In all honesty, we very rarely see such behaviours exhibited at Lakeside. The physical and emotional spaces within nature in themselves reduce anxieties, around which many of the challenging behaviours are focused. As all behaviour is communication we focus on helping students to reflect on their emotions and feelings, and facilitate them arriving at their own strategies in reducing heightened behaviours. Due to the physical space afforded by Lakeside we are able to, as one Educational Psychologist put it, 'ride the storm' of heightened behaviours. With our low student numbers (a maximum of eleven at a time each with a one-to-one support worker), we are able to manage the students and setting so that a heightened student is able to find space to self-calm. If that involves spinning round and round, throwing stones into a pond or smashing a stick against a tree then that is fine. Over time we work with the student to recognise when they are starting to feel heightened and most of our students are now able to remove themselves from difficult social situations and go to their 'safe space' to calm, normally the field, a den, the animal shed or Newt Island. We do have boundaries, be they physical or behavioural, but students know that if they do not put themselves or others at risk, or damage property, then we will give them space. This can take time to be processed by the student, but by us very strongly sticking to these boundaries students know they will be safe.

OUR STUDENTS

Our students are varied in age and specific needs. Each is an individual and is treated as such. Our age range has been 4–63, but has narrowed recently to 5–19 as funding for adult Special Educational Needs and Disability (SEND) groups has become more difficult to secure. As previously stated it is fair to say that all of our students struggle in a traditional school and classroom setting, for whatever reason. Many have diagnoses based around mental health or are diagnosed with Autistic Spectrum Condition (ASC), Attention Deficit Hyperactivity Disorder (ADHD), Oppositional Defiant Disorder (ODD), Pathological Demand Avoidance (PDA), and Sensory Processing Disorder (SPD), whilst others have experienced childhood trauma. Many of our students fall under the category of additional needs referred to as Social, Emotional and Mental Health (SEMH) and thus have anxieties and challenges of varying origins that affect their everyday lives, particularly in a busy school setting where their anxieties surface. Whatever the reason they are with us we look beyond the student we read about on their paperwork to look at the individual in front of us.

On a weekly basis, our students are with us from anything ranging from a half day, so they can have respite from the stresses of mainstream school, through to students for whom schools currently cannot meet their needs, and are thus with us up to three days per week; we are the only provision they may attend. From the point of accessing Lakeside, most students stay with us until a mainstream or special school placement is found or until they are able to return to their mainstream or special school full time, if appropriate. Many of our students are on 'packages', whereby they are not in mainstream school classes, yet do not meet special school thresholds, so they attend several Alternative Provision settings each week. There is a trend that once a referrer has referred to us, they either wish to increase the number of sessions a student attends or they refer further students. Our students work with a one-to-one support worker from the Care Farm, who is their designated key worker, and who builds a trusting relationship with the students; relationships are key.

Specific outcomes required by referrers are as varied as the young people's needs, with the common themes being to decrease anxiety, to be able to feel successful, to increase the students' ability for appropriate social communication, for peer interactions to become positive, and to increase emotional literacy. As a number of our students have received several fixed-term exclusions, permanent exclusions or have been put in 'isolation' in school, they have often lacked the usual playground interactions where the ability for peer negotiation and the rough and tumble of play are honed. This often leads to them struggling when interacting with others. The low-density approach we have, with each student having a one-to-one support worker, allows for supported peer interactions until the time comes when we can step back.

Whilst managing peer interactions is a focus for many of our primary aged students, it is increasing antifragility and raising confidence that is the main focus for our secondary students. For primary students we embed literacy, numeracy and science in to what we are doing. For our secondary students we are an accredited provider for AQA Unit awards, accreditations in hands-on practical subjects like animal care, woodwork and horticulture.

With a diverse staff background, we are keen to match staff and student personalities, proclivities and interests. This helps a student to settle. Once settled, if appropriate, we take a more flexible approach and match students with staff who may challenge the student to expand their interests, with the caveat that if this causes anxiety we return to the original staffing. Staff swap in and out with students on a daily basis depending on activities that are occurring. This gives the Care Farm flexibility so that all students know all staff and can work with them if, for example, their regular staff member is off ill. We are thus building antifragility in to the Care Farm.

Our Partners

Our referrals come from four main sources, (1) local authority SEND Teams, namely Swindon Borough Council and South Gloucestershire Council, but mainly Wiltshire Council, for whom WWT is an approved provider, (2) direct referrals from schools, (3) home schooling and (4) The Independent Psychology Service (TIPS). We are also starting to receive queries from mental health services. Local Authority Educational Psychologists, Speech and Language Therapists, the Communication and Interaction Specialist SEN Service, and members of the Avon & Wiltshire Mental Health Partnership NHS Trust Psychosis Early Intervention Team have all met with their student clients at the Care Farm as it is the setting in which they feel most relaxed. Trainee Educational Psychologists from the University of Bristol are also visiting as part of their placement with the Local Authority. Our positive, open and transparent relationship with Wiltshire Council, particularly its SEND Team, has been key to the development of the Care Farm, and we have liaised with them from early on in the Care Farm's concept. The importance of this latter relationship cannot be emphasised enough.

Day to Day Activities

The day to day operation of Lakeside has a focus on the therapeutic use of animals and horticulture, as well as Forest School activities and meaningful education and work-based experiences in horticulture, nature conservation, woodworking, and site maintenance and development. Wrapped around these are more traditional methods of environmental learning, such a floral and faunal identification, nature walks and bird watching and activities such as camp fire cooking and whittling. Play is particularly important to our primary children, and this provides excellent opportunities to develop collaborative social skills.

The principles of Loose Parts Theory (Nicholson, 1971) are important at Lakeside. Students being able to pick up, move, sort, re-order and recombine natural, tactile materials and objects aids creativity and is a great vehicle for social play, something our students have often missed. Loose parts enable immersive, imaginative learning. This, and building purposefully in natural non-smooth surfaces, such as grass, gravel of varying grades, mud and woodchip that stimulate the senses, help in that reconnectivity to the natural world. Such sensory feedback is essential for our hyposensitive students.

Animal Therapy

Our rescue animals play a significant part in the daily routines for a number of our students. We have five rabbits, six guineas pigs, eleven hens, three goats and two Kune Kune pigs, approximately 60,000 honey bees and my female black Labrador dog, Tilly.

The benefits of animals as a source of therapy are manifold. Students learn about relationships through the animals whilst watching their interaction. Animals are perceived to offer safer, more reliable companionship than unpredictable humans because they will not answer back or judge the individual. Our rescue animals have proved beneficial in that we can talk to students about how the animals were once in settings where they were not being looked after empathetically or where they were being harmed, but now they are in a good place and are happy, and that can happen to humans too.

Due to their diagnosis or home life, many of our students struggle to see things from others' perspectives. By learning to handle the animals gently and appropriately, and giving them space when they need it, students can begin to look at life from another's point of view and can start to develop empathy. They are also encouraged by staff to see the animals as individuals rather than a species or breed, to notice and respect their individual differences in character and appearance. This opens up conversations about bullying, being kind to those who are different and how all animals are individuals with their own equally important needs, be they wild, domestic or human.

Some of our students struggle to communicate verbally. On a second trial visit, a non-verbal pre-school age student said the word 'dog' when he saw Tilly and listened to verbal instructions to not touch her eyes and to focus on her belly. Some of our students struggle to make eye contact or communicate successfully with their peers and adults. Despite this, the guinea pigs can bring them out in a flowing conversation, possibly due to the fact they are constantly communicating themselves via squeaks which encourages students to join in an imaginary conversation. Many students also take much pride in sharing their knowledge of the animals. This gives them opportunities to succeed at communication that they may not receive elsewhere. Furthermore, time spent observing the animals will lead individuals to understand the different expressions and body language being presented by the animals, and therefore what they may need at that moment to keep them happy and healthy. This observational skill can be transferred to humans and increase emotional and empathetic awareness.

Having quiet time brushing the pigs, walking the goats, stroking the dog and handling a rabbit or guinea pig allows children and young people to be more 'in the moment'. If there is something on their mind they are struggling to process this may come out in conversation with the animal and staff are on hand to discuss it further if needed. It is not a staff member's place to offer hugs and physical comfort to students but with the animals they are free to seek the comfort that they need at that time.

Our honey bees have proved particularly therapeutic for one of our students and many hours are spent tending the hive and watching bees enter and exit. The complexity of bee society is another area of learning that students can apply to the human condition. Patience and fortitude can also be fostered with native wildlife, with students having spent many cumulative hours sitting, lying and crouching completely still and silently, coaxing a robin to eat worms out of their hands, for example.

Due to our location on a nature reserve, the native flora and fauna cause much fascination and many are keen to learn about the names of, in particular, the abundant invertebrate life at Lakeside, as well as spending many a minute watching basking grass snakes, foraging woodpeckers, diving great crested newts and a busy weasel. With foxes, otters, deer and badgers on the reserve, animal tracking via footprints and faeces has proved insightful in to the ability of some students to have an incredible eye for detail and subtle changes in the environment. Discussions around native and naturalised species and conservation, as well as directly being engaged on tasks on the reserve, aid in a sense of stewardship of the whole nature reserve, not just Lakeside.

REFLECTIONS

The first pancake is always a blob. (Russian proverb)

Due to the perceived success of Lakeside and the fact we have a waiting list, it became apparent that there was the need for another Care Farm towards the centre of the county. WWT has been fortunate to have been left a legacy of an organic farm and associated paddock, the stable block on which was ideal for the creation of a second Care Farm. We have also been asked by the Local Authority if we will be opening a Care Farm in the south of the county. As part of the strategic thinking behind this, we have been reflecting on lessons learnt from the first four years at Lakeside. Whilst Lakeside most certainly hasn't been a 'blob' there are ways in which we have learnt, to ensure that a new WWT Care Farm is as rounded a pancake as possible from the outset.

As with the majority of decisions at the Care Farm, all staff were involved in the process. The main areas of learning identified are:

STAFF

Having the 'right' staff who thoroughly buy in to the Care Farm ethos and values is critical to its daily operation. What 'right' means is hard to quantify, but non-judgemental staff are essential, as are those who can see when others need help, and gladly offer it. Staff swap regularly mid-session if required. Staff are observant and focused and closely monitor student interactions and act upon them. The mixed demography and backgrounds, perspectives, temperaments, knowledge, experience, skills, and education are vital for cognitive diversity and collective intelligence (Syed, 2019). A horticultural expert in the staff team is essential, as are Forest School trained staff and those with animal care knowledge. Staff training is essential and increases staff confidence, e.g. all staff are provided with training in positive behaviour management, outdoor remote first aid, food hygiene and autism awareness as a minimum.

Our students are keen to learn, if not necessarily keen to be taught, and Care Farm staff are adept at finding and working with the particular 'hook' that will catch the attention and interest of the students with whom they work. Examples of student interests have included Minecraft, Monopoly, aeroplane identification, reputedly the world's hottest chilli (*Carolina Reaper*), Harry Potter, Dungeons and Dragons, dinosaurs, The Simpsons, unicorns and Star Wars. Conversations and activities based around these interests have resulted in a deeper level of engagement than would otherwise have happened.

A 'floating' member of staff, i.e. one that is not allocated to a student, is essential as it acts as a 'safety valve' in the system and allows staff to attend to an incident or accident, and allows staff to take a 'breather' if required. This is particularly needed for those staff who work full time—working at Lakeside six hours a day with a one-to-one student is physically and emotionally draining. To this end, WWT provides, free of charge to staff, sessions with a counsellor should they need to talk to somebody independent about experiences at the Care Farm, or indeed home. There is a considerable emotional labour attached to working at the Care Farm and staff need to have the opportunity to help ease this. Volunteers need to be 'right' and understand the ethos of the Care Farm, follow instructions clearly (even if they don't necessarily at that point in time understand them) and be empathetic of the students at the Care Farm.

Whilst the majority of our days are incident-free, there are days when staff have been subject to physical and verbal aggression, and days where, for whatever reason, one or more students are heightened in their behaviours. This is when the value of having the 'right' staff becomes apparent and the whole staff team pulls together compassionately and empathetically to help to restore balance and keep students safe. We are all reflective practitioners and, as such, we reflect on incidents and frequently update behaviour support plans in the light of this. The value of the end-of-day debrief for growing our collective intelligence is apparent as all staff hear about incidents and successes and are aware of tweaks and changes to practice if required.

One key attribute that has increased amongst all staff over time is confidence; confidence in our ethos, confidence in our practice, confidence in our setting and confidence in ourselves as individuals. As Care Farms' Manager, I frequently question what we are doing, and why and how we are doing it. Cautiously confident is my mindset, ever-mindful that with, for example, the addition of a new student the whole daily dynamic can change and we need to adapt accordingly. Whilst much has been written on its dangers, e.g. Didau (2016), sometimes we have to rely on our gut feelings in a situation, as often that is all we have to go on as we work with highly complex, ever-changing children and young people in a flexible, fast-paced and dynamic outdoor environment.

The development of the recruitment process, from volunteer to casual hours worker to permanent contract has been a success. There has been no staff turnover at Lakeside in what is a very demanding job. Having staff stagger their work starts and end times enables, whilst still covering the core hours, site and animal-related jobs to be completed both before students arrive and after they have left.

STUDENTS: SUPPORT AND ACTIVITIES

The physical setting of the Care Farm and the flexible nature-based learning we undertake suits SEMH (Social, Emotional and Mental Health) profile students more than the EBD (Emotional and Behavioural Disorders) profile. We are much more able to have a positive impact on the former and to help progress them to school placements, if appropriate. We are not a suitable setting for all students and we have to be honest with ourselves and referrers about this. A student-led outdoor environment is not a safe setting for some potential students.

Starting small and growing gradually in terms of student numbers was imperative and we have been clear that there is a maximum number of students we can have on site, otherwise we lose the calm atmosphere we have strived so hard to achieve. We will only grow to the size of the site.

Having a large selection of spare clothing is essential, especially in the winter, as is having a large stock of indoor games, jigsaws, toys and books that allows for supported peer interactions on days of inclement weather.

It is not realistic to expect students to engage in nature-based learning all the time, and that is OK. They are, after all, children. Games such as 'Bird Bingo' and 'Junior Monopoly' have been excellent in developing skills such as turn-taking, rule adherence and sharing, as well as literacy and numeracy.

Transitions in and out of Lakeside at the beginning and end of each day need to be very carefully managed. Many of our students struggle with transitions and it is vital for a successful start and end to the day for each student's transition needs to be met. Some don't like to be reminded it will be time to leave soon, whereas others need five-minute reminders from half an hour before they leave. Managing transitions carefully can be the difference between a student having a positive day or not.

SITE AND INFRASTRUCTURE

The layout of the site is critical in passively managing students, e.g. a second bridge over the ditch from the main building in to the field constructed in our third year has allowed a more flexible flow of student movements and has directly led to incidents being avoided. Zoning in to 'activity', 'play' and 'wild' areas has also worked well. The care of animals and plants at weekends and over school holidays needs careful consideration, as this has financial implications and is difficult on public holidays. Having a Team Leader living very close to the site has proved hugely advantageous to Lakeside.

Space to run within the boundaries of the Care Farm is essential to meet the physical needs of some students. Indeed, space is the key element that has led to a relatively low number of incidents between students, given that many struggle with peer relationships in school and, indeed, may have been excluded as a consequence of them. The advantages of there being space has been highlighted by students, parents/carers, and mental health and psychological professionals. Space is a key element in what we feel makes Lakeside work. It is a resource that is often under-estimated. Linked to this, the layout of the rooms is essential so there can be a free flow of people with no-one feeling 'cornered' or enclosed. On puzzling why a child with autism experienced periods of very heightened behaviour at school but not at Lakeside, an Occupational Therapist concluded that the long sight lines at Lakeside meant that the child could literally see what was coming. This meant they were not surprised by the sudden appearance of peers from around a corner, which lead to rapidly escalating anxiety and associated behaviours.

Being on a nature reserve, or at least enclosed by our own land, has proved beneficial for safety and safeguarding when a student has become heightened and has become a 'runner'. Being set within our own land also means we can go for long walks with no issues with access or permissions.

Having growing beds and surfaces of different heights is inclusive and allows the less mobile to be involved in activities. This, along with surfaces of several types and levels of roughness, has been specifically highlighted by a visiting team of Community Physiotherapists who came to Lakeside to assess its use for their clients.

Time

If space is an undervalued resource, then time is more so. At Lakeside we have time. We have time to work at the student's pace. We have time to explore. We have time to stop and watch. We have time to nurture. Making eye contact, having a drink or using the bathroom at the Care Farm are actions that may be taken for granted but they can only happen for some of our students after months of empathetic support and gentle encouragement. Space and time are the two resources that, on reflection, probably have the most impact on students.

Care Farm II: The Willows

Since the initial draft of this chapter, WWT has opened the aforementioned second Care Farm in the centre of the county. The Willows opened in November 2020 as a direct response to increased need. We were full from the day of opening with the staffing we had in place, and are already approaching the capacity of the site in terms of student numbers. We applied all of the lessons we learnt from Lakeside and the process of opening was smooth, enabling the successful completion of the initial two terms. We are still learning, and if there is to be Care Farm III in the south of the county, we will have learnt yet more from The Willows. We have ensured that new lessons already learnt at The Willows are transferred back to Lakeside, such as the lay-out of the polytunnel to create multi-purpose spaces.

Conclusion

A Wildlife Trust setting up a Care Farm may have raised a few eyebrows, but it was a considered decision that clearly fitted with the ethos of WWT and one of its core strategic aims. Key to Lakeside and The Willows flourishing has been the on-going flexibility and adaptability of all staff, both those directly involved in the daily operations and the members of WWT's Senior Leadership Team, who have provided on-going support and close involvement. We have adhered to our ethos and principles and, always being mindful of new information, have been courageous in decision making. If something has not worked we have reflected and have not been afraid to make changes.

The staff truly have been the key to the success of the Care Farms. Their unstinting compassion and professionalism have ensured that our students are valued and cared for, and are provided opportunities to thrive each and every day. Staff put the needs of the students first and they work to their strengths; our students are at the heart of everything we do.

References

De Bono, E. (1992). *Teach your child how to think*. Penguin.

Didau, D. (2016). *What if everything you knew about education was wrong?* Crown House Publishing Limited.

McCree, M., Cutting, R., & Sherwin, D. (2018). The hare and the tortoise go to Forest School: Taking the scenic route to academic attainment via emotional wellbeing outdoors. *Early Child Development and Care, 188,* 980–996.

Nicholson, S. (1971). How not to cheat children: The theory of loose parts. *Landscape Architecture, 62,* 30–35. https://static1.squarespace.com/static/5af18f19f793926c5c8fc498/t/5b2143b08a922d0a63da9662/1528906923451/Theory+of+Loose+parts.pdf

Syed, M. (2019). *Rebel ideas: The power of diverse thinking*. John Murray (Publishers).

Taleb, N. N. (2012). *Antifragile: Things that gain from disorder*. Penguin.

Fear, Fiction and Facts: Animals in Outdoor Learning Environments

Fiona Cooke

Introduction

Animals are integral to the environment, with a crucial role in maintaining habitats that provide non-traditional learning opportunities. Yet animals are conspicuous only in their absence in discussions in outdoor education facilities, forest schools and alternative learning activities, despite their inevitable presence and fundamental function in those outdoor spaces. This lack of inclusion of animals in outdoor learning presents a concerning gap for education where opportunities are plentiful.

Early positive experiences of animals that offer children the opportunity to develop positive relationships with them, alongside the additional opportunities associated with non-traditional learning environments, influence the ways children grow up interacting with animals and their environment (Harvey et al., 2020). Learning about animals positively influences how people understand and care for their natural environment

F. Cooke (✉)
The Donkey Sanctuary, Sidmouth, UK
e-mail: fiona.cooke@thedonkeysanctuary.org.uk

(Kellert, 2002), improves social skills and empathy (Young et al., 2018) and increases animal welfare and conservation efforts (Chawla, 2009). Outdoor learning presents children with early opportunities to understand danger and develop crucial risk assessment skills in an informed and supervised manner. By essentially excluding animals from the discourse and activities in outdoor learning, we do children a serious disservice in establishing future engagement with their personal and generational health. Crucially, even where children do not develop a specific interest in animals or conservation, understanding the role of animals in nature and society and knowing how to remain safe around animals is a valuable lifelong skill.

This chapter begins with the assumption that the goal is to encourage participation in outdoor learning with children, due to the many benefits that learning outside of the traditional classroom environment offers. Despite being a necessary, natural and consequently integral aspect of the outdoors, animals are rarely discussed within the literature informing outdoor education. When referring to animals in the outdoors, we must be cognisant of the breadth of this concept and that it refers to a wide variety of environments and animal species with differing levels of domestication and wildness. This variation in the types of animals encountered in the outdoors is important, as fear, learning and safety training around animals must very much depend on the idiosyncrasies of the animal under discussion.

Teaching children to distinguish facts about animals, preparing them to learn and presenting them with balanced information is crucial to ensuring they can make rational decisions around animals. The ability to assess risk is a fundamental life skill; and being risk aware rather than risk averse is crucial to effective development and navigation throughout life (Lindon, 2011). However, early animal-focused fear beliefs can negatively influence the way that children engage with animals and their environment into, and during, adulthood. This fear presents barriers to full and active participation in outdoor education and community experiences, potentially reducing opportunities to improve health and wellbeing throughout a person's lifetime.

Children often demonstrate a natural curiosity about animals (Kellert, 1985) yet animal fears and phobias are some of the most common phobias seen in both children and adults (Rosen et al., 2008). Outdoor learning environments are likely to be associated with animal presence of some type, be that insects, wild mammals, companion animals or livestock. This discussion does not explore the nature of phobias or fears, or purport to explain the development of fear, which has multiple complex theoretical backgrounds, instead it considers the impact of animal-related fear on outdoor learners. It seeks to consider ways to integrate learning about animals into outdoor learning during child development, offering opportunities to engage in safe and supervised learning about animals even where proximity may be unwanted or inappropriate.

The Importance of Understanding Animals and the World They Live In

People with an understanding of the natural world and empathy for animals demonstrate increased commitment to animal and environmental conservation efforts (Sandifer et al., 2015; Westgarth et al., 2019), both of which offer social and individual benefits to human health and wellbeing (Wood et al., 2005). They are also at an increased likelihood of engaging and contributing positively towards efforts to improve sustainability issues (Young et al., 2018) and of holding increased pro-environmental values (Pfattheicher et al., 2015). In contrast, a fear of animals can negatively affect conservation efforts and environmental engagement (Johansson et al., 2019). Engaging with learning about animals increases children's empathy towards animals and humans (Taylor & Signal, 2005; Young et al., 2018), and improves their social skills and social competence (Pittinsky & Montoya, 2016). Nature offers children opportunities to understand the complex interplay between the environment and the social structures and behaviours of animals encountered within it. In terms of domesticated animals encountered, direct contact with companion animals may develop the likelihood of pet ownership, creating opportunities to benefit from the myriad of health benefits these bring throughout childhood and into adulthood (Hawkins et al., 2017).

Aside from the positive benefits for conservation and human wellbeing, knowledge of animals also directly improves animal welfare. Negative perceptions of animals increase the likelihood of poor treatment (Cook & Sealey, 2017), whereas an increase in empathy for animals reduces the risk of violence towards them (which is also linked to wider violent offending) (RSPCA, 2018).

DEVELOPMENT OF ANIMAL-BASED FEAR

Fear is an important adaptive response and plays a crucial role in keeping a person or animal alive (Riba, 2013). Fear is triggered by a fear stimulus (e.g. a predator or dangerous animal) causing a sympathetic nervous system response and resulting in fight, flight or freeze responses. The ability to recognise and retain information about dangerous animals holds an evolutionary advantage for humans, both in protecting them from disease (Kasperbauer, 2015) and from potentially fatal encounters (Ulrich, 1993). The perception of animals as dangerous often results in defensive emotional responses of fear or disgust (Davey, 2011), therefore creating avoidance behaviours that perpetuate fear responses and prevent further opportunities for positive associated learning (Dunne & Askew, 2018). Fear and disgust are closely associated with each other in increasing negative responses to animals, with children's fear of animals rising with increased disgust (Muris et al., 2009; Askew et al., 2014). Fear behaviours are negatively reinforced by escape (Muris & Field, 2010), yet avoidance behaviour can affect quality of life and involvement in otherwise everyday activities (Choy et al., 2007). Therefore, despite escape being an effective solution to staying alive in the face of danger, fear responses themselves can inhibit learning and maladaptive reactions reduce learning opportunities.

Both adaptive and maladaptive avoidance behaviours, resulting from fear beliefs, negate learning by reducing opportunities to access new learning and lowering engagement in contexts where animals may be present (Krypotos et al., 2015; Dunne & Askew, 2018). Consequently, this reduces educational opportunities relating to coexistence or conservation (Inskip & Zimmerman, 2009). For example in the UK, over 37% of children have a fear of dogs, with 53% of children choosing to avoid areas where they have seen dogs (Dogs Trust, n.d.). Although fear and disgust emotions are argued by many to be founded in self-preservation (Curtis et al., 2011), perceptions of animals as 'uncontrollable, dangerous, unpredictable and disgusting' also significantly increase fear perceptions of all animals, while a sense of control, predictability and understanding can reduce fear beliefs (Armfield, 2007). Some of the most commonly recognised human fear predispositions relate to spiders, reptiles and insects (Ceríaco, 2012). Preparedness theory (see Åhs et al., 2018) posits that humans are evolutionarily predisposed to be prepared for danger and recognise threat in certain shapes and movements such as those presenting with aposematic signalling (displaying or forming triangle 'warning' shapes) (Souchet & Aubret, 2016). This potential for danger messaging should be taken into consideration when planning teaching and learning activities and materials around animals.

Although fear is a normative response for children and a fear of animals is considered common in young children (Gullone, 2000), fear responses that affect everyday activities can be extremely disruptive to development and can be damaging to engagement in learning opportunities (Abell, 2007). Both heritability and environmental factors affect the development of fears (Remmerswaal et al., 2013), and this must be considered when structuring and introducing outdoor learning activities for children.

Children demonstrate content bias towards, and retain, 'danger' information over and above any other facts they are simultaneously informed of, regardless of culture or age (Barrett & Broesch, 2012). Fear beliefs can be developed in a number of ways, including direct conditioning, verbal information or through experiencing the modelling of fear behaviour (Rachman, 1991). Crucially, children can learn fear responses in one-trial learning events, whether the learning relates to a true danger or otherwise (Barrett & Broesch, 2012). Once fear beliefs have developed, children will avoid animals they fear as well as environments they may be encountered in (Askew & Field, 2007), therefore facing an immediate barrier to outdoor learning opportunities wherein danger may lurk.

Social learning is a more reliable, safe and effective way of learning than individual learning when the risk of error is high (Kameda & Nakanishi, 2002) and thus the sharing of threat information is a central aspect of the aetiology of fear (Rachman, 1991). Children are sensitive to the effects of both verbal and non-verbal information regarding fear and disgust around animals, and can learn fear vicariously. Children will show increased fear acquisition (and consequent avoidance) in response to images of novel animals following the observation of adult or peer fear or disgust responses (Dunne et al., 2018). In fact, children can learn fear responses towards animals from the ages of 15–20 months onwards through only a single visual observation of adult or peer response to animal imagery (Dunne & Askew, 2018). Rifkin et al. (2016) demonstrated that children with limited language structure (aged 3–5 years) develop a fear of novel animals when images are presented alongside verbal threat information, yet the same pairing with positive information does not create significant positive associations. Therefore, outdoor educators have a big responsibility in ensuring that, wherever avoidable these pathways for creating fear responses are not encouraged in children. This consideration will need to be maintained as children mature; children of up to 12 years old exposed to negative parental verbal information about an animal demonstrate significantly increased fear responses (Remmerswaal et al., 2013). These fear beliefs can, however, be decreased using positive vicarious counterconditioning interventions when adults or peers present a positive response to the fear stimuli, or when an expert is available to answer questions (Johansson et al., 2019). This presents opportunities to offer support in outdoor learning environments that cause fear responses.

FEAR AND FOLKLORE

Dangerous animals are usually perceived to be 'outdoor' animals (Barrett, 2005) with narratives depicting danger widely represented throughout the media, where stories of close encounters with large predators inevitably gain broad attention (Bombieri et al., 2018). Children are sensitive to the effects of verbal information from sources such as media outlets (Comer et al., 2008), and additionally, folklore, myths and human values influence the way that animals are perceived, as does different cultural learning about specific animals (Morzillo et al., 2007; Ceríaco, 2012).

Representations of dangerous animals pervade children's literature, with vicious, bloodthirsty wolves (e.g. Little Red Riding Hood, Perrault, 1697), and cunning foxes (as in Br'er Rabbit, Chandler-Harris, 1881) presenting visual and verbal representations of animals that wish to intentionally harm others. Muris and Field (2010) highlight the story of the Jabberwock as such an example, exploring how language and imagery around animals and outdoor creatures can negatively affect the perception of safety in these contexts. Language and narratives used to portray animals significantly influence perceptions surrounding them, with regard to the interpretation of their actions and expectations of how they will behave (Chawla, 2009). Narratives around animals such as spiders and sharks can create fears based on unrealistic scenarios but serve to reinforce fear responses to such animals (Myers, 2007). Although there are also children's stories portraying animals positively (for example, Charlotte's Web, White, 2002), these may not be enough to overcome the impact of the negative information presented in other books. Creating a balanced library for children to learn about animals will help their information gathering and help to balance their views.

Assimilating and Risk-Assessing Animal Information

With the amount of variation in learning that children experience about animals, potential predispositions to fear responses and exposure to external information sources, it is crucial to ensure that children are able to assimilate and apply relevant information in various contexts. This allows children to analyse situations, make risk-based decisions, build their understanding of the natural world and feed their curiosity, alongside developing crucial life skills within non-traditional learning environments. Learning risk assessment skills are particularly important when we consider that the instinct of many people presented with a fear stimulus is the flight response—often involving fast movement, noise or waving arms. None of these actions will keep a child safe when encountering a dog or an aggressive wasp but will increase the risk of that animal responding with unsafe behaviours.

Despite the importance of learning within environments where animals may be present, risk should be acknowledged; children should learn that animals can pose varying levels of risk in varied contexts and that danger can be species-dependent. Learning opportunities around assessing risk are important for child development, providing the foundation for crucial life skills (Lindon, 2011). The ability to analyse risk rationally requires teaching and development through generalisable early learning experiences and understanding about animals. This will ensure that such fears are not encouraged or developed where they present no benefit to the child, and that animals are appropriately represented in outdoor learning environments. Understanding information about animals, their behaviour and how to stay safe around them also provides a sense of control and makes animals more predictable, both factors that reduce animal induced fear responses and increase problem-solving skills in situations involving wildlife (Armfield, 2007; Johansson et al., 2012).

Children automatically categorise animals into different groups (Connor & Lawrence, 2017), which can influence animal welfare and conservation-related behaviour decisions (Serpell, 2004). Information must therefore be presented in a way that spans species categories, to ensure learning is both applicable and broad enough to encompass the animals that children may encounter. The type of information presented to children about animals is crucial to learning and retention. Even when presented with balanced information, context bias leads to the prioritisation of danger information, with any simultaneously presented non-danger information considered only after processing the negative information. Ambiguous information about novel animals is more likely to be interpreted negatively by children than positively, creating higher levels of fear beliefs than positive information (Muris et al., 2010). Where a child is already anxious or fearful, they are at an increased likelihood of interpreting ambiguous information negatively due to interpretation bias (Muris & Field, 2008), but presentation of positive information can be effective in reducing fear (Kelly et al., 2010). However, where children are presented with positive information about novel animals and engage with that information actively with their peers, they are less likely to experience higher fear beliefs than otherwise (Kelly et al., 2010). It is important to carefully consider how information about animals is presented, and, where safe to do so, present balanced information to guide decision-making rather than creating a fear-based narrative (Muris & Rijkee, 2011; Slagle et al., 2013). For example, numerous education campaigns and programmes exist to develop learning about how to act around dogs (e.g. The Blue Dog, 2020) and there is a wide range of literature available to support safe countryside activity participation (e.g. Natural England, 2012).

ADULT'S ROLES: 'YUCK! DON'T LICK THAT'

Young children experience an oral phase (American Psychology Association, 2020) during which they explore items by putting them in their mouths. In response, adults often express verbal disgust such as 'yuck', alongside visual disgust. The negative implications of this in the wider context of learning about animals are significant. Such representations of disgust or fear from adults underpin fear belief development in children and hence the impact of these interactions must be considered in terms of the effects on the child's learning opportunities.

In light of the complexity and pervasion of fear responses to animals, and the potential impact on the outdoor learning opportunities that children can engage in, it is important to consider ways to both reduce the perception of threat and reduce unfounded fear beliefs. Old-fashioned notions of 'just get on with it' or 'facing fears' will not help, and indeed may actually compound the fear response further, even causing generalisation of the fear to wider species and contexts which will further restrict learning opportunities (Dymond et al., 2012).

Teachers are extremely influential role models for children (Bergem, 1990), and their visual or verbal responses to animals are likely to have a significant impact on children's own behaviour and beliefs. Care should thus be taken that such fears are not inadvertently transmitted. Where teachers have their own established fears or phobias of animals, consideration should be made as to whether they are able to prevent that response being recognised by children. Trusted adults need to be aware of the potential impact of fear or disgust responses to animals by peers and mitigate these impacts on individual children wherever possible. In cases where a fear already exists, positive vicarious counter-conditioning and desensitisation may decrease this response to animals. Educators should actively embrace positive narratives around animals and opportunities to provide positive experiences.

In addition to avoiding negative fear belief development in children, adults can also create an understanding in children of the animal as an individual rather than an object or 'group'. Using the pronouns 'him' or 'her', rather than 'it', has been shown to be effective in changing perceptions about animals and allowing children to think about animals as individuals (Young et al., 2018). Encouraging an understanding of the animal's perspective can ensure that children engage further with the experience of the animal, developing empathy for the species and creating engagement with conservation-based support for that animal's habitat (Young et al., 2018). With this information, children are able to consider causes for animal behaviour, consequently making animals more predictable and reducing risk. For example, children will be able to evaluate if animals are behaving in a certain way because they are scared, why they are scared, and therefore respond in a way that reduces the animal's fear and thus the risk posed. This development and encouragement of affective empathy in understanding the emotional experience of another (Eres et al., 2015) can increase engagement with the natural world and enhance social skills, including emotional competence and prosocial behaviours (Telle & Pfister, 2016).

Conclusion

This chapter identifies a requirement to develop methods to engage children in animal-based learning positively, however, advice regarding specific interventions will need to be sought from educational experts (as this requires knowledge of teaching and differentiation according to age, stage of development and individual or group needs). When creating outdoor learning opportunities there must be a clear recognition of the complex interplay of factors that contribute to fear learning. Where possible, these fear factors should be mitigated by teacher, peer and trusted adult role modelling of risk assessment processes, positive interactions and information sharing. It is therefore crucial that teachers and educators support learning about animals and have the tools to do so in learning contexts where fear may be a factor in disengagement.

A fear of animals and the environments they live in will hinder access to the benefits of non-traditional outdoor learning opportunities, and therefore reduce potential learning of additional life skills including empathy, problem-solving skills and prosocial development. There are ways to reduce or balance exposure to negative or neutrally valenced information presented to children and ensure that positive information supports learning, to reduce the development of fear-related beliefs and avoidance behaviours. Negative information about animals is far more easily retained than positive information, and neutral information is more likely to be interpreted negatively than positively. Undoing negative learning about animals is much more complex than preventing it where it is caused by negative narratives, highlighting the importance of proactive teaching to create positive animal-based early learning experiences for children. This places a big responsibility on those leading outdoor education experiences to ensure that information is clearly presented in a way that fairly represents risk. The availability of facts to counter fear or fiction will also help to avoid negative information sharing in relation to animal encounters.

Ensuring that animal fears do not negatively affect outdoor learning experiences is crucial to allowing full engagement in education. By increasing the visibility of animals in outdoor learning, children are offered additional opportunities to engage with wider learning experiences that provide social and environmental benefits. A multitude of opportunities to learn and develop in ways that benefit themselves as individuals, their communities, animals and the environment are available to children when they can access these non-traditional learning contexts with a positive and confident outlook. By understanding which learning experiences may contribute towards fear beliefs that prevent children from fully taking part in outdoor or animal-related learning, and that such fears are valid, the opportunity arises to support their full participation within non-traditional education settings.

REFERENCES

Abell, S. (2007). Fear of animals. *Clinical Pediatrics, 46* (8), 754–755. Sage Publications https://doi.org/10.1177/0009922806290826

Åhs, F., Rosen, J., Kastrati, G., Fredrikson, M., Agren, T., & Lundström, J. N. (2018). Biological preparedness and resistance to extinction of skin conductance responses conditioned to fear relevant animal pictures: A systematic review. *Neuroscience & Biobehavioral Reviews, 95*, 430–437. https://doi.org/10.1016/j.neubiorev.2018.10.017

American Psychology Association. (2020). *Dictionary of psychology*. Oral Stage. https://dictionary.apa.org/oral-stage

Armfield, J. M. (2007). Understanding animal fears: a comparison of the cognitive vulnerability and harm-looming models. *BMC Psychiatry, 7*, 68. https://doi.org/10.1186/1471-244X-7-68

Askew, C., & Field, A. P. (2007). Vicarious learning and the development of fears in childhood. *Behaviour Research and Therapy, 45*(11), 2616–2627. https://doi.org/10.1016/j.brat.2007.06.008

Askew, C., Kübra, C., Liine, P., & Reynolds, G. (2014). The effect of disgust and fear modeling on children's disgust and fear for animals. *Journal of Abnormal Psychology, 123*(3), 566–577.

Bergem, T. (1990). The teacher as moral agent. *Journal of Moral Education, 19*(2), 88. https://doi.org/10.1080/0305724900190203

Barrett, H. C. (2005). Adaptations to predators and prey. In D. M. Buss (Ed.), *The handbook of evolutionary psychology,* (pp. 200–223). New York: Wiley.

Barrett, H. C., & Broesch, J. (2012). Prepared social learning about dangerous animals in children. *Evolution and Human Behavior, 33*(5), 499–508. https://doi.org/10.1016/j.evolhumbehav.2012.01.003

Bombieri, G., Nanni, V., del Mar Delgado, M., Fedriani, J. M., López-Bao, J. V., Pedrini, P., et al. (2018). Content analysis of media reports on predator attacks on humans: toward an understanding of human risk perception and predator acceptance. *Bioscience, 68*, 577–584. https://doi.org/10.1093/biosci/biy072

Ceríaco, L. M. (2012). Human attitudes towards herpetofauna: The influence of folklore and negative values on the conservation of amphibians and reptiles in Portugal. *Journal of Ethnobiology and Ethnomedicine, 8*, 8.

Chawla, L. (2009). Growing up green: Becoming agents of care for the natural world. *Journal of Developmental Practice, 4*(1), 6–23.

Choy, Y., Fyer, A. J., & Lipsitz, J. D. (2007). Treatment of specific phobia in adults. *Clinical Psychology Review, 27*, 266–286.

Comer, J. S., Furr, J. M., Beidas, R. S., Babyar, H. M., & Kendall, P. C. (2008). Media use and children's perceptions of societal threat and personal vulnerability. *Journal of Clinical Child & Adolescent Psychology, 37*(3), 622–630. https://doi.org/10.1080/15374410802148145

Connor, M., & Lawrence, A. B. (2017). Understanding adolescents' categorisation of animal species. *Animals, 7*, 65.

Cook, G., & Sealey, A. (2017). The discursive representation of animals. In A. Fill & H. Penz (Eds.), *The Routledge handbook of ecolinguistics* (pp. 311–324). Routledge.

Curtis, V., de Barra, M., Aunger, R. (2011). Disgust as an adaptive system for disease avoidance behaviour. *Philosophical Transactions of the Royal Society B: Biological Sciences, 366*(1568), 1320–1320. https://doi.org/10.1098/rstb.2011.0002

De Curtis, V., Barra, M., & Aunger, R. (2011). Disgust as an adaptive system for disease avoidance behaviour. *Philosophical Transactions of the Royal Society B, 366*, 389–401.

Dogs Trust. (n.d.). Is your child frightened of dogs? Dogs Trust is here to help. *News.* https://www.dogstrust.org.uk/news-events/news/is-your-child-frightened-of-dogs-dogs-trust-is-here-to-help

Dunne, G., & Askew, C. (2018). Vicarious learning and reduction of fear in children via adult and child models. *Emotion, 18*(4), 528–535.

Dymond, S., Schlund, M. W., Roche, B., De Houwer, J., & Freegard, G. P. (2012). Safe from harm: Learned, instructed, and symbolic generalization pathways of human threat-avoidance. *PLoS One, 7*(10), e47539. https://doi.org/10.1371/journal.pone.0047539

Eres, R., Decety, J., Louis, W. R., & Molenberghs, P. (2015). Individual differences in local gray matter density are associated with differences in affective and cognitive empathy. *NeuroImage, 117*, 305–310.

Gullone, E. (2000). The development of normal fear: A century of research. *Clinical Psychology Review, 20*, 429–451.

Harvey, D. J. et al. (2020). Psychological benefits of a biodiversity-focussed outdoor learning program for primary school children. *Journal of Environmental Psychology.* Elsevier Ltd, 67, p. 101381. https://doi.org/10.1016/j.jenvp.2019.101381

Hawkins, R., & Williams, J. (2017). Scottish Society for the Prevention of Cruelty to Animals (Scottish SPCA) Childhood Attachment to Pets: Associations between Pet Attachment Attitudes to Animals Compassion and Humane Behaviour. *International Journal of Environmental Research and Public Health, 14*(5), 490. https://doi.org/10.3390/ijerph14050490

Inskip, C., & Zimmermann, A. (2009). Human-felid conflict: A review of patterns and priorities worldwide. *Oryx, 43*(01), 18. https://doi.org/10.1017/S003060530899030X

Johansson, M., Hallgren, L., Flykt, A., Støen, O-G., Thelin, L., & Frank, J. (2019). Communication interventions and fear of brown bears: Considerations of content and format. *Frontiers in Ecology and Evolution.* http://urn.kb.se/resolve?urn=urn:nbn:se:miun:diva-38240

Johansson, M., Karlsson, J., Pedersen, E., & Flykt, A. (2012). Factors Governing Human Fear of Brown Bear and Wolf. *Human Dimensions of Wildlife, 17*(1), 58–74. https://doi.org/10.1080/10871209.2012.619001

Kameda, T., & Nakanishi, D. (2002). Cost–benefit analysis of social/cultural learning in a nonstationary uncertain environment. *Evolution and Human Behavior, 23*(5), 373–393. https://doi.org/10.1016/S1090-5138(02)00101-0

Kasperbauer, T. J. (2015). Animals as disgust elicitors. *Biology and Philosophy, 30*, 167–185. https://doi.org/10.1007/s10539-015-9478-y

Kellert, S. R. (1985). Attitudes toward animals: Age related development among children. *Journal of Environmental Education, 16*, 29–39.

Kellert, S. R. (2002). Experiencing nature: Affective, cognitive, and evaluative development in children. In P. H. Kahn Jr. & S. R. Kellert (Eds.), *Children and nature: Psychological, sociocultural, and evolutionary investigations* (pp. 153–178). MIT Press.

Kelly, V. L., Barker, H., Field, A. P., Wilson, C., & Reynolds, S. (2010). Can Rachman's indirect pathways be used to un-learn fear? A prospective paradigm to test whether children's fears can be reduced using positive information and modelling a non-anxious response. *Behaviour Research and Therapy, 48*, 164–170.

Krypotos, A.-M., Effting, M., Kindt, M., & Beckers, T. (2015). Avoidance learning: A review of theoretical models and recent developments. *Frontiers in Behavioral Neuroscience.* https://doi.org/10.3389/fnbeh.2015.00189

Lang, A. (ca. 1889). *The Blue Fairy Book* (London), pp. 51–53. Source: Perrault, C. (1697) Histoires ou contes du temps passé, avec des moralités: Contes de ma mère l'Oye (Paris).

Lindon, J. (2011). *Too safe for their own good: helping children learn about risk and lifeskills* (2nd ed.). National Childrens Bureau.

Morzillo, A. T., Mertig, A. G., Garner, N., & Liu, J. (2007). Resident attitudes toward black bears and population recovery in East Texas. *Human Dimensions of Wildlife, 12*, 417–428. https://doi.org/10.1080/10871200701670110

Muris, P., & Field, A. (2008). Distorted cognition and pathological anxiety in children and adolescents. *Cognition and Emotion, 22*, 395–421.

Muris, P., & Field, A. P. (2010). The role of verbal threat information in the development of childhood fear. "Beware the Jabberwock!". *Clinical Child and Family Psychology Review, 13*, 129–150.

Muris, P., Huijding, J., Mayer, B., Leemreis, W., Passchier, S., & Bouwmeester, S. (2009). The effects of verbal disgust- and threat-related information about novel animals on disgust and fear beliefs and avoidance in children. *Journal of Clinical Child & Adolescent Psychology, 38*(4), 551–563.

Muris, P., & Rijkee, S. (2011). Facing the beast apart together: Fear in boys and girls after processing information about novel animals individually or in a duo. *Journal of Child and Family Studies, 20*, 554–559. https://doi.org/10.1007/s10826-010-9427-y

Muris, P., Van Zwol, L., Huijding, J., & Mayer, B. (2010). Mom told me scary things about this animal! Parents installing fear beliefs in their children via the verbal information pathway. *Behaviour Research and Therapy, 48,* 341–346.

Myers, G. (2007). *The significance of children and animals: Social development and our connections to other species* (2nd ed.). Purdue University Press.

Natural England. (2012). The countryside code (NE326). http://publications. naturalengland.org.uk/publication/987819?category=38017

Pfattheicher, S., Sassenrath, C., & Schindler, S. (2015). Feelings for the suffering of others and the environment: Compassion fosters proenvironmental tendencies. *Environment and Behavior, 48*(7), 929–945.

Pittinsky, T. L., & Montoya, R. M. (2016). Empathic joy in positive intergroup relations. *Journal of Social Issues, 72*(3), 511–523.

Rachman, S. (1991). Neo-conditioning and the classical theory of fear acquisition. *Clinical Psychology Review, 11*(2), 155–173.

Remmerswaal, D., Muris, P., & Huijding, J. (2013). "Watch Out for the Gerbils, My Child!" The role of maternal information on children's fear in an experimental setting using real animals. *Behavior Therapy, 44*(2), 317–324.

Riba, C. (2013). Ethology of fear: Responses, actions, universes. *Catalan Social Sciences Review, North America, 3*: 19–34.

Rifkin, L. S., Schofield, C. A., Beard, C., Armstrong, T. (2016). Adaptation of a paradigm for examining the development of fear beliefs through the verbal information pathway in preschool-age children. *Behaviour Research and Therapy, 87,* 34–39. https://doi.org/10.1016/j.brat.2016.08.013

Rosen, J. B., Pagani, J. H., Rolla, K. L. G., & Davis, C. (2008). Analysis of behavioral constraints and the neuroanatomy of fear to the predator odor trimethylthiazoline: A model for animal phobias. *Neuroscience and Biobehavioral Reviews, 32,* 1267–1276.

RSPCA. (2018). *Building a kinder generation: How the RSPCA will educate the adults of tomorrow to tackle the animal welfare crisis of today.* https://www.rspca.org.uk/documents/1494939/7712578/Prevention+report.pdf/eae6c8c9-758a-ccdc-f69c-66c0bc6ffb1a?t=1555596722243&;download=true

Sandifer, P. A., Sutton-Grier, A. E., & Ward, B. P. (2015). Exploring connections among nature, biodiversity, ecosystem services, and human health and well-being: Opportunities to enhance health and biodiversity conservation. *Ecosystem Services, 12,* 1–15. Elsevier B.V. https://doi.org/10.1016/j.ecoser.2014.12.007

Serpell, J. A. (2004). Factors influencing human attitudes to animals and their welfare. *Animal Welfare, 13,* s145–s151.

Slagle, K., Zajac, R., Bruskotter, J., Wilson, R., & Prange, S. (2013). Building tolerance for bears: a communications experiment. *Journal of Wildlife Management, 77,* 863–869. https://doi.org/10.1002/jwmg.515

Souchet, J., & Aubret, F. (2016). Revisiting the fear of snakes in children: The role of aposematic signalling. *Scientific Reports, 6* (1), 37619. England: Nature Publishing Group. https://doi.org/10.1038/srep37619

Taylor, N., & Signal, T. D. (2005). Empathy and attitudes to animals. *Anthrozoös, 18*, 18–27.

Telle, N. T., & Pfister, H. R. (2016). Positive empathy and prosocial behavior: A neglected link. *Emotion Review, 8*(2), 154–163.

The Blue Dog. (2020). Safe relationships between children and dogs. https://www.thebluedog.org/en/

Ulrich, R. S. (1993). 'Biophilia, biophobia, and natural landscapes'. In S. R. Kellertand E. O. Wilson (eds.), *The Biophilia Hypothesis* (pp. 73–137). Washington DC: Island Press.

Westgarth, C. et al. (2019). Dog owners are more likely to meet physical activity guidelines than people without a dog: An investigation of the association between dog ownership and physical activity levels in a UK community. *Scientific Reports, 9* (1), 5704–5710. England: Nature Publishing Group. https://doi.org/10.1038/s41598-019-41254-6

Wood, L., Giles-Corti, B., & Bulsara, M. (2005). The pet connection: Pets as a conduit for social capital? *Social Science & Medicine, 61*(6), 1159–1173. England: Elsevier Ltd. https://doi.org/10.1016/j.socscimed.2005.01.017

Young, A., Khalil, K.A., Wharton, J. (2018). Empathy for animals: A review of the existing literature. *Curator: The Museum Journal, 61*(2), 327–343. Wiley Subscription Services, Inc. https://doi.org/10.1111/cura.12257

Learning About the World to Save the World: How Learning from Animals May Provide a Means of Promoting Environmental Awareness

Roger Cutting

INTRODUCTION

In the poem, A Swallow, the poet Ted Hughes talks of how the bird's arrival each year heralds the beginning of the summer. Yet, however familiar this event is in England, a further significatory aspect to the poem is that we rarely consider the hidden life of this small bird, in particular the hugely impressive geographical range of the flight that it has made. Hughes lyrically considers this journey, flying out of Africa, across the Sahara where *'mirage heat, Glazed her blues'*, then across the Mediterranean Sea and Southern Europe, to the cooler, verdant, north; to nest eventually under the shaded eaves of a West Country farmhouse. In its evocation of a journey across such beautiful and hostile environments, the poem stands

R. Cutting (✉)
Institute of Education, University of Plymouth, Plymouth, UK
e-mail: roger.cutting@plymouth.ac.uk

© The Author(s), under exclusive license to Springer Nature
Switzerland AG 2022
R. Cutting, R. Passy (eds.), *Contemporary Approaches to Outdoor Learning*, Palgrave Studies in Alternative Education,
https://doi.org/10.1007/978-3-030-85095-1_4

as an effective statement on how little we know and understand about the lives and behaviours of the animals around us (Hughes, 2003). Yet, by coming to understand more about its life, we come to appreciate this small bird all the more. Hughes allows us a brief glimpse through a metaphorical *'crack in the snow-sheet'*; an opening for us to see into this other world, from which the bird appears to have emerged and that we rarely appreciate.

Buller (2012) uses Ruth Padel's poem 'Tiger Drinking by a Forest Pool' to further illustrate the curiously elusive relationship that we have with animals, suggesting that attempts to more fully understand this seemingly complex association may need to lie beyond the rational and scientific. In turn, this '...*opens the door to imagination, to otherness, to myth and a multitude of different ways of knowing*' (Buller, 2012, p. 189). In any form of education, 'doors to imagination', 'otherness' and 'different ways of knowing' should stimulate interest. In a form of education that promotes sustainability and a sense of environmental curation, they are, perhaps, essential. Furthermore, exploring our relationship with the worlds of animals is not only a rich educational resource for the promotion of environmental engagement but may even facilitate greater compassion and care and therefore, agency. This is a point best described in summation by the primatologist Jane Goodall, when she wrote of our relationship with animals in context to our planetary survival and how; '*Only if we understand, can we care. Only if we care, we will help. Only if we help, we shall be saved*' (Lindsey, 1999, p. 6).

Nearly half a century has now passed since the publication of Peter Singer's seminal work, 'Animal Liberation' (Singer, 1975) and in the intervening time, there has been a growing and significant academic interest in our relationship with the non-human animal world. Described by Simmons and Armstrong (2007) as 'the animal turn', it has been a particular interest within the humanities and social sciences. Within these disciplines, there has even been the emergence of new sub-frames of study such as animal geographies (Buller, 2014; Philo & Wilbert, 2000). Applied applications have also been increasingly apparent in social and therapeutic support (Nimer & Lundahl, 2007).

The use of animals in the field of education, particularly in science education, has a more established history. However, Pedersen (2019, p. 1) argues that traditional teaching approaches mean that students are '*taught to utilize, dominate, or control other species*'. Even within the educational sub-frame of outdoor learning, animals are often experienced in captivity, where learning has tended to focus on observation and classification

(Pedersen, 2010a). Bars, glass and Perspex may be interpreted perhaps as the physical manifestations of the social barriers to learning that we have erected.

In 'Earth in Mind', David Orr (2004) notes the title of the book signals the possibility that we have, over generations, assimilated an empathy for the world around us; an idea that he points out E. O. Wilson named 'biophilia'. Orr calls this innate affinity our best hope in such uncertain times. We should put our primary hopes for our future survival, not in abstract ideas of intelligence and progress but rather, in the extent and depth of our affections. It is in our capacity for empathy, for compassion, and love, that we will find a balanced, sustainable future for our children, our ecosystems and our planet.

Therefore, whether education for sustainability is explicit or implicit within the curriculum, to promote the biophilic responses that Orr argues are required, it should necessarily promote emotional intelligence, empathy and compassion. It is in the development and deployment of these innate capacities that animals may have a significant role to play.

The impact that our relationship with animals has in the promotion of a deep appreciation of the natural environment, sense of connectedness to nature, and to even wider environmental understanding has long been recognised. This chapter will initially review the influence of animals on our approaches to teaching about the environment through a review of several key texts that have been widely recognised as inspirational in the development of ideas and teaching strategies, not only education for outdoor learning but also the promotion of sustainability. It will then review the apparent absence of animals in research and practice. It will finally review ways forward in developing teaching and learning strategies that hope to encourage environmental engagement and therefore a greater sense of environmental curation.

Three Things I Hate: 1. Lists. 2. People Who Make Lists. 3. Irony

It's an old joke, but one of the more curious characteristics of news and popular culture websites is the ubiquitous nature and the sheer number of articles based around lists. From best rock albums to the greatest novels, by way of the top ten greatest films, their subjects seem only limited by the imaginations of the compilers. Initially, at least, these seemingly endless lists seem to serve little purpose, other than to fill 'copy' for the publishers and to act as a distraction for those attempting to work on-line. However, and this may be a little generous, they do have a certain capacity to stimulate some thoughtful debate around personal choices and preferences on the specified subjects. To that end, if you were to compile a list of say, the greatest, or at least, most influential books, regarding our relationship with nature, what would it include?

There would, no doubt, be a significant degree of argument and variation over the final list. However, there are probably two volumes that would automatically be selected by most environmental educators and a third, admittedly perhaps a less lyrical read, that would be likely to make most lists as well.

Most would very likely include Henry David Thoreau's 'Walden'. Although not an easy read and, perhaps as Shultz (2015) points out, it may be more revered than read, it is, however, still regarded by many as an iconic work of literature, meditatively exploring the relationships between ourselves and nature and, at the very least, demonstrating '*the rich and full existence of a simple life close to nature*' (Betz, 2015). Whatever the criticisms levelled against the authenticity of his work, it has according to the environmental group Greenpeace (2018), '*inspired generations of environmentalists*' and would be hard not to include.

Another book that would probably appear in most lists would be Aldo Leopold's 'A Sand County Almanac'. Despite, once again, a range of critiques levelled at this work, Dixon (2016, p. 1) describes its influence on environmental ethics as '*tremendous*'. Millstein (2018) quotes a number of writers to illustrate the significant influence that the book has had, one of which, Katz (1995, p. 113), states that '*Leopold's classic essay "The Land Ethic" in A Sand County Almanac is probably the most widely cited source in the literature of environmental philosophy*'. Given its influence on conservation and ideas around our connection to the land and environment, again, it is hard to envisage it not being included in, at least, the top ten books.

Perhaps at this point, in a chapter concerning animals and outdoor learning, it is worth pausing and reflecting on these volumes. For even if the choice is contested and the process of selection is not particularly objective or scientific, these two books are regularly cited as having provided inspiration and insight into the importance of developing deeper relationships with the world around us. These may include the rational but also hint at emotional, even spiritual, relationships. More specifically, each of these books, at some point at least, also explores our complex and nuanced relationship with the animal world. In both volumes, there are renowned, seminally-reflective, sections on human/animal interactions (Quin Liu, 2017) the foremost of which is Leopold's moment of self-realisation, some may suggest self-actualisation, found famously through the dying green fire of a wolf's eyes (Beusterien & Baird-Callicott, 2013). Thoreau's observations and reflections on the animals in and around Walden Pond are similarly deeply symbolic and spiritual and are presented extensively in Wisner's 2017 publication 'Thoreau's Animals'.

Such inspiration from a moment of deep connection with animals is not confined to these two authors. Indeed, other influential environmentalists, contemporary to them, such as Ernest Thompson Seton and Félix Rodríguez de la Fuente have also been identified as coming to a great appreciation of the environment through so-called Significant Life Experiences involving animals. The wolf is a particularly powerful evocation in all four authors' work (Puig & Echarri, 2018).

The final suggestion and a third volume most likely for inclusion on the list for inspiring learning about our connection to the natural environment would unquestionably be Rachel Carson's 'Silent Spring'. A different, more science-based text than the previous two, Carson's book deals with the profound impact that humans have on animal populations and highlights the systemic nature of our relationship with the natural world. The text is regularly cited in a range of different media as the inspiration for the environmental movement. In turn, the realisation of the fragility of the natural environment has moved even the mainstream to appreciate the importance of conservation and, more recently, sustainability (Meyer & Rohlinger, 2012). Aldo Leopold's work influenced the setting up of National Parks and Reserves, Carson's 'Silent Spring' had a similar impact on environmental legislation, perhaps best summarised thus, '*The claim that Rachel Carson's Silent Spring … played a crucial role in outlining the fundamental tenets of modern environmentalism is now almost universally accepted*' (Kroll, 2001, p. 403).

Although both Thoreau and Leopold wrote of the deleterious impact of humans on the natural world, Carson's perspective was more directly scientific, but nevertheless, remains as a key text in the history of environmentalism. In terms of inclusion on a list of greatest environmentally inspiring books, these three may adopt different perspectives and ultimately reach out to different parts of the human mind and spirit, but their focus in doing so is that of our relationship with animals. If we look to more contemporary, lyrical texts, we also find J. A. Baker's 'The Peregrine', or Helen MacDonald's 'H is for Hawk'. For a contemporary and inspirational science-based writer in the vein of Rachel Carson, we find the work of Jane Goodall.

The essential conclusion from this exercise, and this section, is that these inspiring books in the field of environmentalism and environmental engagement have a significant focus on our relationship with animals. Whether spiritual, rational or indeed both, it is this relationship that is quite consistently returned to as an entrée into deeper environmental thought and insight. If our relationship with animals is the source of inspiration for these authors who have in turn inspired a generation, why have the sub-frames of education that purport to help people engage with the world around them, seemingly overlooked its importance?

To ask this question of children's education makes it even more apposite. In the context of children's literature, we commonly see the inclusion of animals. Admittedly they are at times anthropomorphised, or indeed mythical, but the attraction of animals to children's sensibilities seems to be in little doubt. This is a point explored elsewhere in this volume.

Given that animals regularly form such a focus for children's literature, it would appear to be something of an obvious and ready vehicle to promote and inspire in children a deeper connection to nature. Indeed, early book exposure is important in framing and increasing children's knowledge about the world (Ganea et al., 2011). Furthermore, Bradbury (2013) points out the use of children's literature is a powerful approach in helping even young children develop an environmental and global awareness that in turn promotes sustainability and global citizenship. Additionally, Beratz and Hazeira (2012) discusses how important children's literature is in assimilating values, particularly around issues such as sustainability. Even the use of anthropomorphism will influence early years understanding of the nature and science of animals (Geertz, 2016).

However, examples of animals being the primary entrée for educating about the world around us appear remarkably thin on the ground. In outdoor education it may be expected to play a more significant role, and yet, here again, one has to search quite extensively to find activities and approaches, perhaps with the exception of mini-beasts, that involve animals. Concepts around an animal centred pedagogy seem very far and few between and yet, such an approach would appear to have significant potential for not only connecting students to the natural environment but also in promoting its care.

ANIMALS IN LEARNING

Every generation of teachers has faced the significant task of developing and implementing approaches to learning that empower the next generation. However, today we face such profound global challenges that the significance of education in the promotion of sustainability and environmental awareness is now widely recognised. Since the first intergovernmental conference on environmental education, resulting in the Tiblisi Declaration of 1977, there has been genuine development and widespread adoption in mainstream education, of approaches that promote a connection to, and therefore a responsibility for, the natural environment. While these various pedagogical approaches have evolved through various guises over the last 44 years (Scott, 2009), there has been one seemingly constant theme, and that has been a recognition of the interrelationships that we have with other parts of the biosphere and how intertwined and interdependent the relationship is between humans and non-human animals (Sjögren et al., 2015).

This relationship seemingly has particular resonance for young children, as animals appear to represent a strikingly important component of environmental awareness. For example, recent work from Finland suggested that children's concerns around environmental issues did not appear to centre on their own health and well-being, but rather they were concerned more about the deleterious impact of such issues on animals. Their concerns around climate change were more focused on the plight of polar bears, the issue of plastics is seen through its effect on marine life (Soryte & Pakalniskiene, 2019).

As outdoor learning, specifically, gains traction in schools, the concern is that the pedagogical approaches employed reflect this new environment and realise the opportunities for effective teaching (Waite, 2011). The concern is that while the walls may be dissolved, teaching approaches, along with their allied social and political frameworks, remain. Outdoor learning is seen as a mechanism for not only developing and enhancing behavioural characteristics such as confidence and resilience but also, in more recent times perhaps, as a means of developing a greater understanding and appreciation of the natural world.

This increasing interest in outdoor learning, both nationally and internationally, has facilitated a significant body of research work. However, a brief review of the research carried out shows an interesting omission. Since 2000, two of the leading peer-reviewed journals in outdoor learning have published nearly 1000 research papers (approximately one a week). Research to inform the development and effectiveness of outdoor learning appears to concentrate primarily on relationships within and between the student/s and the natural environment. Popular topic areas include initiatives such as Forest Schools and the taught programmes of outdoor, or field studies, centres. It is interesting to note that only one paper in nineteen years of research in these two journals, deals with learning and animals.

At a time when the Care Farm movement and animal-assisted therapies, both discussed elsewhere in this volume, are playing an increasingly important role in education and social support, animals are curiously absent from the research literature. Papers review 'nature therapies' and the important benefits to be gained by people being out in the natural environment, but animals seem quite often to be invisible within those environments. Attempts to connect to nature therefore appear somewhat ill-defined and suggest a connection to only aspects or parts of nature. Moreover, a common theme often discussed within the literature is the importance of a sense of 'place' in outdoor learning and 'place-based learning'. Often such considerations rarely consider the importance of animals, despite regularly using terms such as ecology, environment and ecosystem. Curiously, an appreciation of the actual functioning of such systems requires an understanding of the importance of animal ecology. Yet, when the living environment of places is considered, it is more likely to be the floristic rather than the faunal. Furthermore, few explore the efficacy of a more animal centred approach for promoting compassionate education and thereby enhancing the proposed, deeper, aims of environmental and outdoor learning.

Of course, another of the key aspects of sustainability education is the emphasis that it places on systems thinking (Orr, 2017). Developing strategies that stress the interrelationships within the human and the natural world is perceived as key to developing a mindset that no longer looks for simple, linear approaches to highly complex and interwoven problems. The interrelationships and effects that regulate or adjust a system have become the focus of such approaches. Of course, outdoor learning, where the student is placed in some form of the external environment beyond the confinement of a classroom, is also regarded as an allied approach to sustainability education. It may promote a connection to place, it may encourage a more sensory form of learning leading to a more emotional association to the environment. The ideas of systemic thinking seem ideally suited to an outdoor education particularly given that one of its primary aims is the promotion of our connection to the living world. Indeed, the literature is full of pedagogical approaches and activities that are specifically designed to heighten the sense of environmental connectivity. Yet, a cursory glance through, rather intriguingly, shows a curious absence of animals. Common-place activities sometimes promote an understanding of certain biological principles, such as camouflage, or predator/prey relationships, but generally, these are through role-playing, or games. Beyond what are generically termed 'mini-beasts' living animals are fairly low in terms of visibility in most outdoor learning activities.

The static nature of plants is an obvious reason as to why outdoor learning activities are often based around them. This is not to say that learning in the outdoors about plants or using them in teaching narratives has little value, quite the reverse. Their stillness, beauty and seasonal change are all incredibly important characteristics for teaching. However, given the ideas around systems thinking, it seems incongruous that such an important element of the natural world in seemingly absent, namely animals.

Animals are certainly more difficult to study in that they may seem at least to be absent. Their transience and elusiveness make them significantly more difficult to study. Yet, to ignore them is to almost wilfully misrepresent the nature of the living world, where plant-animal interactions are such an essential characteristic. The living world can only be understood by considering the role of animals and yet so rarely do they seem to be considered. In turn, this is not only an issue around the understanding of how the natural world operates, but it is also missing a potential means to promote the very sense of connection to of the environment that outdoor learning encourages.

The revolution in outdoor learning with children has seen more emotive and creative approaches replace those of the more 'point and tell' variety and are undoubtedly both qualitative improvements as well as far more enjoyable and engaging. However, looking at the earlier published works from the 1980s suggesting activities for children, the nature-based activities do include those that explore the animal kingdom, but mainly from a role-play perspective with children imagining the reactions of animals to events. This is not necessarily an approach shared with activities related to plants and trees. In more recent times, there has been more consideration of animals in outdoor learning with some texts including complete sections on the animal kingdom (Porter, 2018). However, it is interesting to note that science and outdoors texts seem curiously bereft on the topic, even including those purporting to take an original and creative approach (Cutting & Kelly, 2015).

As Forest Schools programmes have grown and the move to educate outdoors has gained increasing traction, it is curiously ironic that animals, particularly mammals, remain out of the mainstream teaching approaches. Children may be able to make wooden spoons, but may not be able to recognise a particular bird-call.

If we are to promote agency in future generations, this curiously lopsided approach to the teaching of the natural world seems to be missing an opportunity to engage children and young people effectively. There is no implied criticism levelled at initiatives such as Forest Schools programmes, they have been extremely successful in the promotion of outdoor learning and the outdoors, for some, being an effective therapy. However, one wonders about the qualitative difference that a child would have with a tree compared to that with another sentient creature.

It is important to stress that this chapter is not a call for more visits to animal holding facilities, such as zoos, sanctuaries and wildlife parks, but rather one that suggests adaptations, or additions, to outdoor pedagogy. These include simply building activities around listening to bird song, planting for insects, or building potential nesting sites for hedgehogs or other small mammals. Indeed, sometimes even the simple recognition of the existence of animals in the natural environment would be a positive step.

However, it is the case that many animals are held in captivity in holding facilities, such as zoos, aquaria, and sanctuaries. The undoubted ethical considerations of zoos and animals being held in captivity are contentious and are never far away, nor should they be, yet the constraints of this chapter do not allow an exploration of this debate. However, while animals appear largely absent from research into outdoor learning in the natural environment, there is a significant research literature concerning learning during visits by children to see animals in captivity. In so far as visits to such sites may constitute 'the outdoors' in senso stricto, it is difficult to distance observations of animals in captivity from the prevailing anthropocentric sense of humans being in environmental control.

Visitors to zoos may view exotic animals from around the globe. However, one of the primary risks of such visits, to see exotic species, is to give the impression that animals live elsewhere, well, certainly the interesting ones. Of course, the animal kingdom is all around us and outdoor learning has an important role in emphasising this. There are increasingly impressive resources available online to develop such teaching approaches, produced by a wide range of organisations, including the RSPCA and the RSPB. A crucial point here and one that reinforces the seeming absence of animals as learning resource in learning programmes general and outdoor learning specifically is that beyond some general taxonomy in Key Stage 2, animals and their welfare are largely absent from the National Curricula of England, Wales and Scotland. This of course does not unduly undermine its importance, as in the National Curriculum for England in 2000 the word 'sustainability' appeared 29 times. By 2013, it had fallen to zero (Cutting & Kelly, 2015). However, education for sustainability initiatives have continued despite this. Therefore, the emphasis chosen for teaching may be beyond the banality of government documents and the contextual positioning of education is perhaps what hinders our approach to the living world.

When considering the nature and transmission of ideas around promoting a more sustainable world through education it is almost inevitable that questions arise over the anthropocentric approaches of much of mainstream education (Pedersen, 2010a). Placing humans as the central focus in this way is problematic for sustainability as it narrows wider, alternative perspectives, resultantly emphasising human needs over planetary. Such humanist perspectives not only hinder our full appreciation of nature of the issues the world faces, but may also continue to promote a utilitarian perspective of the planet, that places ecosystems under our control and that ultimately perpetuates, or even worsens the situation.

Post-human perspectives go some way in at least recognising humans as animals within the biosphere and a Systems Thinking approach puts the onus not on the individual, but rather on the relationships that surround us (Sterling, 2001). It is here, in our relationships with the animals with which we share the biosphere where we may well find the greatest traction for new approaches that promote, not only a rational acceptance of the importance of sustainability but also a deeper, more emotional, engagement with the world around us. Perhaps moving us forward in the journey of education for sustainability. Here animals can, perhaps, play an important role.

It was not through the observation of animals in captivity that leads to the lyrical writing of Thoreau, or a visit to an aviary that led J. A. Baker to write 'The Peregrine'. It was rather the sight of animals, fleetingly glimpsed at times in their natural environment. This was the inspiration for both, and their writing has, as a result, been an inspiration for others. It is the multi-dimensional nature that situated learning provides that is key here. Observing animals from behind bars, or more recently Perspex screens is a primarily one-dimensional experience. Being physically close to animals, with no barriers, or sharing a habitat with animals is a multi-dimensional experience and a richer one for it.

In conclusion, we have a curiously complex relationship with animals. Our attitudes to farm animals, our relationships with pets and our association to wildlife may, on occasion be pragmatically contradictory. However, compassion is rarely absent. The closer we are to animals, both physically and perhaps importantly, emotionally, the greater the sense and feeling of compassion appears to be. The protection and safeguarding of the physical environment is often promoted in terms of our responsibility to the 'next generation', that the planet is somehow a bequeathment from one generation to the next. This has its antecedence in the various definitions of 'sustainability'. Yet, while a worthwhile sentiment, it does however, lack the sense of urgency that contemporary data around the Sixth Great Extinction suggest is required. With over 500 species of land animals alone likely to go extinct in the next 20 years (Carrington, 2020) profound and detrimental change to the planet is a problem that we as a generation will experience. No longer is it the exotic species that are under threat, but the more common mammals (Díaz et al., 2019; Pavoine et al., 2019), once common woodland song-birds (Birdlife International, 2020) and pollinating insects (Cardoso et al., 2020). Animals and insects once common in our own localities and lives are increasingly scarce. It is perhaps through the plight of the animal kingdom that the most effective sustainable and environmental agency resides.

This chapter began by looking at the importance of animals in some of the most influential books around environmental thought and education. It is perhaps appropriate then to conclude by considering the words of a fictional animal character. In one part of the children's book 'The Wind in the Willows', in itself a marvellous evocation of the countryside and the natural world, Badger explains to Mole that he did not truly build his house in the Wild Wood. He actually lived in a series of tunnels that he had merely cleaned out. The original tunnels had once been part of a human city. This great city had subsequently become abandoned and over time, the Wild Wood had re-established. He concludes that people and cities come and go but badgers, like nature, are patient and eventually prevail. While this lyrical passage reminds us of the resilience of nature and its capacity for recovery, it was written in the world of 1908. The changes and pressures the world of 2020 faces are considerably more profound and the potential contribution from education in promoting a sustainable world are proportionately more urgent. If we are to find educational solutions, perhaps we should look beyond the somewhat functional utility of environmental curation, but rather to a wider form of environmental compassion. If we are to effect positive change through a broader and more emotional engagement with the environment, then our relationships with animals provides an effective gateway. Given the empathetic and immediate nature our relationship with animals, if we are to promote such a form of environmental compassion, perhaps we look little further than those influential environmental authors such a Leopold, Thoreau and Carson, who inspired a generation by identifying the importance of animals in our learning and appreciation of the world around us. A lesson perhaps that we as educators need to relearn.

References

Beratz, L., & Hazeira, H. A. (2012). Children's literature as an important tool for education for sustainability and the environment. *International Electronic Journal of Environmental Education, 2*(1), 31–36.

Betz, M. (2015, July 12). Walden Pond still inspires 170 years later. *The Philadelphia Inquirer.* https://www.inquirer.com/philly/opinion/currents/20150712_Walden_Pond_still_inspires_170_years_later.html Accessed 23.01.20

Beusterien, J., & Baird-Callicott, J. (2013). Humor and politics through the animal in Cervantes and Leopold. *Comparative Literature Studies, 50*(1), 43–63.

BirdLife International. (2020). IUCN Red List for birds. Retrieved February 10, 2020, from http://www.birdlife.org

Bradbury, D. (2013). Bridges to global citizenship: Ecologically sustainable futures utilising children's literature in teacher education. *Australian Journal of Environmental Education, 29*(2), 221–237.

Buller, H. (2012). "One slash of light, then gone": Animals as movement. *Études Rurales, 189,* 139–153.

Buller, H. (2014). Animal geographies 1. *Progress in Human Geography, 38*(2), 308–318.

Cardoso, P. S., Barton, K., Birkhofer, F., Chichorro, C., Deacon, T. F., et al. (2020). Scientists' warning to humanity on insect extinctions. *Biological Conservation.* https://doi.org/10.1016/j.biocon.2020.108426

Carrington, D. (2020). Sixth Mass Extinction of Animals Accelerating Say Scientists. *The Guardian.* https://www.theguardian.com/environment/2020/jun/01/sixth-mass-extinction-of-wildlife-accelerating-scientists-warn. Accessed June 1, 2020.

Cutting, R. L., & Kelly, O. (2015). *Creative teaching in primary science*. Sage.

Díaz, S., Settele, J., Brondízio, E. S., Ngo, H. T., Agard, J., Arneth, A., ... Garibaldi, L. A. (2019). Pervasive human-driven decline of life on Earth points to the need for transformative change. *Science, 366*(6471).

Dixon, B. (2016). Deriving moral considerability from Leopold's A Sand County Almanac. *Ethics, Policy & Environment, 19*(2), 196–212. https://doi.org/1 0.1080/21550085.2016.1195191

Ganea, P. A., Ma, L., & DeLoache, J. S. (2011). Young children's learning and transfer of biological information from picture books to real animals. *Child Development, 82*(5), 1421–1433.

Geertz, M. S. (2016). (Un)Real animals: Anthroporphism and early learning about animals. *Child Development Perspectives, 10*(1), 10–14.

Greenpeace International. (2018). https://www.greenpeace.org/international/story/11658/a-brief-history-of-environmentalism/

Hughes, T. (2003). *Ted Hughes. Collected poems*. Faber and Faber.

Katz, E. (1995). The traditional ethics of natural resource management (pp 101/116). In R. L. Knight & S. F. Bates (Eds.), *A new century for natural resource management*. Island Press.

Kroll, G. (2001). The "silent springs" of Rachel Carson: Mass media and the origins of modern environmentalism. *Public Understanding of Science, 10*, 403–420.

Lindsey, J. (1999). *Jane Goodall. 40 years at Gombe. A tribute to four decades of wildlife research, education and conservation. Stewart*. Tabori & Chang Inc.

Meyer, D. S., & Rohlinger, D. A. (2012). *Big Books and Social Movements: A Myth of Ideas and Social Change Social Problems, 59*(1), 136–153.

Millstein, R. L. (2018). Debunking myths about Aldo Leopold's land ethic. *Biological Conservation, 217*, 391–396.

Nimer, J., & Lundahl, B. (2007). Animal-assisted therapy: A meta-analysis. *Anthrozoös, 20*(3), 225–238. https://doi.org/10.2752/089279307X224773

Orr, D. W. (2004). *Earth in mind. On education, environment and the human prospect* (10th Anniversary Ed.). Island Press.

Orr, D. W. (2017). *Foreword in EarthEd: Rethinking education on a changing planet*. Worldwatch Institute. Island Press.

Pavoine, S., Bonsall, M. B., Davies, T. J., & Masi, S. (2019). Mammal extinctions and the increasing isolation of humans on the tree of life. *Ecology and Evolution, 9*(3), 914–924.

Pedersen, H. (2010a). *Animals in schools. Processes and strategies in human-animal education*. West Lafayette. Purdue University Press.

Pedersen, H. (2010b). Is 'the Posthuman' Educable? On the convergence of educational philosophy, animal studies, and posthumanist theory. *Discourse: Studies in the Cultural Politics of Education, 31*(2), 237–250.

Pedersen, H. (2019). The contested space of animals in education: A response to the "Animal Turn" in education for sustainable development. *Education Sciences, 9*(211).

Philo, C., & Wilbert, C. (2000). *Animal spaces, beastly places.* Routledge.

Porter, H. (2018). *Educating outside: Curriculum-linked outdoor learning ideas for primary teachers.* Bloomsbury Education.

Puig, J., & Echarri, F. (2018). Environmentally significant life experiences: The look of a wolf in the lives of Ernest T. Seton, Aldo Leopold and Félix Rodríguez de la Fuente. *Environmental Education Research, 24*(5), 678–693.

Quin Liu. (2017). Animals in Walden. *English Language and Literature Studies., 7*(3), 43–47.

Scott, W. (2009). Environmental education research: 30 years on from Tbilisi. *Environmental Education Research, 15*(2), 155–164.

Shultz. (2015). The moral judgments of Henry David Thoreau. *The New Yorker.* American Chronicles October 19. Retrieved February 23, 2020, from https://www.newyorker.com/magazine/2015/10/19/pond-scum

Simmons, P., & Armstrong, L. (2007). Bestiary. An introduction. In P. Simmons & L. Armstrong (Eds.), *Knowing animals.* Brill.

Singer, P. (1975). *Animal liberation.* The Bodley Head.

Sjögren, H., Gyberg, P., & Henriksson, M. (2015). Human-animal relations beyond the zoo: The quest for a more inclusive sustainability education. *Pedagogy, Culture & Society, 23*(4), 567–615.

Soryte, D., & Pakalniskiene, V. (2019). Why it is important to protect the environment: Reasons given by children. *International Research in Geographical and Environmental Education, 28*(3), 228–241.

Sterling, S. (2001). *Sustainable education: Re-visioning learning and change.* Schumacher briefing; 6. Totnes: Green Books.

Waite, S. (2011). Teaching and learning outside the classroom: Personal values, alternative pedagogies and standards. *Education 3-13, 39 (1)*, 65–82.

Wisner, G. (2017). *Thoreau's animals.* Yale University Press.

Animals as Catalysts for Learning, Personal Growth and Enlightenment

Ben Hart

Introduction

When first born we necessarily explore our new environment through our senses. Even before birth, we have a perceptible sensory awareness, recognising shapes of light and the differing melodies of human voices. Dehaene (2020) suggests that we are born hard-wired, with the capacity to learn through recognition and understanding as an important part of an evolutionary inheritance. It is from birth that we are at our most receptive; unfettered by past or future, we are free of pre-conceptions. Plotkin (2003) refers to this as innocence in the newborn child and suggests that this accepting, non-judgemental innocence is the embodiment of receptivity. It is from this early point that we begin to develop relationships with the world around us. As we grow and explore, we discover that we share the world with other sentient creatures and it is at this point, perhaps, that our connection with other animals develops. The nature of this

B. Hart (✉)
The Donkey Sanctuary, Sidmouth, UK
e-mail: ben.hart@thedonkeysanctuary.org.uk

© The Author(s), under exclusive license to Springer Nature Switzerland AG 2022
R. Cutting, R. Passy (eds.), *Contemporary Approaches to Outdoor Learning*, Palgrave Studies in Alternative Education, https://doi.org/10.1007/978-3-030-85095-1_5

relationship will determine if and how we will learn from our animal companions.

Throughout history, we appear to have had a unique relationship with animals that is beyond the merely functional. From the cave paintings, the parietal art, and the mobiliary art forms of the Palaeolithic, it appears evident that animals were valuable to humans for more than their meat and skins. Many early shamanistic cultures thought of animals as guides, in this world and the next. Their close connection to the environment meant that early humans respected animals for their wisdom of the natural world. Perhaps from our very earliest history animals were regarded as teachers from whom much could be learnt.

Our ancestors have worshipped animal gods or half human-animal gods. Whether they were Egyptian, Hindu, Celtic or Pagan, stories of animal gods have influenced and even perhaps, guided human thinking (Gilhus, 2006; Peruzzetto et al., 2013). Additionally, throughout history animals in stories have also informed, inspired and educated (Spencer, 2020). In Aesop's Fables, for example, all manner of teaching on morals were in the form of stories based on the behaviour and activities of animals and we can see such antecedence in modern literature.

Today our children's lives are filled with animals, be they in nursery rhymes, or caricatures of animals on clothes and toys. We read them storybooks whose main characters are animals and we have any number of soft toy animals to provide comfort and calm throughout our early years. We find them in television programmes, films and games. Blockbuster films with animal characters are so standard that we do not raise an eyebrow at talking donkeys, singing mice, helpful reindeer, emotional horses or cunning dogs. These, albeit anthropomorphic, animal creations mean that at least the form of animals continues to have a role in our education. Yet this appears to take place almost unnoticed.

Throughout childhood, we grow up with animals, who in fictional forms at least, show human emotions and motives and, as a result, develop considerable affection for animal characters. We, therefore, bring animals into the lives of our children, only to later diminish their status, not only as teachers but even as sentient beings. Later we demote them still further from the level of educated, sentient teachers, to simple commodities even, at times, subjecting them to all manner of abuse and welfare restriction (Singer, 1975). At some point in our development, it seems we withdraw from our natural animal connections.

Beyond our developmental relationships with animals, there is research-based evidence that suggests there are physical advantages of growing up and living with animals. Early studies appeared to indicate several ways in which our relationship with companion animals is beneficial (Beck & Meyers, 1996: Bekoff, 2007). Many of these appear related to a reduction in emotional stress. This results in a number of recorded physiological adjustments, such as improved blood pressure and improved recovery times from cardio-vascular illness for those who own pets. Furthermore, children also appear to experience health benefits, as they see pets as members of their families and as such they provide significant emotional support (Monsen, 2001). Further studies, perhaps unsurprisingly, also indicate that children who live with pets are likely to be more confident, more empathetic, socially orientated, suffer lower rates of depression and have higher levels of self-esteem (Friedmann et al., 1980). This is not to suggest that pets act as therapists or mentors for children, and we can reasonably suspect that they do not see their pets as such. However, it would seem to be the case that animals and our close relationship with them, has the potential, at least, to provide a passive, and therefore fairly elusive, range of physical and emotional health benefits (Herzog, 2010).

This chapter is not concerned with the deliberate use of animals in therapy settings. It will, however, explore the nature and effectiveness of learning opportunities that animals create simply by our interaction with them. The chapter will deal explore some of the contemporary research and publications around our relationship with animals, but primarily it will provide observations and insights gained from many years of practical experience in animal behaviour and human behaviour change.

Human-Animal Relationships

Even the naturalist Charles Darwin seems to have been influenced heavily by his relationships with his dogs Polly and a half-bred retriever, Bob. These dogs influenced Darwin's thoughts not only of the consciousness of dogs but even more controversially, on what he and other Victorian writers described as their morality. Certainly, Darwin recognised similarities of behaviour and even emotion within the complexity of the animal kingdom. These ideas around emotions in animals were expressed most clearly in his 1872 book The Expression of Emotions in Animals and Man (Daston & Mitman, 2005, p. 65).

However, even without such carefully observed research, it appears that we also learn from animals in a non-structured way. This learning takes place through our simple interaction with them. Animals provide the opportunity for us, as individuals, to enter into an entirely non-judgemental relationship; to be vulnerable and honest about who we are. It allows us to form a higher expression of ourselves. Perhaps an animal's unreservedness in their response to our behaviour provides a sounding board. Animals behave honestly, expressing their emotions through their behaviour in real-time. The suppression of emotion in animals can be trained, but for the most part, is under a form of stimulus control and outside the boundaries of trained behaviour. Animals, in the way Plotkin (2003) describes young children, are just themselves, active and reactive to whoever is in front of them.

For illustrative purposes, here I will rely on my personal observations from working with both animal behaviour and human behaviour change principles. It is the case that human beings generally hate to feel that they are being manipulated. When we are trying to influence the behaviour of another person, we are keen to express our thoughts and solutions to any problems. Often our 'solutions' will not be contextualised or appropriately nuanced, and may not take into account the individual's situation, environment, history or even personal character. I fear that often talking has come to have a far greater onus than listening. It is often not our ability to act or provide guidance that fails us but rather it is our inability to listen. As a species, humans have come to rely heavily on language as a method of communication. Therefore, our focus on words distracts us to a point where perhaps we begin to misread, or even not notice, more subtle forms of communication. Our reliance on spoken language often overrides our ability to appreciate the micro-signalling of body language or verbal tone. These elusive, nuanced forms of communication provide so much more information than mere words. Without the confusion of spoken words, therefore, animals have a more significant advantage in their ability to read such languages. It is these characteristics that perhaps provide animals with distinct advantages in delivering honest, transparent, and timely communications.

The connection that we may experience with animals might also have an evolutionary origin. Lieberman (2013) suggests that we are evolutionarily 'wired to connect'. Social and emotional pain that we may feel is not only recognised as a threat to our survival, but the existence of social pain *'is a sign that evolution has treated social connection like a necessity, not a luxury'*. It would appear that humans are highly social creatures and that this characteristic is an inherited evolutionary behaviour. There was an evolutionary advantage for our ancestors to align themselves to others of similar social characteristics and learn how to predict the behaviour of other humans through our social interactions. This strategy provided clear advantages for survival.

If social interaction is an evolutionary behaviour and the human community an advantage to survival, it would seem that similar advantages would be gained through the transference of these characteristics to animals. The relationship between dogs and humans has a bond which can be traced back at least 15,000 years to the Bonn-Oberkssel dog. At this Upper Pleistocene archaeological site in Germany, two humans found in a grave had a dog buried with them. Analysis revealed that the dog was deliberately buried with the humans and, although young when it died, the dog had suffered from canine distemper between ages 19 and 23 weeks. The dog could not have survived the disease to that age without considerable human support, This suggests that perhaps 15,000 years ago, some humans were already developing emotional bonds with their dogs rather than simply a utilitarian ownership (Janssens et al., 2018).

The evolutionary advantages of social behaviour are, of course, not the preserve of humans alone. The recognition of such social behaviours in other mammals may suggest that they may also be hardwired for connection. There are recognisable and significant advantages to survival around parental nurture and membership of the pack or herd. Such connectedness has been crucial in the evolution of mammals. It appears that there is a latent evolutionary ability for humans and animals to develop social relationships. The potential of a connection at a more emotive level perhaps requires further exploration of the characteristics of the nature of the mind.

Lieberman (2013) believes that one of the great evolutionary features of the human mind is the process of 'mentalising'; the ability to think what the other person is thinking. This so-called hard wiring for social projection is the basis for the theory of mind in humans. This is the ability to learn to think with other people's minds, and has clear evolutionary advantages. To put ourselves in other people's minds and to see, even appreciate, different perspectives would have given us unique insights and would have cemented social relationships and hierarchies.

From the development of the human theory of mind and our ability to understand what others are thinking, it is perhaps only one small step to consider human minds being able to understand the minds of other species. However, to what level and to what extent such projection may operate to is open to conjecture.

While scientists now generally agree that animals can feel emotions, what they feel or how they feel is still a mystery. Is the dog really feeling guilty because they raided the waste bin during the owner's absence from the house? Or, just as likely, have they have just been smart enough to learn that offering submissive body language avoids confrontation and punishment when they register our angry, disapproving body language?

One of the complicating factors here is our tendency to anthropomorphise, as discussed earlier in relation to literature and modern media. We, initially at least, simply afford animals with human behaviour traits. We have to accept that we can only judge animal experiences of the world based on our world-view. This fact means that we tend to interpret the behaviour of our animals with our anthropocentric filter.

Without a greater formal understanding of animal behaviour and cognition, most humans naturally view animal behaviour through their personal perceptions. Hence, when a human views an animal's behaviour, that behaviour is unconsciously filtered and interpreted to fit certain beliefs, cultural norms, wishes, desires, fears and expectations. Again, from a personal perspective, as a behaviourist, I have seen exactly the same expression of an animal's behaviour be interpreted, by different people, as both positive and negative.

It is common even to see the whole character of the same animal be viewed entirely differently by different people. While one person may consider a donkey's character or behaviour as fearful, confused, and nervous, at the same time a different observer will observe the same animal's behaviour as naughty, bad, and deliberately deceiving.

The origins for such variation in such interpretations are complex and, no doubt, have explanations in social, cultural and developmental psychology. Here, however, a key observation is that such interpretations create an opportunity to view our behaviour through the mirror of our animals. Thirty years ago as a young agricultural student, I observed the 'disobedient behaviour' of the livestock in my charge and labelled them as unreasonable, annoying or just stupid. Now, with greater understanding, when I look back, I see that same behaviour differently. I now marvel at both the learning ability and problem-solving skills of those same animals. The animals' behaviour has not necessarily changed, but my interpretations of it have.

What Is the Animal-Human Bond, and How Does It Help Us Develop as Humans?

It may be apposite at this point to address the fact that sometimes people do terrible things to animals. Not all children who grow up with a pet treat that pet well or develop great empathy. Furthermore, our recognised empathy and connection to animals does not negate factory farming, poaching of endangered species, and neglect and the mistreatment of animals in countries around the world.

Our increasing need for cheap and available food at a global level may be one reason for these abuses, with farm animals being seen more like units of income rather than sentient creatures. Similarly, poverty is one of the drivers for poaching and poor farming. Perhaps, in the so-called high-income countries, our ability to relate to animals is becoming more restricted as we become increasingly disconnected from them. The modern world is reducing our animal contact time through growing mechanisation, increasing farm sizes, urbanisation and technology use. The fewer opportunities there are for animals touch our lives, the easier it is for us to absent ourselves from methods that mistreat them.

When working in more impoverished communities worldwide, it has struck me how difficult it is to ask for the treatment of animals to be elevated to a higher position in practice. When owners struggle to secure the physiological needs of their children for food, water and warmth, there is a conflict between resources for their children or their donkey. The fear and insecurity that so many people around the world live in make it very difficult to elevate animals to a level of social well-being beyond their own and that of their dependants.

However, this is not to say that people in impoverished circumstances do not learn from their animals or that they do not value their animals. Undoubtedly, challenging environments make it difficult to prioritise the well-being of and interaction with animals. The fact that many people living in such harsh conditions do so gives more weight perhaps to the theory that our need for social connection with animals is essential to the human mind.

It is perhaps only the affluence that is enjoyed in western societies that has facilitated the rise in veganism, animal rights, and higher welfare food standards. Without the uncertainty of poverty, our deeper, emotional, relationship with animals is remembered. However, while economics and environmental prosperity have an enormous influence on the way we feel about animals, what we learn from them remains an intriguing characteristic.

Given how different economic and social environments influence our relationships, the nature of the connection between humans and animals is hard to define. The American Veterinary Medical Association (2021) broadly describes it as any situation where an interchange, at any level, takes place. It goes on,

> *The human-animal bond is a mutually beneficial and dynamic relationship between people and animals that is influenced by behaviors considered essential to the health and well-being of both. The bond includes but is not limited to the emotional, psychological, and physical interactions of people, animals, and the environment. The veterinarian's role in the human-animal bond is to maximise the potential of this relationship between people and animals and specifically to promote the health and well-being of both.* (p. 1)

Put more succinctly, Vanfleet and Faa-thompson (2017) state that the importance is '*the concept that relationships exist between two or more entities and that they are built on mutual influence, what one does affects the other* (p. 2).

These two definitions align very closely with my own experiences as an animal behaviourist. The bond between both human and animal is mutually beneficial and reflects the character and behaviour of both parties. The human-animal relationship also affects the emotional, psychological, and physical well-being of both.

Being around animals allows us to learn about ourselves. However, the degree of learning that takes place will depend upon the individual's environment, their journey and exploration of their experiences. Sometimes the connection with animals can be profound. If the animal provides a non-judgemental feeling of safety for a person, then they may have the opportunity to feel validated for who they are, potentially for the first time.

In our modern world, where there is so much pressure to perform and to conform, it is easy to feel that we are not good enough. There is an explicit danger of children growing up feeling inadequate or incapable. Social media and a celebrity culture provide unrealistic images of achievement, happiness and success. In a world where instant online comparisons may be made to others' lives, it is perhaps, easy to see why so many people feel judged.

Experiencing the perceived non-judgemental unconditional approval of an animal seems to validate our existence. A brief moment of feeling essential and connected to another living being without rigid controls of therapy or coaching but simply to spend quality time with an animal can be a disarmingly simple way to find value in ourselves.

Achieving learning, growth and enlightenment with animals is often unintentional. We grow and learn because we take inspiration from them. We feel better from being around them, and the clarity of mind that brings allows us to focus on what is important. We slow down and become fully present and mindful to experience our animal more. If we pay attention, the constant reflection of our behaviour from our animal tells us when we are off track. When we are distant or angry, their behaviour reflects this, and we have to control our emotions if we want the reward of the social connection our brain so desperately requires.

Learning Because of Behaviour Issues

It is clear, as a practitioner, that when working with animals that have behaviour issues, owners who are seeking to help their animal have a significant opportunity to learn about themselves.

If we have an animal with behavioural problems, when working with that animal we must explore the human role as part of the problem. In doing so, we will likely take some ownership for the cause or continuation of the problem. In doing so, there is an innate acceptance of our part in the animal's behaviour. If, as suggested, our behaviour is reflected in that of our animals, it follows that we must change our behaviour to expedite a change in those animals.

We are naturally curious about what is occurring in the minds of our animal companions. The social connectedness that we feel with animals and our ability to anthropomorphise inevitably leads us to ask questions about how an animal is thinking, feeling or experiencing their world. The search for answers to these questions leads us to an ever-closer relationship. As our bonds strengthen, we begin to feel the emotions that our animals feel. Even though we can never fully understand how an animal experiences such emotions, we can sense their expression of sadness, depression, joy, boredom or playfulness, and we can feel these for ourselves.

We know when animals are mentally struggling, we know when they are fearful or anxious, and, as we develop greater empathy, we do not want them to experience those emotions. Again, through my work, I have found that people often blame their animals for being naughty or deliberately acting in a way that is seen as deviant. However, using these incorrect labels of an animal's behaviour is in itself a stage of human growth. For helping people have a better relationship with their animals often involves helping them to have a better relationship with themselves first, and then improving the communication between the two of them. When working with a client, it is often necessary to explore their understanding of animal emotions and to look at their motivations within the relationship. If we blame an animal for expressive behaviour, it becomes almost impossible to look at ourselves as a cause of that behaviour. However, blaming the animal is very much an anthropocentric state of mind and needs to be challenged before the person can move on to helping their animal. It is in this personal reflection that profound learning can take place.

If I have an owner who is outcome led and in whom the achievement of goals is a measurement of their self-esteem and ability, they may bring that desire to their relationship with their animal. The goal-orientated approach focuses on success rather than the animal's experience and leads the owner pushing the animal past the threshold of their comfort zone. Through the process of classical conditioning, this constant pushing of the animal's boundaries beyond their fear thresholds causes the animal to associate the human to the negative emotions experienced during the interactions.

Horses, donkeys and mules do not know their owner's ambition or the degree of success that is attributed to the final achievement of a goal. The conflict between the ambitious owner and mindful animal can only be mutually resolved if the owner learns to put their goal-driven behaviour aside, at least while working with the animal. As the owner learns to pay more attention to enjoying the journey and the animal's experience of the interaction, the relationship develops a positive focus.

Practical experience has provided several occasions to witness that, once the owner has become aware of their behaviour and experienced a paradigm shift in their behaviour, the experience of valuing the journey begins to prevail in other areas of the owner's life.

I recently asked a friend, who is a successful CEO, how he thought his family dog had changed his life. He told the story of being tired one evening after work and 'feeling grumpy'. Once home he took their young, mixed-breed, hairy rescue dog out for training. Despite his usual focus and attention on his owner's training, this evening the dog wouldn't work or listen. Instead, the young dog spent the session just jumping up at his owner, perhaps trying to appease his tired, tense human. My friend recognised his mistake and said: 'I never did that again.' In effect, his dog was teaching him about emotional control and appropriate response.

Just being with animals that have behaviour issues creates the opportunity to start a learning journey. The need to help another animal ease their discomfort and suffering seems to motivate us more than trying to alleviate our discomfort. My behaviour experience has consistently shown me that, as we begin to explore behavioural issues in our animals, we inevitably begin to explore our personal behaviour. This exploration of our behaviour for the benefit of an animal appears to be another stage of human growth. It is worth emphasising again, that moving on from blaming the animal to accepting responsibility for the situation is key to both helping the animal and for greater emotional freedom for the individual.

Having taken responsibility for an animal's behaviour, we seem willing and able to prioritise time to our animal's needs, more so than we are to our own personal development. Somehow, it seems that helping ourselves is quite often perceived as selfish but assisting another animal with a behaviour issue is an essential priority.

Of course, the more we understand ourselves, the greater opportunity we have to understand others. The more we know the minds of others, the more we know our own minds.

Working with an animal that has a behaviour issue creates a path of learning. The animal becomes the catalyst for change. To help the animal we need to explore new perspectives and ask the questions that the animals cannot ask for themselves. We need to deploy a range of empathetic skills at the same time reflecting on our own positioning.

Of course, often the animal does not have a behavioural issue, but rather is being trained in preparation for life in domestication. The very act of training our dog or equid for veterinary intervention, travelling, safe handling, hoof care or nail clipping all create a challenge. Bringing up any young animal or living with a rescue animal means that we need to explore how to prepare them for life with us and how we prepare for being with them.

Ultimately, our relationship with animals comes down to our ability to communicate. Our ability to communicate comes down to our ability to empathise and understand them and ourselves. As we improve our non-language communication skills, we have to enhance our understanding of the mind of another non-human animal. Being able to communicate well, by observation, listening and expressing ourselves, is a critical factor of deeper authenticity.

There can be no doubt that our interaction with animals has a vast range of possibilities for learning and personal growth. Opportunities come in a variety of forms, but the difference between this form of animal learning and those of animal-assisted therapies is the unstructured nature of learning the absence of a third party, an interpreter, filtering and deciding on the lesson outcomes.

It is interesting to note that animal therapy has been developed from observing the natural benefits of interaction with animals and formalising this process. However, we set out knowing the goal of treatment is to improve ourselves in some way. Perhaps the fact that the therapy facilitator and client know we are working on changing ourselves changes the effects we experience, much like the observer effect in physics.

When we are just with animals, change happens not as a reason for the interaction but as a consequence of caring for an animal or trying to improve their lives. We make our own agenda and find our own lessons through the need for social connection and love. We don't affect the results we get by setting out to observe change; we just travel together on a journey that may lead to change; there is no pressure to change. Our need for deep social connection and talent for anthropomorphism means our relationship with animals creates a non-judgemental opportunity for creeping self-reflection and changing our intrinsic thought patterns.

Much of what we know about being human has come from the scientific observation of animals and their behaviour. We have much to learn from animals. The benefits of children in particular merely being around animals is now widely documented. However, to hunt, farm, kill and eat animals, humankind has to use our ability to doublethink. This curious human characteristic allows us to love, respect and even worship the animals we choose as teachers and companions, and then to justify killing and eating them. In the accepting innocence that we see in the eyes of animals, we can reflect perhaps, on how much we still have to learn about our own nature as a species.

References

American Veterinary Medical Association. (2021). *Human animal bond*. https://www.avma.org/one-health/human-animal-bond

Beck, A. M., & Meyers, N. M. (1996). Health enhancement and companion animal ownership. *Annual Review of Public Health, 17,* 247–257.

Bekoff, M. (2007). *The emotional lives of animals: A leading scientist explores animal joy, sorrow, and empathy and why they matter.* New World Library.

Daston, L., & Mitman, G. (2005). *Thinking with animals, new perspectives on anthropomorphism.* Columbia University Press.

Dehaene, S. (2020). *How we learn: The new science of education and the brain.* Penguin Books.

Friedmann, E., Katcher, A. H., Lynch, J. J., & Thomas, S. A. (1980). Animal companions and one year survival of patients after discharge from a coronary care unit. *Public Health Reports, 95,* 307–312.

Gilhus, I. S. (2006). *Animals, gods and humans: Changing attitudes to animals in Greek, Roman and early Christian ideas.* Routledge.

Herzog, H. (2010). *Some we love, some we hate, Some we eat: Why it's so difficult to talk about animals.* Harper Collins.

Janssens, L., Giemsch, L., Schmitz, R., Street, M., Van Dongen, S., & Crombé, P. (2018). A new look at an old dog: Bonn-Oberkassel reconsidered. *Journal of Archaeological Science, 92,* 126–138.

Lieberman, M. (2013). *Social: Why our brains are wired to connect.* Oxford University Press.

Monsen, R. B. (2001). Children and pets. *Journal of Paediatric Nursing, 16*(3), 197–198. https://doi.org/10.1053/jpdn.2001.25268

Peruzzetto, A., Metzger, F. D., & Dirven, L. (Eds.). (2013). *Animals, gods and men from east to west: Papers on archaeology and history in honour of Roberta Venco Ricciardi.* BAR International Series.

Plotkin, B. (2003). *Soulcraft: Crossing into the mysteries of nature and the psyche.* New World Library.

Singer, P. (1975). *Animal liberation: A new ethics for the treatment of our animals.* New York Review.

Spencer, J. (2020). *'I Was An Ass': Writing about animals in the age of revolution.* Oxford University Press.

Vanfleet, R., & Faa-thompson, T. (2017). *Assisted play therapy.* Professional Resource Exchange Inc.

'All They Need to Know Is Tigers Are Awesome': The Place of Animal Pedagogies in Twenty-First-Century Schools

Rowena Passy, Katherine Gulliver, and Beth Gompertz

INTRODUCTION

Writing in 2010, Pedersen argued that there has been a 'silence' (p. 241) in educational research around the nature of animal-human relationships for two principal reasons. The first is that Western education is founded on the humanist tradition, which we take to be a broad approach that aims to encourage human flourishing, underpinned by Enlightenment thinking that a rational, scientific approach to problem-solving will lead to social progress and improvement. Although millions of people have been lifted out of poverty by economic growth, there is a view that such an approach is no longer appropriate in the 21st century that is marked by environmental and humanitarian crises (Mirchandani, 2020). Carson's

R. Passy (✉) • K. Gulliver • B. Gompertz
Institute of Education, University of Plymouth, Plymouth, UK
e-mail: R.Passy@plymouth.ac.uk; katherine.gulliver@plymouth.ac.uk;
beth.gompertz@plymouth.ac.uk

© The Author(s), under exclusive license to Springer Nature
Switzerland AG 2022
R. Cutting, R. Passy (eds.), *Contemporary Approaches to Outdoor
Learning*, Palgrave Studies in Alternative Education,
https://doi.org/10.1007/978-3-030-85095-1_6

1962 publication *Silent Spring* demonstrated how deeply flawed an anthropocentric notion of improvement can be, and her account of ways in which human activity was leading to widespread poisoning and destruction of non-human life remains profoundly disturbing. The point has been further brought home by the 2020–2021 pandemic that has demonstrated how wildlife habitat destruction leads to changes in animal populations which, in turn, increase the risk of zoonotic diseases (Gibb et al., 2020) such as Covid-19 (Carrington, 2020).

The second, linked reason given by Pederson is that in the West, young people are socialised into a capitalist system that is focused on the notions of growth, expansion and productivity, and there is little room within this process for animals other than in relation to consumption and/or production (Pedersen, 2010, pp. 241–242). Pupils in England are taught to aspire to passing exams and progressing to the next level of education, with the ultimate aim of accessing an economically-rewarding job; less obviously they are taught to compete rather than collaborate, that sustainability is a niche subject and different subject areas are compartmentalised rather than connected (Daniel Smith, 2020). In addition, careers advice is now 'patchy' in schools (Christie, 2017, p. 404), with the advent of austerity politics from 2010 meaning fewer specialist advisers and networks to support students with a diversity of choices (e.g. Passy, 2012). The metric of graduate income level ('Graduate Outcomes') is now an important contributor to the English university league tables, emphasising the desirability of financial outcomes to extended education. Together, these factors contribute to an individualistic approach to career development (see Graeber, 2019) and help to create an absence of discussion around the possibilities offered by alternative, compassionate and/or charitable employment routes.

Over the past ten or so years, however, there has been some international resistance to test-dominated forms of education, and outdoor learning, seen as practical and experiential learning activities conducted outside (Passy et al., 2019), is an important part of this resistance. Gilchrist et al. (2016, p. 1) report that learning in natural spaces has undergone 'something of a renaissance' for three main reasons: test-dominated systems fail to provide a rounded education that engages students' curiosity and wider sense of morality; for several reasons, children are spending less time outside than their forebears, which is a contributory factor to rising levels of obesity and mental ill-health in young people; and children's relative detachment from the outdoor environment seems to mean they have less emotional commitment to and assume less responsibility for the natural world (Gilchrist et al., 2016, pp. 3–6). As policy-makers have begun to absorb the implications of these developments, outdoor learning in England seems to be shifting from a bottom-up approach, with a wide range of services offered by public, private and charitable organisations, towards a more coherent approach of policy-based funding to support schools in taking children outdoors (Passy et al., 2019); the government has pledged to spend £10 million on this between 2019–2022 (HMG, 2018, p. 75). Other examples of a more coordinated approach across the UK can be seen in the growth of the Institute of Outdoor Learning regional research hubs, which support research across the sector; the Council for Learning Outside the Classroom taking a leading role in coordinating the sector's response to the Department for Education about Covid-19; an increasing number of universities now offering different aspects of outdoor learning in their initial teacher education and Master's courses; and the Royal Horticultural Society's success in recruiting 26,000 member schools and groups in their long-standing Campaign for School Gardening (https://www.rhs.org.uk/schoolgardeningdonations).

But within these positive developments, there is an absence; animals are largely missing from research and practice in outdoor learning, as our colleague Roger Cutting (e.g. 2019) has often commented. There has, however, been an 'animal turn' in different branches of environmental education, humanities and social science that explores the place and role of animals in the natural world, and this has helped to challenge the notion that humans are a separate—and superior—species (Russell & Spannring, 2019, p. 1137). Scholars within environmental education have suggested raising levels of human-animal interaction as a direct way of encouraging understanding of humans' place in the world 'within the larger context of the anthropocene' (Dolby, 2019, p. 403) and, as people with long-term involvement with animals—Passy is a farmers' daughter and was a qualified riding instructor (BHSI) before shifting to academia; Gulliver is a lifelong dog lover; Gompertz studied ecology before adopting education as a career, has never been without a dog and now lives on a farm—we agree that including this kind of education in schools could support children and young people's development.

Equally, we are aware that pedagogies involving animals, or 'animal pedagogies', in schools have had little research attention. Anecdotal evidence suggests that they tend to be facilitated through visits and trips, or confined to farm schools and those that keep pets on the school grounds.

The English National Curriculum currently has elements associated with animals in science, but this learning tends to be focused on animal classification and life cycles, and another potential avenue of bringing animals into learning via the Personal, Social and Health Education (PSHE) curriculum is a matter of choice for individual teachers. If animal pedagogies are to be engaging, informative and meaningful to young people, they need to be based on secure subject knowledge and careful thought with respect to aims, content and technique before introduction to the classroom.

This chapter is an exploration into animal pedagogies, focusing on our research into the views of employees from animal or conservation charities and organisations on the type of learning young people should, or could, experience. In the next section we report on the research methodology. This is followed by a discussion on the two main areas of learning suggested by our research participants, and we bring the chapter to a close with reflections on pedagogical principles and approaches in relation to learning with and about animals.

Project Methodology

The aim of the research was to interview 20 national and international animal charity employees, with a focus on:

- exploring animal welfare and conservation issues that participants believed children and young people should know about.
- discovering the pedagogical approaches they employed in schools and local communities.

This was the first phase of a project that we intend to develop over the academic year 2020/21 and was scheduled to involve research into animal pedagogies and activities within primary schools in England. We anticipated that interviews with animal charity and other experts would provide different perspectives on key animal welfare and conservation issues as a foundation of practical, expert knowledge for subsequent phases of the project; twenty interviews would enable us to access views from a wide range of organisations. Our ethics application, which focused on voluntary participation, confidentiality, anonymity, and secure data management and protection, was passed by the departmental ethics committee, ready for the project to begin … in the first month of the national Covid-19 lockdown. At this point, 20 interviews seemed to be a highly ambitious target.

Using search engines and local knowledge, we created a database of 80 national and international animal charities and related organisations; of these, seven had no educational programme, so were discounted. An email was sent to each of the remaining organisations' contact, giving a short explanation of the project and inviting them to participate via an online Zoom interview. Those who volunteered were sent an information sheet and consent form, asking for permission to audio-record the semi-structured interview with a voice recorder that was separate from the Zoom platform. Questions centred around participants' views on animal conservation, animal welfare and animal pedagogies.

Many of the responses from charities and organisations highlighted the difficulties related to income loss and staff shortages that they were facing during the pandemic; some were closed, and others replied that they were only responding to emergencies related to animal care. Nonetheless, 18 responded positively to our invitation to an interview, and two more provided a written response to the interview schedule. Of these 20 respondents, six were charities or organisations that operated only in the UK and 14 were international, most operating from several centres in different countries across the world. Our sample included respondents from a National Park, zoos and animal sanctuaries as well as animal welfare and conservation charities. A few had a specific interest in one species while others focused on the welfare of domestic pets, but the majority had a wide range of interests that covered different aspects of animals' welfare and conservation in a number of different contexts. All were engaged in education; some had a reach of several million young people and others a few hundred. We were profoundly grateful for their generosity with their time, their expertise and their enthusiasm in the midst of acutely challenging circumstances, and understood their wholehearted participation as a measure of the topic's importance.

Interviews were transcribed verbatim by a transcription service, read through and coded into themes separately by the three researchers. We then discussed and agreed on the two themes to be included in this chapter, which reflected views expressed in different ways by all or most interviewees. Quotations are non-attributed to maintain participants' anonymity and have been selected as illustrative examples of participants' views.

Theme 1: One Health for Animal Conservation and Welfare

Asking *why* we should look after animals' welfare and conserve their habitat is a question that reaches to the heart of this type of education, and is one that our research participants believed could be answered at global and local levels. Almost all spoke either directly or indirectly about the One Health approach, which maintains that the health of human, animal and planetary life is interconnected. It is a term used across different academic specialisms and contexts, is based on a collaborative multi- and interdisciplinary approach, and involves organisations and institutions around the world in researching, understanding and educating on ways that aim at optimising the health of humans, animals and the environment (Stadtländer, 2015). This approach has become increasingly important as the effect of a growing human population is felt in planetary terms; new, formerly pristine areas now support human life, land-use changes with deforestation and intensive farming practices, and international trade and population movement are increasing. All of these contribute to an increase in the speed at which diseases can spread across the globe (see https://www.cdc.gov/onehealth/basics/index.html).

Our interviewees were in agreement, however, that educating children about impending disasters can lead to a feeling of helplessness or eco-anxiety (Fawbert, 2019), and all had a positive way of demonstrating the interconnectivity between humans, animals and environmental sustainability. The following interview extract is an example of their approach:

> One of the key messages I'm trying to get across at the moment … is the idea that conservation is not just about that species. It has significantly wider implications. Primate conservation has implications for rainforest health. Rainforests give us our oxygen, our water, our medicines … [they] play a massive role in protecting us against climate change. If we cut them down, we can't do that. In fact then you make it worse because then you're releasing all the stored carbon that those trees were sequestering for us (Interviewee 10, international charity).

Furthermore:

> Large species help us to tackle climate change. It sounds like an odd thing to say but elephants and gorillas, they eat the big fruit and they disperse the seeds of the big fruit. The big fruit comes from the biggest trees and the biggest trees hold the most carbon … those trees can't disperse their seeds

without those seed dispersal agents. If those seed dispersal agents aren't there, you're going to get a significant reduction in the number of those trees in the forest. You'll get other trees but they won't play the same role as those really big ones did. So you're changing the whole makeup of the forest which means it changes the services that it provides (Interviewee 10, international charity).

The idea of One Health is complemented by One Welfare. This was mentioned by the majority of our interviewees and is an approach that focuses on the interconnection between animal welfare, human wellbeing and the environment. It has a focus on keeping animals in systems that are environmentally friendly; its influence can be seen in attempts, for instance, to create greater understanding in farming of the value of high welfare, or to ensure that pets are well looked after (García Pinillos et al., 2016). An example of how One Welfare and One Health connect was related to factory farming by one interviewee:

Land use affects the habitats of animals, so it could be that the soya that goes to feed your factory-farmed chicken involved cutting down a rainforest … It could also be that while you're growing that soya or that corn, you're using lots of insecticides which have a damaging effect on animals … agriculture has a massive impact on the natural world in terms of destroying habitats for animals and putting poisons their way, and in turn, it has an effect on our health (Interviewee 1, international charity).

Other interviewees related One Welfare to bringing wild animals into captivity, arguing that this was good for neither the animal nor for the environment from which they had been taken:

… a pet has a history and if it's a wild animal, that will involve transporting that wild animal from the wild … The whole idea of just taking things out of one place and putting them in another, what happens to the other place? Does it work as well without this creature in place? From a welfare issue, it's [about] understanding that animals are often badly treated in getting them to where they are (Interviewee 13, international charity).

These short extracts demonstrate the clarity of these organisations' message to young people that animal, human and planetary life are interconnected, and is consistent with their view that young people should be introduced gradually to the complexities and sensitivities that arise from trying to ensure health for all. Another area of agreement was that primary aged children tend to be more open to learning with and about animals than those in their teens:

> ... from some of the evidence out there, it appears that children are more open to learning about animals, kind of in the seven to twelve ... age band. They start to develop empathy and attachment around [the] age of nine to ten. So there's ... some evidence that they have a more clear interest in nature at around that age (Interviewee 8, international charity).

The key for our research participants was engaging young children through their emotions and encouraging a love for animals and the natural world that would endure over time:

> There is a phrase which the American writer Stephen Jay Gould coined, he said: 'We will not fight to save what we do not love'. That's basically at the heart of all the work I do. We need to actively fight to protect nature. Nature is this enormous nebulous concept, it's utterly impossible to go, "I love nature", because it's just big. You need to find a gateway species, you need to find your way in ... A lot of the wildlife and conservation groups rely upon the charismatic megafauna, the elephants, the dolphins, the whales, the lions, the tigers, that sort of thing to try and seduce us into falling in love with nature (Interviewee 9, UK charity).

Or, as another interviewee put it: at an early age, 'all they need to know is tigers are awesome' (Interviewee 10, international charity).

Theme Two: More than Welfare and Conservation

The second major theme raised by our research participants related to introducing children and young people gradually to the complexities and sensitivities of One Health and One Welfare as a way of supporting their social and moral development. Interviewees argued that reflecting on the human place in the world:

> ... helps them [young people] place themselves in a bigger ethical picture ... we live in a society, which seems to me to becoming increasingly driven by individualism ... By looking beyond themselves through the lens of animals, they start to have a more universalistic view of the world and it's not just utilitarian. It's not, 'What I can get for me?'; it's, 'What I can do for the

natural world?' in this case, but it could also translate into, '[What can I do] for other humans?'. So, there is something about having a slightly bigger picture of the world than just being very egocentric (Interviewee 6, UK conservation organisation).

All agreed that the foundation of encouraging this type of thinking is for children and young people to understand that animals are sentient. Almost all interviewees cited the importance of children learning about the five welfare needs of animals that are enshrined in the UK Animal Welfare Act of 2006, which stipulates that keepers of all animals should care for their health, behavioural, dietary, environmental and companionship needs (see, for example, https://www.pdsa.org.uk/taking-careof-your-pet/looking-after-your-pet/all-pets/5-welfare-needs).   However, while it may be relatively straightforward to educate on the physical needs of animals

> … the challenging thing is to teach children about the need to care for the animal's psychological needs. [Our] programme is set up to get the children to think about the animals as sentient beings who can suffer, and [to] think about animals in that way. In order to do that you have to use a bit of … anthropomorphism, which the scientists tend to shy away from. It's absolutely necessary and it's fundamental to how children learn … Children start by relating things to themselves, so if you want to get children to imagine a dog as a sentient being, they would have to image how they would feel in the dog's shoes. It's an anthropomorphic process. I used to be frightened of anthropomorphism because I'm a biologist myself, but it needs to be done (Interviewee 4, international charity).

Anthropomorphism is an important part of humane education (Bires & Schultz, 2014), which is founded on compassion, a feeling that arises when we are aware of another's distress and want to alleviate the source of that distress. Similar to the One Health and One Welfare approaches, humane education seeks to generate an understanding that all living things are interdependent and should be treated with respect, and to foster empathy—the ability to identify with others' emotional states, whatever these might be. Compassion and empathy are both complex feelings that develop over time and are learned primarily from role models (Jalongo, 2014). Some (e.g. Dolby, 2019) argue that there has been a decline in empathy in the past twenty years among young people, and Dolby highlights the value of utilising discussions around/encounters with animals in nurturing a capacity for empathy with university students. Equally there was agreement among interviewees that, as the idea of animal sentience is established, and as young people develop their capacity to put themselves in others' shoes/paws/hooves, animal pedagogies can be widened in scope, introducing a social and moral dimension into discussions about human responsibilities and the difficulties of balancing what are often competing interests. Interviewees drew on their own practical experience to describe the subjects that they have explored with young people over the years, and one that was often cited related to human/animal conflict and sharing precious resources:

> ... ample rainfall links to less human/wildlife conflict and ... everyone's happy, everyone has enough food, wildlife and people. But during times of drought we start to see an increase of human/wildlife conflict as elephants stray outside of the ... protected areas into other areas and, if they see a juicy watermelon crop, they are inclined to help themselves. So, a lot of the work we've been doing is putting strategic electric fences in certain areas where we can alleviate that human/wildlife conflict ... [Our] community outreach and educational aspects all help provide this positive message around conservation and why we need wildlife ... trying to help communities not get so frustrated but, as I say, it's a complicated matter. It's about human population, population growth, and the pressure on all these that also we have to share (Interviewee 7, African charity).

The point about sharing is a deeply moral one, positioning animals as equal to humans in their five welfare needs and insisting on the obligation of humans to take responsibility for the local wildlife population's health. Others pointed out the complexity of these issues at a more domestic level:

> ... the longer we work in the field the more we understand that there are underlying causes to human behaviours. And that's so important. Somebody may be appearing to neglect their animal, it might be because of poverty, it might be because of previous abuse in the family. There's all sorts of different things that underline the way we behave and we need to understand and be empathetic to those if we want to really help in the long term ... there are so many different perspectives on animal welfare and conservation that it's important for a student to understand there are multiple perspectives (Interviewee 8, international charity).

Understanding multiple perspectives is given an extra affective dimension by centring discussions around animals:

> Using animals to help talk about these topics is really impactful. They put a face to something, they ignite a level of interest and emotion that probably wouldn't be there if the same subject was discussed in a regular lesson (Interviewee 19, international charity).

These educators encourage young people to think about and discuss other ethical issues such as animal welfare in food production, the boundary (if any) between resource utilisation and exploitation of the natural world, and understanding the arguments of people who, for example, support animal rights, animal liberation and/or animal conservation perspectives. Discussions such as these help to develop young people's confidence in their views and support them in becoming citizens who can exercise sound judgement based on moral understandings (Allison et al., 2012). One interviewee argued that this type of discussion

> ... really does help to develop 21st-century skills ... The four Cs are critical thinking, creativity, collaboration, communication. And those four are so important to improving our problem solving and decision-making skills that, you know, you could then apply that to any environmental or social justice issue, or health issue in the world (Interviewee 8, international charity).

Interviewees reported that an important aspect of this type of education was ensuring that young people were given information about how to take action at a local level and, if possible, to see the difference that they were making. As one commented, the tigers in Sumatra can seem a long way away from everyday life in the UK, but children can make a difference by picking up elastic bands left by postmen that can injure or kill wildlife, making holes for hedgehogs in their garden to ensure they can travel across their 'patch' and/or putting up bird boxes. Older students can think about the implications of buying cheap chocolate and cheap meat with the understanding that 'every consumer can affect these by voting with their feet' (Interviewee 19, international charity). Thinking about the consequences of their actions in relation to animal welfare and conservation can be an important part of young people's development as (or if) they seek to find ethical lifestyles in the midst of a consumer-dominated world. And, as a number of interviewees commented, young people need information but also the time and space to figure things out for themselves; telling them what to think and how to behave has a limited effect in the long term.

Many interviewees saw a link, too, between cruelty to animals and violence to other humans, arguing that the compassion and empathy learned through animals can be utilised to reduce issues such as bullying and create a kinder atmosphere within schools; this is another aspect of humane education discussed above. One interviewee brought all these ideas together in a succinct description that summed up the multiple benefits that they believed could be derived from animal pedagogies:

> … if you encourage human kindness and humane thinking, it can reduce bullying, it can improve kids' self-esteem, it can improve their work and their interest in things. The kids that get involved and are active end up doing better, so there's all sorts of benefits to mental health from caring about animals. And some kids who have trouble relating to people can learn to do it, partly through animals first. And they can learn responsibility and right and wrong. And a lot of kids like animals and are interested in [them], so it's a great subject for getting them to write and think and add up and whatever … Compassion is indivisible and if you get kids caring about animals, they end up caring about people too (Interviewee 1, international charity).

Conclusion: Lessons from Those Who Care

Project interviewees were all convinced that including animal pedagogies into school learning can have wide-reaching benefits for children and young people, and we needed little persuasion to accept their arguments— it's difficult to resist the promise of a kinder, healthier and more compassionate world, and we too have a deep-seated love of animals. However shifting away from an anthropocentric approach to education towards an holistic, One Health, One Welfare approach is no simple task; anthropocentrism is a hard habit to lose in an education system that has been built up over the centuries to serve human purposes and that apparently serves capitalism so well. Added to that is the separation (segregation?) of many adults and children from animals and/or the natural world through urbanisation, a global phenomenon that can contribute to both children and adults being deeply afraid of domestic and/or wild creatures when they happen to meet. At a school level, ignorance or fear of animals among teachers may contribute to avoidance of animal pedagogies, particularly in a crowded curriculum that leaves teachers with little space for reflection or developing new approaches. While not insurmountable, these are significant challenges to both the idea and the practice of animals becoming part of everyday school learning.

One important way into animal pedagogies is through anthropomorphism, as our interviewees suggested. Telling stories is the way that we make sense of things, and children of all ages love stories; stories about animals can serve the dual purpose of engaging interest and piquing curiosity, all the more so if young people can identify in some way with the anthropomorphised animal(s) involved. Curious people are more likely to want to find out more about whatever is being discussed, providing an opening for an increasingly sophisticated engagement with wider topics, which in turn, as our interviewees have demonstrated, opens avenues for discussions about an ethical, examined (Grosz, 2013) life. We need now to develop principles for animal pedagogies that are founded on the insights provided by our interviewees, and build on their and others' work to strengthen resistance to test-dominated education and encourage a more collective, compassionate approach to life.

REFERENCES

Allison, P., Carr, D., & Meldrum, G. (2012). Potential for excellence: Interdisciplinary learning outdoors as a moral enterprise. *Curriculum Journal, 23*(1), 43–58.

Bires, N., & Schultz, D. (2014). Foundational humane education: promoting love of nature and affinity for animals in schools and communities. In M. R. Jalongo (Ed.), *Teaching compassion: Humane education in early childhood.* Springer.

Carrington, D. (2020, August 5). Deadly diseases from wildlife thrive when nature is destroyed, study finds. *Guardian.* https://www.theguardian.com/environment/2020/aug/05/deadly-diseases-from-wildlife-thrive-when-nature-is-destroyed-study-finds

Carson, R. (1962/2000). *Silent spring.* Penguin Books.

Christie, F. (2017). The reporting of university league table employability rankings: a critical review. *Journal of Education and Work, 30*(4), 403–418. https://doi.org/10.1080/13639080.2016.1224821

Cutting, R. (2019). I'm so tired of learning from this nature stuff. *Presentation at the Peninsula Research in Outdoor Learning conference,* January 18. https://www.plymouth.ac.uk/research/peninsula-research-in-outdoor-learning/resources

Daniel Smith, J. (2020). Teach the future. *Forum, 62*(2), 213–217.

Dolby, N. (2019). Nonhuman animals and the future of environmental education: Empathy and new possibilities. *Journal of Environmental Education, 50*(4–6), 403–415. https://doi.org/10.1080/00958964.2019.1687411

Fawbert, D. (2019). 'Eco-anxiety': How to spot it and what to do about it. *BBC Three.* https://www.bbc.co.uk/bbcthree/article/b2e7ee32-ad28-4ec4-89aa-a8b8c98f95a5

García Pinillos, R., Appleby, M., Manteca, X., Scott-Park, F., Smith, C. & Velarde, A. (2016). One Welfare—A platform for improving human and animal welfare. *Veterinary Record.* https://doi.org/10.1136/vr.i5470

Gibb, R., Redding, D., Qing Chin, K., Donnelly, C., Blackburn, T., Newbold, T. & Jones, K. (2020). Zoonotic host diversity increases in human-dominated ecosystems. *Nature,* 584. https://doi.org/10.1038/s41586-020-2562-8

Gilchrist, M., Passy, R., Waite, S. & Cook, R. (2016) Exploring schools' use of natural spaces, in C. Freeman, & P. Tranter (eds.), *Risk, protection, provision and policy,* Vol. 12 of Skelton, T. (ed) *Geographies of Children and Young People.* Springer. https://doi.org/10.1007/978-981-4585-99-6_18-1

Graeber, D. (2019). *Bullshit jobs: The rise of pointless work and what we can do about it.* Penguin.

Grosz, S. (2013). *The examined life: How we lose and find ourselves.* Chatto and Windus.

Her Majesty's Government. (2018). *A green future: Our 25 year plan to improve the environment.* https://assets.publishing.service.gov.uk/government/uploads/system/uploads/attachment_data/file/693158/25-year-environment-plan.pdf

Jalongo, M. R. (2014). Humane education and the development of empathy in early childhood: Definitions, rationale, and outcomes. In M. R. Jalongo (Ed.), *Teaching compassion: Humane education in early childhood.* Springer.

Mirchandani, R. (2020). Five global issues to watch in 2021. *United Nations Foundation blog.* https://unfoundation.org/blog/post/five-global-issues-to-watch-in-2021/

Passy, R. (2012). Widening participation, Aimhigher and the coalition government: Narratives of freedom and efficiency. *Power and Education, 4*(1), 83–95.

Passy, R., Bentsen, P., Gray, T., & Ho, S. (2019). Integrating outdoor learning into the curriculum: an exploration in four nations. *Curriculum Perspectives, 39,* 73–78.

Pedersen, H. (2010). Is 'the posthuman' educable? On the convergence of educational philosophy, animal studies, and posthumanist theory. *Discourse: Studies in the Cultural Politics of Education, 31*(2), 237–250. https://doi.org/10.1080/01596301003679750

Russell, C., & Spannring, R. (2019). So what for other animals? Environmental education research after the animal turn. *Environmental Education Research, 25*(8), 1137–1142. https://doi.org/10.1080/13504622.2019.1687639

Stadtländer, C. (2015). One Health: people, animals, and the environment. *Infection Ecology & Epidemiology, 5*(1), 30514. https://doi.org/10.3402/iee.v5.30514

'When you have this intimacy with it, you do want to protect its environment.' The Role of Emotions on a Zoo Visit in Engaging Visitors in Wildlife Conservation

Susan Warren

INTRODUCTION

Zoos have long provided places for humans to spend time with exotic animals. Their origins date back to the menageries and cabinets of curiosities, which emerged during the era of European exploration and colonisation. During these times, collections of animals captured from the wild were displayed as symbols of human victory and dominance and provided a spectacle for entertainment. By the eighteenth and nineteenth centuries, menageries were well established throughout the world.

Over time, and in response to changes in the political, social and environmental contexts, zoos have evolved and repurposed themselves as centres for conservation. The education of zoo visitors has become central to

S. Warren (✉)
University of Exeter, Exeter, UK

© The Author(s), under exclusive license to Springer Nature
Switzerland AG 2022
R. Cutting, R. Passy (eds.), *Contemporary Approaches to Outdoor
Learning*, Palgrave Studies in Alternative Education,
https://doi.org/10.1007/978-3-030-85095-1_7

83

this conservation role, with zoos aiming to: (1) increase visitor knowledge and awareness of endangered species; and (2) encourage visitors to change their behaviours to support the conservation of these species and the wider natural world. Despite this reimagining of the role of the zoo, their existence continues to attract criticism from some quarters, due to the captivity and confinement of animals. However, with over 700 million visitors worldwide to zoos and aquariums each year (Moss et al., 2014), from a range of socio-demographic backgrounds, these organisations have huge potential to engage with and influence a very large audience.

In their efforts to change visitor behaviours, zoos have primarily adopted a community-based social marketing approach. This involves promoting a specific behaviour to visitors, which the zoo has identified as important in helping to address a particular wildlife conservation issue. For example, the campaign 'Don't Palm Us Off', encouraged visitors to Zoos Victoria (Australia) to petition and shop for sustainably produced palm oil, as part of the effort to stop the destruction of rainforest habitats by the palm oil industry.

This social marketing-based approach to behaviour change is a familiar one and has provided the main framework for the UK and other western government responses to environmental challenges (Jones et al., 2013). It places the onus on the individual to change their behaviour to address the challenges of human-induced climate change and biodiversity loss. The popular science book 'Nudge' (Thaler & Sunstein, 2008) epitomises this approach.

'Nudge' draws on psychology and consumer behaviour studies to influence the choices and behaviours of an individual. Whilst it does not tell consumers what to do, it steers and influences them through the manipulation of the context in which the decision is made. 'Nudges are not mandates. Putting fruit at eye level counts as a nudge. Banning junk food is not' (ibid., p. 8).

However, whilst social marketing techniques have been in operation within government policy and campaigns since the early 2000s, the trajectory of environmental problems has continued upwards, with continued loss of habitats and species, and increases in greenhouse gas emissions.

The inability of social marketing to effect positive change for the natural world—at the necessary rate or scale—has led environmental social scientists and some environmental organisations to question the value of this approach, and to explore other ways which might be more successful in changing our interactions with the natural world. Through this critique and exploration, the role of emotions in influencing our decision making has come to the fore. This can be exemplified by the 'Values and Frames' approach (Crompton, 2010), where the development of an individual's values and attitudes towards the natural world can enable them to become more environmentally aware and active in helping to address environmental challenges. This has the potential to secure longer-lasting changes in behaviour, over a wider spectrum of activities, without being repeatedly 'nudged' to do so.

More widely, this emotionally-centred engagement with the natural world reflects calls within human-animal studies for a more relational approach between humans and animals/nature. Highlighting the enduring paradigm of human-domination over nature as the fundamental source of our disconnection from and destruction of the natural world, a relational approach seeks to de-centre the human in favour of a more egalitarian and empathetic conceptualisation of human-animal relationships.

The nature of a visit to the zoo lends itself towards an exploration of an emotionally-centred approach to engaging visitors in behaviour change. Individuals have opportunities for close-up experiences with (often) exotic animals, which they can see, smell, hear and in some cases touch, with the potential to evoke a range of emotional responses. A small body of research within psychology has explored visitors' emotional responses to animals encountered at the zoo (for example Clayton et al., 2011). However, until now, this research has not been utilised to explore an alternative approach beyond social marketing to engaging zoo visitors in behaviour change. To address this, I undertook a novel doctorate research study at the Wild Planet Trust's Paignton Zoo, Devon, UK between July 2015–June 2019, to explore this alternative, emotionally-centred approach to behaviour change, as a means of framing and supporting the visitor experience at the zoo. The remainder of this chapter describes this research and its findings.

Exploring Visitors' Experiences with Animals at the Zoo

New Methods of Enquiry at the Zoo

Approaches to visitor studies at the zoo are firmly rooted in the research tradition of natural sciences, employing quantitative methodologies to generate statistical data as a means to capture the impact of aspects of the zoo visit. In relation to visitor behaviour change, this approach focuses on identifying the number of individuals undertaking a specific behaviour, pre-determined by the zoo, as a result of the visit. A small body of psychologically-based studies has broadened approaches to the study of visitors' experiences. However, this too has focused on a quantitative approach, using psychometric measurement scales to quantify visitors' emotional responses to their encounters with animals. In seeking to deliver the zoo's educational mission, these approaches have not enabled an in-depth exploration of *why* visitors respond in particular ways to their experiences with animals at the zoo, and *how* these responses influence their feelings and behaviours (both during and after the zoo visit) towards these animals, their conspecifics in the wild, or the wider natural world.

To better understand the why and the how, I used a qualitatively-based, and novel, ethnographic approach, to enable visitors to provide: personal, in situ accounts of their emotional responses in their own words; the reasons for their responses; and descriptions of how these influenced their feelings and behaviours, both during and beyond the zoo visit.

The specific objectives of this study were to explore and understand: (1) visitors' emotional responses to the animals they encountered on their visit to Paignton Zoo; (2) how these responses stayed with visitors after their zoo visit to influence their pro-environmental attitudes and behaviours; and (3) how the zoo could help increase visitors' engagement with animals and involvement in pro-environmental behaviours.

How This Research Was Conducted

Participants were recruited using Paignton Zoo's online publications and social media channels. Fourteen separate visitor groups were recruited to the study (with a total of 41 participants). These groups were comprised of individuals, couples, families, or friends, and participants ranged in age from 4 to 74 years. Some participants were zoo members, either at Paignton Zoo or another UK zoo, and visited their local zoo on a regular (at least monthly) basis. Others did not have a zoo membership and were infrequent visitors (at least a year between zoo visits). The qualitative methodological framing of this research study did not require a statistically robust cohort of participants, which could provide a representative, generalisable sample. Instead, the focus was on gaining access to participants who were concerned or involved in some way in the research aim/objectives.

The approach involved two elements of data collection. During the zoo visit, a 'go-along' interview (Kusenbach, 2003) was carried out with each of the 14 visitor groups. This mobile method provides a relaxed and informal approach, where participants find it easier to verbalise their feelings and attitudes. I accompanied each of the visitor groups for all or part of their zoo visit, asking all group members questions about their emotional responses to the animals they encountered and observing their interactions with these animals. Up to three weeks after the zoo visit, I visited or spoke with the same visitor groups to follow-up on this zoo experience. Using semi-structured interviews, participants were able to reflect on their emotional responses at the zoo, the influence of these responses on their feelings towards endangered animals, and their engagement in pro-environmental behaviours. Ways in which the zoo could support their interest and engagement in pro-environmental behaviours were also discussed. These interviews provided a co-creative space to explore how the zoo could help to mediate visitor-animal encounters and increase visitor engagement in pro-environmental behaviours. All of the interviews (both at the zoo and after the zoo visit) were audio-recorded and transcribed verbatim. I conducted a detailed thematic analysis (Cope & Kurtz, 2016) of these interview transcripts using the data management software NVIVO 11.

Emotional Engagement with Animals at the Zoo

Four key themes were identified through the thematic analysis, which highlight the potential for emotional engagement between visitors and animals, and the influence of these emotional responses on visitors' pro-environmental behaviours.

Theme 1: Emotional Responses at the Zoo Are Varied and Are Influenced by Several Factors

Participants' encounters with animals at the zoo elicited a wide range of emotions, which were categorised into ten different types of emotional response. Two main aspects influenced the nature of these responses: (1) past experiences of animals and the zoo, which participants 'brought with them' to the zoo; and (2) elements present at the moments of encounter during the visit (Fig. 1).

Past experiences of animals and zoos   **During the zoo visit**

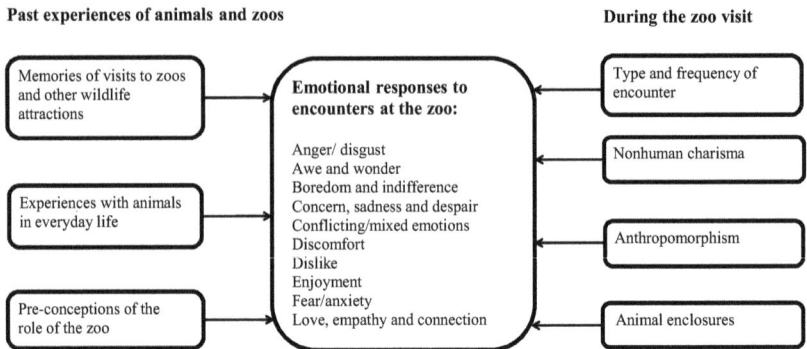

Fig. 1 Emotional responses to animals at the zoo and the key factors influencing these

Past Experiences of Animals and Zoos

Participants' memories of previous encounters with animals at zoos or other wildlife attractions conveyed a sense of immediacy, even after the passing of many years. Sensorial and emotional memories of firsthand encounters in these settings remained strong and clear. They served to inform or even dominate participants' responses during the go-alongs, particularly in relation to emotions of 'enjoyment', 'love, empathy and connection', and 'dislike and disgust'. As Alice explained, as we approached the zoo's two Bactrian camels:

> When I was a child, I was spat at by one and that was that … we don't get too close, disgusting things! Alice

Whilst encounters with animals at the zoo were not an everyday occurrence, many participants had had experiences with domestic pets on a more regular basis. These influenced their emotional responses to animals at the zoo from within the same phylogenetic family, in particular with regard to cats and reptiles, eliciting responses commonly in the categories of 'love, empathy and connection', and 'dislike and disgust'. For Christina, her intimate knowledge of her own cat informed her response as she watched the adult male lion:

I feel a connection because of my own cats, cos I love my cats and I can just see the way they walk, particularly I've got a big grey cat called Morris and he walks and move just like these large versions. Christina

Whilst participants highlighted the enjoyment, appreciation and value they attached to embodied encounters with animals at the zoo, previous 'virtual' animal encounters also played an important part in mediating their emotions during the zoo visit. Once again, the longevity of previous experiences was evidenced, with participants recalling books and films from their childhood when encountering particular animals during the visit:

I kinda think back to 'The Lion, the Witch and the Wardrobe' and Aslan and I would just love to hug a big maney lion. Karen

Participants' pre-conceptions of the zoo concerning entertainment and wildlife conservation also influenced their emotions. All participants expressed enjoyment at being on a 'day out' at the zoo. Some also expressed emotions of 'concern, worry and sadness' in relation to the captivity and confinement of animals they encountered. In contrast, those who appeared more familiar with the work of the zoo, and identified the important role of the zoo in wildlife conservation, were more confident about the welfare of the animals at the zoo.

During the Zoo Visit

Aspects present during the moments of encounter at the zoo also served to influence participants' emotional responses. Participants greatly valued and enjoyed getting close to, and sharing space with, animals during the zoo visit. Deborah explained how being in close proximity enabled her to feel an emotional connection with the animals:

I think for me it's probably about the intimacy you can have with them because you know you can get close to them. Deborah

Participants who visited a zoo at least monthly, affording them frequent opportunities for close-up encounters, described the impact of these repeated encounters on their emotions:

I used to spend hours sitting with her (an orang-utan), so that's why I just love orang-utans, because I spent a lot of time looking at her and her looking at me. Diane

However, whilst unusual, repeated encounters did not always serve to build emotional bonds with animals. Anthony described the impact of coming to the zoo over many years in contrasting terms:

I think you've seen them for so many years you just want them to do something that bit more interesting, cos it's the same thing isn't it. Anthony

The perceptions of animals as having or exhibiting non-human charisma (Lorimer, 2007) triggered strong emotional responses in many participants. The perceived charismatic aspects of both lemurs and red pandas elicited many expressions of 'love, empathy and connection', and were variously described by participants as 'fluffy', 'cute' and 'cuddly'. In contrast, other species, particularly reptiles, triggered equally strong, but negative emotional responses of 'dislike' and 'fear/anxiety', as witnessed in Christina's encounter with a monitor lizard:

That is horrible. It's evil. It's like something from a sci-fi movie, it's unreal. Christina

In addition to their perceptions based on aesthetics, participants also sought to relate to animals through anthropomorphism. This attribution of human traits, emotions or intentions to animals served to influence participants' emotions in contrasting ways. Encounters with a 'meditating' gorilla; a 'philosophical' crocodile; and a 'litter-picking' black hornbill, all served to enhance enjoyment and engagement with these animals. However, emotions of 'concern' and 'sadness' were expressed in relation to animals thought to be sad, lonely or unhappy. This was particularly true in the case of the zoo's elderly and solitary African elephant, Duchess.

Participants' encounters took place with animals living in a range of enclosures, of varied design and size. Exhibits perceived to be more 'natural' added to their enjoyment of the encounter. However, despite the naturalistic look of the enclosures, the size of some enclosures was a major source of concern and sadness, related to the perceived wellbeing of the animals living there. Spending time with her family watching the great grey owls, Julie commented:

I do sometimes feel sad for the owls though … they don't have any flying room. Julie

Theme 2: Encounters at the Zoo Can Build Strong and Lasting Emotional Connections

Up to three weeks after the zoo visit, the participants had the opportunity to reflect on how the visit had influenced their feelings towards endangered wildlife. For most participants, their encounters with animals at the zoo stayed with them beyond the zoo visit. Emotions of 'anger and upset/disgust', 'concern, worry and sadness' and 'empathy' were expressed in relation to the wellbeing and future existence of conspecifics of the animals encountered at the zoo, living in the wild. This was particularly the case for those who visited the zoo frequently i.e. at least once a month. In considering the extension of her emotions beyond the animals at the zoo, Jennifer described how she felt about seeing animals at the zoo, and then hearing stories about their death in the wild:

> *…it does make you think differently about them, and then when you hear a story you think "Oh my god, all those animals."* Jennifer

However, whilst uncommon, some participants described how their feelings at the zoo failed to persist beyond the visit:

> *…I mean walking around the zoo looking, particularly at ones that you know are endangered, you do feel sad for them and you do feel we as humans have obviously gone wrong somewhere, but then you come away from the zoo and it does sort of leave your mind, it sort of stays in the zoo…* Heather

Theme 3: Emotional Connections with Animals Are Important in Driving Pro-Environmental Behaviours

Participants identified that their feelings towards animals they encountered at the zoo motivated them to carry out a range of pro-environmental activities, including: waste reduction and recycling; financial donations; and choosing environmentally friendly products, for example chocolate bars made with sustainable palm oil. These types of behaviours are typical of the ones which Paignton Zoo and others are keen to encourage amongst their visitors. As Kenneth described:

…so we do as much as we can (to help support wildlife), we don't waste very much, and we recycle. Kenneth

For some, their emotional connection with animals at the zoo had a significant influence on behaviours over and above those typically understood or promoted as pro-environmental actions by Paignton Zoo and other zoos. Deborah described the motivation behind her decision to make major changes to her shopping practices, moving beyond the purchase/avoidance of specific products, to reappraising the procurement of all her purchases, based on their environmental impacts:

…I think when you see the animal there and you have this intimacy with it then you do want to protect its environment … and if there is anything I can do to help them, I will. Deborah

Like Deborah, the strength of Angela's emotional connections with the animals at the zoo was the driving force behind her activities as an advocate for wildlife conservation in her local community: talking to her friends, family, work colleagues and shopkeepers:

…regarding palm oil and things, I talk to people in shops you know, the shopkeepers, 'What about this soap? Has it got palm oil in?' If not, it would be a selling point if you could say that it hasn't (got palm oil) and so, yeah, I do those things. Angela

Moving further beyond 'typical' pro-environmental behaviours promoted by the zoo community, many participants also described how time at the zoo, and their emotional connections with the animals, encouraged them to pursue an interest in wildlife: learning more about animals they saw, and the threats to their future survival:

…definitely since I've started going to the zoo, I've thought about it an awful lot more than I would have done before, and also finding information out and perhaps watching programmes that I wouldn't have watched before, reading a book that I wouldn't have read before, you know I think it has made a difference to me in that respect, it's made me think about it an awful lot more. Janice

In considering their feelings about endangered species, and their ability to enact the changes necessary to secure a positive future for endangered wildlife, many participants also discussed how they felt helpless, hopeless, angry and frustrated. This lack of personal agency arose when they considered the potential impact of their efforts, in comparison with the role of wider political and economic systems:

> *For me, there's a slight sense of helplessness. You know you can do your bit at home, you can eat less diverse food and you can try and lead a more simple life that doesn't impact, but it does feel slightly helpless when it's, it's the supermarkets, it's the pharmaceuticals, the big boys, it's the oil, you know. Where do you go with that?* Rashmi

Theme 4: Developing and Retaining Emotional Connections

Participants identified three main ways the zoo could help them to develop and retain their emotional connections with the animals at the zoo, and their conspecifics in the wild, and to become more actively involved in pro-environmental behaviours. These were: (1) helping them to understand the threats to wild animals; (2) being given opportunities to talk with zoo staff and volunteers; and (3) having opportunities to see and connect with the zoo animals after their visit.

Understanding Threats to Wild Animals

A number of participants expressed a desire for the zoo to provide more information and imagery regarding the nature of threats to endangered wildlife. Highlighting the seriousness of the situation was felt to be compelling in terms of motivating people to take action:

> *...it'd be good to know about what's happening (for endangered species), how bad it's getting, their population and (that) 20 years from now they could all be extinct if we don't do something now. And that has more effect on me I think, how bad things are for them.* Christopher

However, in discussing their desire for this approach, participants were very aware of the potential conflict with the expectation of the zoo visit as a 'fun day out', and the appropriateness of portraying these challenging issues to children and young people, a key audience for the zoo.

Opportunities to Talk with Zoo Staff and Volunteers

Many participants were keen to have more a personalised experience during their visit, through having time to talk with zoo staff and/or volunteers to find out more about the animals at the zoo, the zoo's conservation work, and how to help with wildlife conservation:

> *I think there are lots of willing folk out there, but they've never been properly approached. And if they (the zoo) had an hour here and there on certain days, it would just be wonderful ... I know they send people off and I would love to hear firsthand from the people involved about their conservation work overseas.* Andrea

In considering their lack of personal agency in tackling threats to endangered species, participants were also keen to gain a better understanding of the work of Wild Planet Trust to advocate for pro-conservation policy and practice. This could help visitors feel supported in their actions, and help to ameliorate their feelings of helplessness, hopelessness, anger and frustration concerning the efficacy of their individual behaviours.

Opportunities to See and Connect with Animals after the Zoo Visit
Participants identified the importance of attending to visitor engagement not just during the zoo visit, but also beyond the boundary of the zoo. They expressed a desire to stay in 'virtual touch' with the animals following the zoo visit, to help ensure the persistence of the zoo experience over time and space. This was identified as important in retaining and enhancing their emotional engagement with the animals at the zoo: getting to know and understand the animals better through more frequent engagement. Amy described how her son's emotional connection with animals had benefited from a YouTube channel provided by a North American zoo:

> *We used to look at loads of different videos of different animals (at the zoo), and they had a little video blog as well about animals that had just been born, how they were doing, and that had an impact on my son and his interest and love for wildlife.* Amy

Discussion

The Importance of Attending to the Emotional Dimension of Visitors' Encounters with Animals at the Zoo

At the core of the emotionally-centred 'Values and Frames' (Crompton, 2010) approach to behaviour change is the reframing of our relationship with the natural world, such that individuals have strong positive emotional connections with non-human others. This emotional connection to nature can help secure more environmentally aware and active citizens, without recourse to 'nudging' them to undertake particular behaviours (Crompton, 2013). More broadly, recent research in environmental psychology has also identified a positive relationship between an individual's emotional connection with nature and pro-environmental behaviours (Martin et al., 2020).

My research illustrates the capacity of relational engagement to motivate actions, which can be understood in terms of active citizenship. Repeated encounters with animals at the zoo motivated some participants to act as advocates for wildlife conservation in their local communities and to make significant changes to their lifestyles. In addition, framing behaviour change from an emotionally-centred approach aids the reappraisal of other behaviours resulting from the zoo visit, notably participants pursuing an interest in wildlife. While these types of behaviour do not have a direct link to supporting endangered species, they can be understood in terms of their influence on participants' emotional engagement with animals at the zoo. They have the capacity to build an individual's interest in, and care for, these animals and their conspecifics in the wild, which can then serve to motivate actions in support of wildlife conservation in the future. My research also revealed the differential capacities of, and complexities within, visitor-animal encounters at the zoo in nurturing relational engagement between humans and animals. This serves to illustrate the challenge which the zoo seeks to address through its visitor engagement programme. The agency of the animals encountered at the zoo can only do so much to encourage empathetic and caring responses. In light of this, it is vital that the zoo considers its practices of visitor engagement and how it can mediate visitors' encounters with animals.

Practices of Visitor Engagement at the Zoo

There are several actions which the zoo could undertake to support positive emotional connections with its animals and increase visitors' willingness to carry out actions in support of wildlife conservation. Underlying all these actions is a desire from the visitors to engage with, and understand more about, the animals at the zoo, their conspecifics in the wild, and the conservation work of the zoo. Much good practice exists in some zoos, particularly with regard to visitor engagement with staff and volunteers, virtual encounters with animals beyond the zoo boundary, and on- and off-site information provision. This study serves to highlight the importance of these factors in relation to supporting and developing positive emotional connections with animals during and after the zoo visit.

Additionally, this study has revealed two aspects which are not so prevalent in relation to the behaviour change agenda at the zoo. Firstly, the provision of information and images of threats to wildlife would help visitors fully appreciate the threats faced by endangered species. This is an area little explored in zoo visitor research. The dominant assumption within human-animal studies and zoo-based visitor practices is that empathetic emotions are the key pathway to enhancing attitudes and behaviours towards animals and the wider natural world. However, an alternative scholarship has argued that other emotions, in particular anger, are more strongly involved in securing moral concern for animals (Kasperbauer, 2015). A study exploring the tolerance of visitors at Chester Zoo to an exhibition depicting challenging issues of environmental and wildlife destruction identified the potential value of moving towards 'a more personally (for the visitor) challenging agenda' (Esson & Moss, 2013, p. 93). Whilst this presents a difficult challenge to the culturally embedded expectation of the zoo as a 'fun day out', its capacity to help further emotional connection and motivate action should be further explored.

Secondly, within the social marketing model of behaviour change, the focus is on the individual as the agent of change to address environmental challenges. However, given visitors' awareness of the scale of the impact of the actions of government and business on the environment, they would welcome knowing more about the zoo's conservation advocacy work in the wider world. For example, the Wild Planet Trust works closely with local businesses to improve environmental performance, and has recently undertaken political lobbying in support of Marine Conservation Zones. However, it is important that the Trust also communicates this to visitors, alongside continuing to advocate for policies and practices which are less detrimental—and ideally beneficial—to the natural world.

More broadly, the strong influence of preconceived notions, experiences and perceptions of animals, points to a much bigger challenge faced by those seeking to engage and educate visitors about animals. Spaces and places of human-animal encounter must look to provide ways for people to experience and appreciate animals in new and different ways. This is especially important for the multitude of species which are not, from our perspective, either cute or cuddly. Everything from the design and layout of a zoo, through to the information provided to visitors, has a part to play in opening up and challenging peoples' perceptions and attitudes. Always placing the charismatic and cuddly centre stage in the zoo, whilst others are placed in less immediately accessible spaces, can serve to reinforce which animals we like, love and value. In contrast, providing exhibits and opportunities to interact with the less charismatic can help to open visitors' hearts and minds to new ways of relating to these species. Highlighting their capabilities, uniqueness and their similarities to us, for example a need for home, family, food and safety, are all important if we are to achieve greater relational engagement and understanding between humans and the vast range of non-human animals.

Conclusion

Research in environmental education and psychology has identified the importance of embodied experiences of nature in helping to secure positive and caring relationships with the natural world, in terms of both attitudes and behaviours. The forms of 'natureculture' which are advocated as places for embodied encounters centre on 'green spaces' including parks, nature reserves, and 'wilderness' areas (for example Crompton, 2010; Soga & Gaston, 2016). The natureculture provided by the zoo is conspicuous by its absence in this literature.

In relation to desired outcomes of empathetic and caring engagements with the natural world, my research, by bringing a new conceptual framing, has provided new ways of understanding human-animal interactions at the zoo. This new evidence identifies the capacity of the zoo to build relational engagements between humans and nature, in particular with endangered wildlife. Zoos remain contested spaces, however, for many city dwellers, where a visit to the zoo may be their 'best nature experience' (Falk et al., 2007), the zoo has a role to play within this mosaic of naturecultures. It has the capacity to secure relational engagements, and thus emotional proximity, with geographically remote animals. This is arguably unique in comparison with the work of other environmental organisations and could be further capitalised upon to support pro-environmental behaviours.

Acknowledgements Thanks to: The Wild Planet Trust and the University of Exeter for their sponsorship and support of this research; the research participants; and Dr Anna Sansom for help in editing and proofing this paper.

References

Clayton, S., Fraser, J., & Burgess, C. (2011) The role of zoos in fostering environmental identity. *Ecopsychology, 3*(2), 87–96.

Cope, M., & Kurtz, H. (2016). Organizing, coding, and analyzing qualitative data. In N. Clifford, M. Cope, T. Gillespie, & S. French (Eds.), *Key methods in geography*. Sage.

Crompton, T. (2010). *Common cause. The case for working with our cultural values*. WWF-UK.

Crompton, T. (2013). Behaviour change: A dangerous distraction. In R. Crocker & S. Lehmann (Eds.), *Motivating change: Sustainable design and behaviour in the built environment*. Routledge.

Esson, M., & Moss, A. (2013). The risk of delivering disturbing messages to zoo family audiences. *The Journal of Environmental Education, 44*(2), 79–96.

Falk, J., Reinhard, E., Vernon, C., Bronnenkant, K., Heimlich, J., & Deans, N. (2007). *Why Zoos and Aquariums Matter: Assessing the Impact of a Visit to a Zoo or Aquarium*. Silver Spring MD: American Association of Zoos and Aquariums.

Jones, R., Pykett, J., & Whitehead, M. (2013). *Changing behaviours. On the rise of the psychological state*. Edward Elgar.

Kasperbauer, T. J. (2015). Rejecting empathy for animal ethics. *Ethical Theory and Moral Practice, 18*(4), 817–833.

Kusenbach, M. (2003). Street phenomenology. The go-along as ethnographic research tool. *Ethnography, 4*(3), 455–485.

Lorimer, J. (2007). Nonhuman charisma. *Environment and Planning D: Society and Space, 25*(5), 911–932.

Martin, L., White, M., Hunt, A., Richardson, M., Pahl, S., & Burt, J. (2020). Nature contact, nature connectedness and associations with health, wellbeing and pro-environmental behaviour. *Journal of Environmental Psychology, 68*, 101389.

Moss, A., Jensen, E., & Gusset, M. (2014). *A global evaluation of biodiversity literacy in zoo and aquarium visitors*. WAZA.

Soga, M., & Gaston, K. (2016). Extinction of experience: The loss of human-nature interactions. *Frontiers in Ecology and the Environment, 14*(2), 94–101.

Thaler, R., & Sunstein, C. (2008). *Nudge: Improving decisions about health, wealth, and happiness*. Yale University Press.

PART II

New Frontiers: Contemporary Research into Outdoor Learning

'A Sea of Men': Supporting Men as Fathers Through Outdoor Learning Experiences

Ian Blackwell

INTRODUCTION

This chapter explores how activities on offer through dads' groups, when delivered with sensitivity and attention by outdoor learning professionals, can disrupt traditional, problematic masculine behaviours, leading fathers to develop caring, responsible parenting skills and to be more emotionally expressive while maintaining acceptable male performances. I offer an insight into the emerging literature on the symbolic 'situatedness' of fathering practices (Creighton et al., 2015; Marsiglio et al., 2005; Schoppe-Sullivan & Fagan, 2020; Wissö, 2018), the 'geographies of masculinity' (Gorman-Murray & Hopkins, 2015; Ward et al., 2017), and the subsequent impact on identities and behaviours, but my main aim is to contribute to calls to debate the role of outdoor learning in tackling the tenacious issues of patriarchy, gender inequality and hegemonic masculinity that are not only inherent in society but also prevalent across the outdoor education sector (Humberstone, 1995; Kennedy & Russell, 2020).

I. Blackwell (✉)
Plymouth Marjon University, Plymouth, UK

R. Cutting, R. Passy (eds.), *Contemporary Approaches to Outdoor Learning*, Palgrave Studies in Alternative Education, https://doi.org/10.1007/978-3-030-85095-1_8

MANLINESS, THE 'HANDS-ON' DAD AND OUTDOOR LEISURE ACTIVITIES

The image of the ultra-active, rugged, frontiersman-adventurer roughing it out in 'the wilderness' is a central trope in the construction of hegemonic, heterosexual Western manhood (Coakley, 2006; Kimmel, 1995). Likewise, for men as fathers, the international literature repeatedly emphasises that fathers' caregiving with infants and young children is characterised by physical activity and rough-and-tumble play, heightened Challenging Parenting Behaviour, intensive sport, leisure and outdoor interests, and a higher level of risk-taking activity than mothers (John et al., 2013; Such, 2009). In addition, socio-cultural expectations, media images and contemporary narratives of what the 'good dad' looks like, combined with the persistent temporal demands of working men, bear on fathers to be more physically active, outdoorsy and 'hands-on' given their limited free time (Creighton et al., 2015; Earley et al., 2019). As such, active play, outdoor activities, sport and leisure time pursuits remain a highly significant part of Western fathering practices and thus continue to contribute to how men create and sustain masculine fathering identities and behaviours (Brandth & Kvande, 2018; Brussoni et al., 2013; Coakley, 2006; Harrington, 2009; Kay, 2009).

Writing in the 1970s, Hantover was alert to the importance of outdoor activities for male identity when he argued that the Scouting movement: 'provided adult men, denied by their occupations, an opportunity to validate the traditional image of masculinity... [because] adult men need the opportunity to perform normatively appropriate male behaviour.... What acts a man performs and how well he does them truly make a male a man' (Hantover, 1978, p. 78—see also Goffman, 1977). Thirty years on, Willms (2009) argues that leisure, the outdoors and sport are arenas where men hope 'to reclaim some foundation of masculinity that may have been threatened or dissipated through modern life' (Willms, 2009, p. 127). For men as fathers, leisure-time pursuits serve as useful occasions to be involved with children while performing, negotiating and validating their male identity without having to make a choice between 'domesticating masculinity or masculinizing domesticity' (Gavanas, 2004, p. 255). These activities, therefore, sustain masculine ideals of fathering because they provide 'a context in which [men] can successfully avoid the dilemma of feminizing the fathering role' (Trussell & Shaw, 2012, p. 380) and 'can differentiate between fatherhood and motherhood, and simultaneously make fathering seem manly, heroic and appealing' (Gavanas, 2004: p. 255).

Goodsell (2005), in his study of father-child excursions, highlights the extent to which outdoor activities 'connect [men] with good fatherhood' (Goodsell, 2005, p. 39) but he cautions that: 'to load [such] places with images of enjoyment, cooperation, and emotional closeness potentially risks—or at least suggests—lack of the same in the immediate places in which narrators spend the great majority of their time... [and] it is easy [for fathers and children] to maintain a façade while there' (Goodsell, 2005, pp. 39–40) so masking the actualities of the father-child relationships. As a result, regardless of the realities of their everyday relationship with their child, men may use such occasions deliberatively to orchestrate their identity work as fathers—to create positive paternal meanings and memories, and to validate their own image of good fathering practices (Goodsell, 2005). Furthermore, Coakley (2006) argues that fathers (in his study of upper-middle class US families) who buy equipment such as 'kayaks, camping gear, rock climbing equipment, and other recreational toys that can be enjoyed with children' are using leisure as a strategy to 'add masculinized activities to the periphery of the domestic sphere, thereby avoiding the task of actually changing the culture and dynamics of lived everyday family life' (Coakley, 2006, p. 158). I conclude that men implicitly recognise that places, and the leisure activities they choose to do there, present cultural and symbolic resources that they may draw on to reinforce differentiation from notions of femininity (Gavanas, 2004; Gorman-Murray & Hopkins, 2015).

My assessment of the 'new caring dad' may sound punitive to some but it is important not to be drawn into an uncritical acceptance of the 'good dad' narrative. As Höfner et al. (2011, p. 680) state: 'the fragmentation of male identity is also provoked by the fact that fatherly identity is produced in opposition to several significant others like one's own father, partner, peer group members, etc'. This means fathers may counter-identify, sometimes antagonistically, with others in order to cement their masculine parenting credentials. For some it is a counter-identification with their own father—the 'old school', absent, emotionally-distant breadwinner (Dermott, 2014; LaRossa, 1988; Williams, 2008). They may also counter-identify with the mother / maternal, as Andrea Doucet's study of stay-at-home Canadian fathers found. She points out how 'care-giving such as promoting their children's physical and outdoor activities, independence, risk-taking, and the fun and playful aspects of care' (Doucet, 2018, p. 196) were used to differentiate paternal from maternal caring practices. Furthermore, it is apparent that some men use their hegemonic privilege as successful fathers in harmonious, dual-income households to undermine not-so-successful fathers: these 'hegemonic new dads ... [enjoy] the best of both worlds at little significant cost and much convenience, e.g. by projecting aggression, domination and misogyny onto other, subordinated groups of men' (Henwood & Procter, 2003, p. 340). So perhaps we should 'view ideas surrounding a caring masculinity ... as a broadening of hegemonic masculinity, rather than an entirely new form' (Hunter et al., 2017, p. 1).

In summary, taking part in activities in the outdoors has, for many decades, offered men opportunities to demonstrate clear-cut, heterosexual, masculine credentials (Coakley, 2006; Coles, 2009; Connell, 1995; Kimmel, 1995; Willms, 2009). On entering fatherhood, men may adapt this behaviour to accommodate the arrival of a child by adopting a modified masculinity that is displayed through father-child rough-and-tumble play, leisure activities and outdoor pursuits (Brandth & Kvande, 2018; Kay, 2009). Thus traditional, sometimes problematic masculine behaviours, can continue to be enjoyed throughout fatherhood, and indeed are widely encouraged, secure in the comfort of the normative, Western (predominantly bourgeois) narrative of the 'hands-on' dad (Coakley, 2006). So, while I accept many contemporary fathers are emotionally-connected parents (Dermott, 2014; Miller, 2011) and active contributors to gender equality (Holter, 2014), and that past repressive masculine norms and cultural homophobia across a range of leisure settings are undergoing significant, permanent, positive change, especially since the turn of the millennium (Magrath et al., 2020), I think it is fair to say that there remains a long journey ahead.

So What's the Problem?

The first issue lies within the outdoor education sector itself. Although Barbara Humberstone attempted to ignite a debate about gender in our sector over two decades ago (Humberstone, 1995), the question of how to address hegemonic masculinity, sexism, harassment, male power and patriarchy—'the storm clouds' (Kennedy & Russell, 2020, p. 7) at the heart of the outdoor sector—has only recently re-emerged as something that requires urgent attention (Gray & Mitten, 2018; Kennedy & Russell,

2020; Warren, 2016). Indeed, the sector is called to task for 'its sexism and heterosexism ... problems [that] have been baked into the very structure of the outdoor field itself since action, risk, challenge, adventure, and leadership are all core foci of most established outdoor organizations..., and these all are typically associated with masculinity' (Kennedy & Russell, 2020, p. 4).

Leading on from this sectoral challenge, the second issue must be how we successfully engage men in rewarding outdoor experiences without our male participants falling into repressive, problematic masculine behaviours and staff (intentionally or unintentionally), reinforcing these behaviours as we struggle to find a suitable response. The challenge is for us as practitioners, in essence, is how do we manage masculinity in the field? Across the outdoor education sector, examples are needed to illustrate how we can support progressive, reflective masculinity (Kennedy & Russell, 2020)—this chapter is one such contribution. In the next section I will illustrate how regular, outdoor learning activities, for male carers and their children that take place in local green spaces, while they might appear pleasant, unremarkable events, in fact, offer dads unique opportunities to trial alternative, caring performances of masculinity in the company of other men. I also want to demonstrate how female outdoor learning staff are subtly supporting progressive performances of fathering identities.

Background and Methodology

Fatherhood scholars (Doherty et al., 1998; Lamb, 2010; Marsiglio & Cohan, 2000; Palkovitz & Hull, 2018; Schoppe-Sullivan & Fagan, 2020) have advocated for several decades that fathering research should take a broad conceptual approach that aims to capture the multifaceted nature of fathering alongside the ecologically rich contexts of men's lived experiences, including the diverse physical and social spaces where men enact their fathering (Creighton et al., 2015; Gorman-Murray & Hopkins, 2015; Marsiglio et al., 2005). While there is no unifying, agreed conceptual model that captures this ambitious multidimensionality of fathering, the phenomenon of identity has been widely applied as a useful explanatory theoretical construct (Habib, 2012; Pasley et al., 2014; Schoppe-Sullivan & Fagan, 2020). As 'men construct, negotiate and reconstruct masculine identities through "local" interactions within their social and cultural contexts' (Dolan, 2014, p. 825), place and what happens there are relevant because 'the material and symbolic characteristics of one's environment or situational context... encourage or inhibit the enactment of identity' (Adamsons & Pasley, 2013, p. 168). Community-led dads' groups, as local spaces where father figures come together with their children for an activity, are unique settings in which to observe a group of men parenting solo for several hours without the fathers' partners present. As a researcher, I am interested in exploring how dads make use of these places to perform, modify and validate their identities, and the role of staff, children, mothers and indeed the *locale* in supporting this identity construction (Doucet, 2011).

This research is an ethnographic study of four community-based dads' groups in southern England. Data collection took place between June 2018 and September 2019. Two groups take place indoors and are funded through local Children's Centres; two are 'Dangerous Dads' groups which focus on outdoor activities based on Forest School principles.[1] 51 informal, semi-structured interviews with fathers (n = 24), mothers (n = 7), children (n = 8) and staff (n = 12) and eight field observations (17 hours) were undertaken by the researcher in total. This chapter is limited to a discussion of the data from interviews with six female staff who run the Dangerous Dads groups. I followed an informal interview schedule and covered a range of topics, such as the purpose of the group and the impact they had observed on those attending. Confidentiality is protected using pseudonyms for people and places. The analytical process was informed by a thematic analysis (Braun & Clarke, 2006) and Saldana's eclectic coding method (Saldaña, 2015), and organised using NVivo11 software.

MANAGING MASCULINITY: FIRE CIRCLES, FOOD AND FATHERS' CONVERSATIONS

In the context of the woodland spaces where the dads' group activities take place, the female leaders interviewed (Emma, Lucy, Lynn, Philippa, Rose and Sally) are alert to gender, heightened by being in the minority:

---

[1] These are part of *The Dangerous Dads Network*, a social enterprise that I established in 2007 in partnership with the national charity *Action for Children*. The 'Dangerous Dads' model is one based on active, fun and challenging events for father figures from all backgrounds and ages, with their children, daughters as well as sons (www.dangerousdads.org. uk). While I am involved in the Network, the life stories of interview participants were unknown to me prior to the study.

'When I first started, I was stood there on Day One with 48 dads, it was a *big* first group, and I realised that it was two women who were about to run this group, and I thought: 'Ooh am I doing the right thing?', kind of 'hmm', but actually, no, it's absolutely fantastic. (Lynn)

Although rare, the staff recount the need to directly intervene on occasion to tackle male excessiveness, such as building huge fires. As Philippa describes 'there's testosterone going around the place, so you might need to rein it in slightly ... but that's only happened, like, one or two occasions'. More often the staff are less conspicuously responding to the demands of the group. Rose recounts how, being the only woman present, she has to push against traditional gendered expectations:

'Occasionally the child comes to me for a bit of juice, and I go: 'Ask your dad,' and the dad does it. It's like everyone's conditioned for the maternal figure to get the drink ready. Well, why? ...it's just little things like that happened quite a lot. (Rose)

These data extracts illustrate the importance staff place on the sessions as 'powerful' (Sally) opportunities to shift traditional gendered beliefs by putting responsibility on the fathers and tackling out-dated 'conditioned' views of what constitutes the maternal.

The fire circle emerges as a central point for encouraging conversations about fatherhood. As Emma says: 'the fire is a nice alternative to bring people together so, when [dads] start cooking around the fire, that is really ... bonding. Isn't it?'. Likewise, Sally consciously supports conversations between the dads around the fire:

'... if you're all sitting round a fire ... a lot of people often comment on things ... I quite often start with that actually, as a bit of a, you know: 'Tell me something amazing that you've done outside from your childhood' or whatever it might be, fire's very powerful isn't it? It can bring out a lot. (Sally)

Rose recounts a similar experience:

'... so it was when the children had run off and the dads were with each other that they were able to talk because ... you're around the fire, you're looking at the fire or doing the whittling, so it's easy to have silence and it's easy to have those conversations without it feeling quite so in your face. That's when it happened, yeah. (Rose)

Emma acknowledges that 'it takes longer than it does for the mums. The mums will make friends in one session, then they'll be going out for a coffee the next day [laughs] … whereas the dads it takes a few meetings'. In response to their personal experiences of men and masculinity, the female group leaders actively work to encourage the dads to chat around the fire as they are aware, not only of the potential for male stoicism and inexpressiveness, but also the undercurrents within hegemonic masculinity to male-male aloofness (Scoats & Robinson, 2020). As Rose says:

> Something I didn't expect was the fathers talking to each other as fathers … they were chatting about lots of things including, you know, my precocious 8 year old and what she's up to: 'oh yeah, well don't worry, I went through that. Actually it gets better,' that kind of stuff was happening which was really beautiful. That was probably when I stepped back and did a bit of cooking. (Rose)

From the limited research we have of dads' groups in the UK (Dolan, 2014; Gilligan et al., 2012; Hanna, 2018; Robertson et al., 2016), the role of the session leaders appears invaluable in encouraging men to feel at ease discussing issues of emotional concern amongst a peer group, behaviours typically scorned by traditional masculine norms. In Dolan's (2014) study of a dads' group in the West Midlands, he reports how staff carefully managed the sessions:

> 'Being a man' in this context encouraged men to distance themselves from certain aspects of traditional masculinity, such as impulse and aggression, and to value characteristics such as intimacy and affection that also allowed them to talk openly about their love for their children. (Dolan, 2014, p. 826)

In the outdoors, the fire-circle is carefully selected as the venue to encourage interaction between the dads, who often do not know each other, as 'you're maybe not facing … it's not confrontational' (Sally) while also being respectful of men's preference for silence at times. In response the female leaders orchestrate opportunities for men to share parenting experiences and bond as a group via carefully crafted questions, getting them cooking together or 'stepping back' (Rose) leaving the dads to chat amongst themselves. The women are, thus, continually sensitive to choreographing interventions and spaces that encourage openness, sharing, co-creation and meaningful conversations between men in order to encourage respectful listening and dialogue about the expectations, meanings, constraints, challenges and potential of new forms of fathering without judgement from others.

Managing male Sensibilities and Building Dads' Confidence

Group leader Lucy describes how one of her roles is also to facilitate closer bonding between the fathers and their children at their Forest School site:

> I quite like giving them the time because that's about them building those relationships, you know, so we don't want to be too, sort of, you know, pushy on that side, saying: 'You can do this or that', and give them ideas, it's actually nice just watching them develop [relationships] with their child. (Lucy)

The female facilitators are acutely aware that secure masculine performances are important to men, and that dads will want to appear confident and skilled in front of their child in relation to tool-use, fire-lighting and other Forest School activities:

> … it was definitely something about women being in charge so that if *I* show you [dad] how to do something in a really safe way with your children, I can explain it in a really soft way and say: 'Oh *I know* you know how to do it. You *clearly* know how to do it … if you were to do it with your children, this is the safe way of doing it. Have you ever thought you could minimise that risk by doing it this way?'… So it was less about me as a woman telling the man they didn't know how to do it and more about 'Oh, as a Forest School ethos, this is how you might like to do it in front of your children so that they remain safe' … I think the men who came to our [dads' group] weren't bush-crafty types, there were a couple who kind of thought they were like nifty with the fire or whatever, but *most* of them were pretty much useless when it came to lighting a fire and so, instead of being useless in front of their child … I asked them to not do it until I showed them, so they all started with the same ground level: 'I'm going to teach you how to teach your child safely', so it didn't matter if they knew how to do it or not, they could all learn to do it in a Forest School set-up so it was done to maximise success for the child … and they all managed to do it in front of their child, so the child never saw them not able to light a fire. (Rose)

Not being too directive is something staff elect to moderate in front of the dads. A more typical patriarchal response would be to exert 'power-over' behaviours, such as mocking the ones who lack skills (Pleck, 2004). Emma knows she is a competent woman and, consequently, is consciously mindful in judiciously approaching the subject of tool use:

> I didn't fully think it through, and then, when I had to stand up in front of a sea of men and say 'right this is what we are going to do, these are the fire rules and this is how safety works, and this is how you gonna use a bow-saw' … I felt a bit odd and having to put that across … I think we've, we've got it better now because, we, I'm able to say, 'I *know* you probably are used to using tools, but we're able to show you how to safely use them with your children' which actually is something that men do shy away from, quite often. (Emma)

This illustrates well how the staff are aware of being women in leader-ship positions with superior outdoor skills to the men. In Western cul-tures, fire skills and tool-use are seen as highly masculine activities (Brandth & Haugen, 2005). In addition, the female group leaders are aware of the need not to undermine the father's male credentials in front of others, especially their child. In response, as women in front of 'a sea of men' (Emma), the female staff are choosing to manage their language—to be 'softly' spoken, not 'too pushy', and minimise intergender competitive-ness—in order to avoid unsettling masculine sensibilities. As a conse-quence, they are actively and skilfully supporting successful performances of fathering identities by perceptively conducting themselves in ways that encourage emotional openness, social interaction with peers, the acquisi-tion of skills, and closeness between fathers and children. On a final note (for now)—that women are, as ever, still having to be constantly alert to gender, manage their conduct and veil their superior skills in order to deal with potential male sensibilities totally unbeknown to the male partici-pants, illustrates how much still remains to be done for gender equality.

Conclusion

Dads' groups are homosocial settings that, when done well, offer an inter-section of play with public displays of intimate, embodied solo fathering that are important in supporting men to build their confidence as parents (Doucet, 2011; Wilson & Prior, 2010). While Dolan (2014), in his study of a dads' group, saw 'no "undoing" of well understood and expected expressions of masculinity' (Dolan, 2014, p. 15), others have argued these gatherings offer opportunities to 'solidify', 'embrace', 'shore up and further develop [men's] identities as fathers' (Hanna, 2018, p. 78) through peer interaction. Dads' group sessions can help fathers develop an emotional openness, dads build trust and rapport with the other dads, they can speak openly about issues, and share a concomitant sense of respectful identities which provide validation that their experiences are common. While these initiatives can introduce fathers 'to new forms of social and cultural capital thereby expanding their repertoire of acceptable (and beneficial) ways to "be a man"' (Robertson et al., 2016, pp. 18–19), I have established that new forms of fatherhood also benefit from the sensitised collaboration of those proximate to the fathers to ensure that progressive, nurturing identities are validated, celebrated and embedded.

In this chapter, I have explored dads' groups in outdoor settings. The interview excerpts highlight the diversity of emotional and sensitised work of female outdoor learning professionals (Gray & Mitten, 2018). The staff are cognisant that these are men who are developing a fathering identity and they recognise that they have a role in the dads' journey into becoming confident parents. The female group leaders are working hard, unknown to the dads themselves, to encourage more open, caring fathering identities. They are sensitive to the possibility of traditionally gendered behaviours yet do not shy away from tackling these issues. Outdoor learning staff are, therefore, actively but subtly involved in affirming more nurturing, emotionally-open paternal practices. Rather than being troubled by or hostile to the idea of working with dads, as some sectors seemingly are (Ferguson & Hogan, 2004; Ghate et al., 2000; Page et al., 2008), these outdoor practitioners welcome fathers, actively scaffold opportunities for dads to model positive parenting behaviours, and sensitively reassure the dads that they are becoming competent, skilful and have the resources to be a 'good dad'. As such their work offers a shaft of welcome light out from 'the storm clouds' (Kennedy & Russell, 2020, p. 7).

I have demonstrated that the outdoor learning sector can support male father figures as caring contributors on the co-parenting journey, thus disrupting problematic masculine templates. Sessions for dads and their children, when carefully facilitated by those alert to the issues of less progressive masculine behaviours, can be locations where outdoor learning staff can help cultivate and stabilise a more expansive and generative fathering identity. Staff working in the outdoor learning sector should be reassured that they can make use of their existing resources, in particular natural settings, fire circles and simple outdoor activities, to support men to re-examine counterproductive masculine conceptualisations of fatherhood amongst their peers. Whilst a small-scale project located in a particular subset of outdoor education, I hope this chapter contributes to the wider issues and on-going debates. I also hope that others working in outdoor learning settings have similar stories and practices to share.

REFERENCES

Adamsons, K., & Pasley, K. (2013). Refining identity theory to better account for relationships and context: Applications to fathering. *Journal of Family Theory Review, 5*, 159–175.

Brandth, B., & Haugen, M. S. (2005). Text, body, and tools: Changing mediations of rural masculinity. *Men and Masculinities, 8*(2), 148–163.

Brandth, B., & Kvande, E. (2018). Masculinity and fathering alone during parental leave. *Men and Masculinities, 21*(1), 72–90.

Braun, V., & Clarke, V. (2006). Using thematic analysis in psychology. *Qualitative Research in Psychology, 3*(2), 77–101.

Brussoni, M., Olsen, L. L., Creighton, G., & Oliffe, J. L. (2013). Heterosexual gender relations in and around childhood risk and safety. *Qualitative Health Research, 23*(10), 1388–1398.

Coakley, J. (2006). The good father: Parental expectations and youth sports. *Leisure Studies, 25*(2), 153–163.

Coles, T. (2009). Negotiating the field of masculinity: The production and reproduction of multiple dominant masculinities. *Men and Masculinities, 12*(1), 30–44.

Connell, R. W. (1995). *Masculinities*. Polity Press.

Creighton, G., Brussoni, M., Oliffe, J., & Olsen, L. (2015). Fathers on child's play: Urban and rural Canadian perspectives. *Men and Masculinities, 18*(5), 559–580.

Dermott, E. (2014). *Intimate fatherhood: A sociological analysis*. Routledge.

Doherty, W. J., Kouneski, E. F., & Erickson, M. F. (1998). Responsible fathering: An overview and conceptual framework. *Journal of Marriage and the Family, 20*(3), 277–292.

Dolan, A. (2014). 'I've learnt what a dad should do': The interaction of masculine and fathering identities among men who attended a 'dads only' parenting programme. *Sociology, 48*(4), 812–828.

Doucet, A. (2011). It's just not good for a man to be interested in other people's children': Fathers, public displays of care and 'relevant others. In E. Dermott & J. Seymour (Eds.), *Displaying families*. Palgrave Macmillan.

Doucet, A. (2018). *Do men mother? Fathering, care and domestic responsibility.* University of Toronto Press.

Earley, V., Fairbrother, H., & Curtis, P. (2019). Displaying good fathering through the construction of physical activity as intimate practice. *Families, Relationships and Societies, 8*(2), 213–229.

Ferguson, H., & Hogan, F. (2004). *Strengthening families through fathers: Developing policy and practice in relation to vulnerable fathers and their families.* The Centre for Social and Family Research.

Gavanas, A. (2004). Domesticating masculinity and masculinizing domesticity in contemporary US fatherhood politics. *Social Politics: International Studies in Gender, State & Society, 11*(2), 247–266.

Ghate, D., Shaw, C., & Hazel, N. (2000). *How family centres are working with fathers.* Joseph Rowntree Foundation.

Gilligan, P., Manby, M., & Pickburn, C. (2012). Fathers' involvement in children's services: Exploring local and national issues in 'Moorlandstown'. *British Journal of Social Work, 42*(3), 500–518.

Goffman, E. (1977). The Arrangement between the Sexes. *Theory and Society, 4*(3), 301–331.

Goodsell, T. L. (2005). Fatherhood and the social organization of space: An essay in subjective geography. In W. Marsiglio, K. Roy, & G. L. Fox (Eds.), *Situated fathering: A focus on physical and social spaces* (pp. 27–47). Rowman & Littlefield Publishers.

Gorman-Murray, A., & Hopkins, P. (Eds.). (2015). *Masculinities and place.* Ashgate.

Gray, T., & Mitten, D. (Eds.). (2018). *The Palgrave international handbook of women and outdoor learning.* Palgrave Macmillan.

Habib, C. (2012). The transition to fatherhood: A literature review exploring paternal involvement with identity theory. *Journal of Family Studies, 18*(2–3), 103–120.

Hanna, E. (2018). *Supporting young men as fathers: Gendered understandings of group-based community provisions.* Palgrave Macmillan.

Hantover, J. P. (1978). The Boy Scouts and the validation of masculinity. *Journal of Social Issues, 34*(1), 184–195.

Harrington, M. (2009). Sport mad, good dads: Australian fathering through leisure and sport practices. In T. A. Kay (Ed.), *Fathering through sport and leisure* (pp. 67–88). Routledge.

Henwood, K., & Procter, J. (2003). The 'good father': Reading men's accounts of paternal involvement during the transition to first-time fatherhood. *British Journal of Social Psychology, 42*(3), 337–355.

Höfner, C., Schadler, C., & Richter, R. (2011). When men become fathers: Men's identity at the transition to parenthood. *Journal of Comparative Family Studies, 42*(5), 669–686.

Holter, Ø. G. (2014). "What's in it for men?": Old question, new data. *Men and Masculinities, 17*(5), 515–548.

Humberstone, B. (1995). Bringing outdoor education into the physical education agenda: Gender identities and social change. *Quest, 47*(2), 144–157.

Hunter, S. C., Riggs, D. W., & Augoustinos, M. (2017). Hegemonic masculinity versus a caring masculinity: Implications for understanding primary caregiving fathers. *Social and Personality Psychology Compass, 11*(3), e12307.

John, A., Halliburton, A., & Humphrey, J. (2013). Child–mother and child–father play interaction patterns with preschoolers. *Early Child Development and Care, 183*(3–4), 483–497.

Kay, T. A. (Ed.). (2009). *Fathering through sport and leisure.* Routledge.

Kennedy, J., & Russell, C. (2020). Hegemonic masculinity in outdoor education. *Journal of Adventure Education and Outdoor Learning.* https://doi.org/10.1080/14729679.2020.1755706

Kimmel, M. S. (Ed.). (1995). *The politics of manhood.* Temple University Press.

Lamb, M. E. (Ed.). (2010). *The role of the father in child development* (5th ed.). John Wiley & Sons.

LaRossa, R. (1988). Fatherhood and social change. *Family Relations, 37*(4), 451–457.

Magrath, R., Cleland, J., & Anderson, E. (Eds.). (2020). *The Palgrave handbook of masculinity and sport.* Palgrave Macmillan.

Marsiglio, W., & Cohan, M. (2000). Contextualizing father involvement and paternal influence. *Marriage and Family Review, 29*(2–3), 75–95.

Marsiglio, W., Roy, K., & Fox, G. L. (Eds.). (2005). *Situated fathering: A focus on physical and social spaces.* Rowman & Littlefield Publishers.

Miller, T. (2011). *Making sense of fatherhood: Gender, caring and work.* Cambridge University Press.

Page, J., Whitting, G., & Mclean, C. (2008). *A review of how fathers can be better recognised and supported through DCSF policy.* Department for Children, Schools and Families.

Palkovitz, R., & Hull, J. (2018). Toward a resource theory of fathering. *Journal of Family Theory & Review, 10*(1), 181–198.

Pasley, K., Petren, R. E., & Fish, J. N. (2014). Use of Identity Theory to inform fathering scholarship. *Journal of Family Theory Review, 6*(4), 298–318.

Pleck, J. H. (2004). Men's power with women, other men, and society: A men's movement analysis. In P. F. Murphy (Ed.), *Feminism and masculinities* (pp. 57–68). OUP.

Robertson, S., Woodall, J., Henry, H., Hanna, H., Rowlands, S., Horrocks, J., Livesley, J., & Long, T. (2016). Evaluating a community-led project for improving fathers' and children's well-being in England'. *Health Promotion International.* ISSN: 1460-2245. https://doi.org/10.1093/heapro/daw090

Saldaña, J. (2015). *The coding manual for qualitative researchers.* Sage.

Schoppe-Sullivan, S. J., & Fagan, J. (2020). The evolution of fathering research in the 21st century: Persistent challenges, new directions. *Journal of Marriage and Family, 82*(1), 175–197.

Scoats, R., & Robinson, S. (2020). From Stoicism to Bromance: Millennial men's friendships. In R. Magrath, J. Cleland, & E. Anderson (Eds.), *The Palgrave handbook of masculinity and sport* (pp. 379–392). Palgrave Macmillan.

Such, L. (2009). Fatherhood, the morality of personal time and leisure-based parenting. In T. Kay (Ed.), *Fathering through sport and leisure* (pp. 89–103). Routledge.

Trussell, D. E., & Shaw, S. M. (2012). Organized youth sport and parenting in public and private spaces. *Leisure Sciences, 34*(5), 377–394.

Ward, M. R. M., Tarrant, A., Terry, G., Featherstone, B., Robb, M., & Ruxton, S. (2017). Doing gender locally: The importance of 'place' in understanding marginalised masculinities and young men's transitions to 'safe' and successful futures. *Sociological Review, 65*(4), 797–815.

Warren, K. (2016). Gender in outdoor studies. In B. Humberstone, H. Prince, & K. A. Henderson (Eds.), *Routledge international handbook of outdoor studies* (pp. 360–368). Routledge.

Williams, S. (2008). What is fatherhood? Searching for the reflexive father. *Sociology, 42*(3), 487–502.

Willms, N. (2009). Fathers and daughters: Negotiating gendered relationships in sport. In T. Kay (Ed.), *Fathering through sport and leisure* (pp. 124–144). Routledge.

Wilson, K. R., & Prior, M. R. (2010). Father involvement: The importance of paternal solo care. *Early Child Development and Care, 180*(10), 1391–1405.

Wissö, T. (2018). Researching fatherhood and place: Adopting an ethnographic approach. In E. Dermott & C. Gatrell (Eds.), *Fathers, families and relationships: Researching everyday lives* (pp. 89–108). Policy Press.

The Scenic Route to Academic Attainment via Emotional Wellbeing Outdoors

Mel McCree

INTRODUCTION

For several years now there has been an increasing pressure on children in many UK schools to succeed academically. To apply such pressure and to put such emphasis on children's academic performances will almost inevitably make apparent their unequal capabilities. Not matter the pacing, some children will fall behind with all the resulting, negative connotations, of isolation and sense of failure that such events simply precipitate.

This chapter describes a project around learning at the children's own pace and supporting affective, restorative learning processes (Rose et al., 2012; Roe & Aspinall, 2011). It set out to explore and critically evaluate the idea that, for disadvantaged young children, outdoor learning can expedite improvement in achievement at school (Dillon & Dickie, 2012). Uniquely, at the time, this was a longitudinal project across an extended time-frame, however, subsequently the body of evidence to support

M. McCree (✉)
Bath Spa University, Bath, UK
e-mail: m.mccree@bathspa.ac.uk

R. Cutting, R. Passy (eds.), *Contemporary Approaches to Outdoor Learning*, Palgrave Studies in Alternative Education,
https://doi.org/10.1007/978-3-030-85095-1_9

117

long-term restorative outdoors intervention has improved (Malone & Waite, 2016).

The project considered how nature connection, wellbeing and academic development are influenced by outdoor learning. We also sought to understand how the children felt and saw their world and acted within particular contexts. We asked specific questions that explored the relationship between outdoor experience and academic performance. Essentially, exploring potential changes in attitudes and behaviour and, if so, how these expressed themselves in formal school settings.

In 2015, therefore, a small county-town school with 320 pupils with an age range of 5 to 11 was approached to take part. Situated in Wiltshire (south-west England) the pupils included a social mix of families, with around 26% eligible for Free School Meals (FSM) (similar to the national average of 26%) and nearly 13% of pupils receive Special Educational Needs (SEN) support (the national average being 13%).

The outdoor learning project was designed and implemented by the Wiltshire Wildlife Trust Youth Wellbeing team who have a successful record of developing outdoor projects with children and their work spans both formal and informal learning, both in and out of school. This outdoor project was located in woodlands and involved the children in a range of Forest School type activities. It was year-round, including school holidays.

The children who took part were chosen by the headteacher as those 'struggling to thrive' and therefore likely to underachieve (Head, Y1). The headteacher further defined them as 'economically and emotionally disadvantaged and with special education needs (including behaviour difficulties)' (Head, Y1). Their home lives included known elements of stress, trauma and complex family relationships.

METHODOLOGICAL APPROACHES

For three years, the research followed 11 children who took part in the project, aged five—seven on entry to seven—ten years old on exit. The research design applied mixed methods and adopted elements from the child-centred Mosaic approach (Clark & Moss, 2001). To achieve this, creative child-centred interviews and evaluation events were used, based on employing two-stages of participation and community reflection (Gallacher & Gallagher, 2008). Qualitative data sets were also collected using published measurement scales (Laevers, 2005; Cheng & Monroe,

2012), fieldwork observation, focus groups, questionnaires and wider interviews. Quantitative data were also collected and compiled from school administrative records. Baseline and post-project questionnaires were collected at the point of entry in 2013, and exit in 2016, from children, parents and staff. The children completed a child-appropriate 6 question 'smiley' questionnaire, with writing assistance, at entry and exit ($n = 11$) and verbal comments were noted. Class teachers and staff involved with study children completed questionnaires ($n = 7$ at entry, $n = 7$ at exit). Parents were hard to reach and achieved a low response rate ($n = 3$ at entry, $n = 0$ at exit). They were positively involved in the halfway evaluation event, reflecting the emergent findings back to the school. Focus groups and informal discussions were also held with parents at the halfway point and the conclusion of the study. The combined qualitative data were analysed thematically using grounded theory (Strauss & Corbin, 1998).

The mixed-method approach allowed for a balanced methodology and the evaluation criteria corresponded to the desired outcomes of the school, parents and the funding educational charity. These outcomes formed the focus of interest and included the overall academic performance in a set of National Curriculum (England) subjects, including Mathematics and English. They also included wider social parameters such as metrics on attendance data. More evaluative data were collated on attitudes to school and learning drawn from parents and teachers.

The methodology was tested in Year 1 and then refined in Years 2 and 3. Full consent was confirmed before the study from all participants. Ethical guidelines from the British Educational Research Association (BERA) were followed and liaison support from a trusted pastoral member of staff was offered throughout to ensure parents' ongoing awareness and a safe way to raise concerns or initiate a withdrawal. An initial discussion session with the children developed under-standing about participation, consent and withdrawal. Children who joined the project after this date were not part of the study cohort, and children who left before the end of the 3 years were removed. Regular check-ins with the children ensured that they knew they did not have to engage with the researcher on any given day and that they could withdraw fully if they wished. Children sometimes exercised their rights to not answer questions, being otherwise engaged and not wanting to be interrupted by research activities.

RESULTS: INVOLVEMENT, CONNECTION AND WELL-BEING

Observations were made using Leuven scale measures (Laevers, 2005). This tool is based around two key indicators namely children's 'involvement' and 'wellbeing'. Involvement refers to the degree to which a child engages in activities and is therefore an important component in learning processes. Wellbeing refers to both an emotional sense of being at ease with one's self and from being free of emotional tensions and this in turn relates to self-confidence and self-esteem.

High levels of both wellbeing and involvement on the sessions were sustained throughout the project (at or above a level 4 on a Leuven scale). A second comparative measure of engagement was taken by the session leader with a similar result of a level 4 or above sustained throughout.

The Connection to Nature Index (Cheng & Monroe, 2012) was used on exit with both the cohort and the whole school, the mean average differences between the school (3.9), the study cohort (4.5) and a national survey (4.05) (Bragg et al., 2013; RSPB, 2013) indicates that the intervention strengthened the children's connection to the rest of nature. This is perhaps not surprising given that there was so much affordance for connection in a nature-based programme with rich species diversity and availability of natural materials to play and to construct with on-site (Malone & Waite, 2016; Austin et al., 2015).

RESULTS: ACADEMIC ATTAINMENT AND ATTENDANCE

Data drawn from teachers' records showed that the cohort made a variety of academic improvements, with continued improvement in all three of the subject areas (reading, writing and mathematics). Writing attainment progressed and improved by 18% (compared to 6% in the total year groups). Reading and maths attainment both showed improvements of 27% each compared to 13% reading and 15% maths in the total year groups.

Of course, improvement is to be expected as part of attending school and maturing and the findings do need to be seen in the context of improved attainment across the whole school. We cannot attribute any sole causality to the project, yet the study cohort fared well in comparison to their peers.

Attendance data showed a positive difference for the study cohort (2.4% mean average) compared with the whole school (1.1% mean average). Attendance for the study cohort was below the whole school in Years

0 and 1, peaked above in Year 2 and settled at a similar level as the school in Year 3. This suggests that the project needed to be long term to make a sustainable difference. The findings show a positive impact on attainment and attendance for the study cohort.

QUALITATIVE ANALYSIS THEMES

Data were analysed from session-based fieldwork, school-based interviews, focus groups and Mosaic approach events. Across the three years that the programme operated, the identified themes emerged, deepened and were refined. Some faded, others became more defined. Here was simply present the themes viewed by Year 3. These were 'self-regulation and resilience through emotional space', 'nurture', 'physical adventure', 'free social play', 'nature discovery', 'socially confident learners' and 'choice and independence'. These themes are inter-dependent both in their nuances and in the school-based themes such as 'behaviour perceptions'. Other themes observed with-in school were 'new perspectives' and 'whole school culture change'.

SELF-REGULATION AND RESILIENCE THROUGH EMOTIONAL SPACE

A longitudinal project by its nature provides a great deal of data and here, again for brevity, we concentrate our discussion on the theme found to be the most significant; 'self-regulation and resilience through emotional space'. 'Emotional space' here means the provision of a physical space in which the children are free to express their emotions. Reports from the children, session staff and project practitioners stated that this was the most constructive contribution to their wellbeing, and the children demonstrated a clear development in this area over time. We regard this important finding as a meta-theme, with others as vital ingredients towards the children achieving self-regulation and resilience, steadily growing in strength as evidenced by the halfway evaluation and final year.

The children expressed a strong attachment to attending the project and evaluated the experience as positive. However, negative emotions featured strongly in how the children said they often felt.

The children found ways to self-regulate within the sessions, for example through fantasy-play and den-building, tool-mastery and social physical play. The different choices they made reflected their different characters and needs, and in turn the different meanings they derived from the experience. Children exhibited challenging behaviour at times, particularly in Year 2, and were excluded from the sessions on one or two occasions. The source of the problems was similar for both; their relations with other children, yet for different reasons. Eventually, the sessions became a safe space where they played out their emotions and overcame social conflicts. These findings emphasise the importance of this social time with adequate affordances in place, both physical and emotional, for children to find ways to develop positively, inter and intra-personally. It was not unusual to present attachment disorders or a need to play out dysfunctional domestic situations. As time went by the children knew they had space and permission to express themselves in such ways and to find their way to self-regulate; they were learning the parameters of what was acceptable.

There were many instances where children would do something alone rather than with the group. They would seek one-to-one attention from an adult, take their space and then re-join the group once they felt able. The ending of the valued sessions remained a flashpoint for the children even into Year 3, suggesting that they appreciated the time to unwind from their often complex lives, and found some endings difficult.

Nurture

Firstly, creating stable ongoing relationships with a skilled, attuned practitioner lay a strong foundation for the children to feel nurtured and thrive. Further, ensuring that the basic needs of the children were met remained a priority throughout the project and a vital part of a positive session, such as bringing spare clothes for children who didn't have enough to keep them warm. When the children were first getting used to being outside, the popularity of hot drinks and snacks around the fire was not surprising yet essential. There was a tangible transformation in their behaviour when their basic needs were met. A hot meal on a cold day and a welcoming base camp area enabled the children to feel secure in their new environment and its regular provision had a nurturing effect on the group. This simple provision is not to be underestimated. In Year 1, drinking hot chocolate was the most popular activity for all the children and held significance throughout. There were only a few sessions at the end of the project in Year 3 where the practitioner did not include hot chocolate and the children commented upon this in their final interviews. By Year 3, it seemed that the children had a solid and positive relationship with, and trust in, the session leaders, the place, their peers and in themselves. It also appeared that perhaps some nurture needs were being met with a wider species connection. 'I like getting juicy blackberries', said Child C in Year 3. 'Fruit gives you energy and it's free!'

Physical Adventure

Over time, the children increased their roaming range across the main session site, in parallel with an observable increase in confidence and ownership of the space. They named places or gave them specific associations and regularly initiated exploration to find new secret corners which they could claim. By Year 3 they knew the woods very well and could find their way around a large part of them. This confidence and trust also enabled the adults to give a wider roaming radius to the children.

A final significant aspect of this theme is the physical experience. Physical activities scored highly as the children's first preference and were consistently voted as popular activities in each yearly evaluation. Child A's case study shows his clear satisfaction of the same, regular, repeated physical adventurous play and this was echoed by all the children in their actions each week. Children frequently tested their bodily limits, and then pushed beyond them. In short, they learnt about their physicality through free play.

Free Social Play

This theme evolved from shared time and space and is associated with 'choice and independence', 'physical adventure' and 'nature discovery'. The site had a clear agency and role within the children's play; 'It's a special place because we had fun there and that's for us to remember' (Child 1, Y3). The social experience was important in various ways. Social interactions affected each experience and its learning potential strongly. The need for friendship and positive social interactions was paramount with a strong preference for sharing time and space with friends over other activities. An apparent need to assert positions and leadership was observed in Year 1 group dynamics. In subsequent years, this was still a flashpoint but was mediated most strongly through the children's social play more than adult intervention.

Nature Discovery

There was an element of taught ecological education within the project, although always led from the children's interests or choice of activities such as pond dipping or making bird-boxes. Additionally investigating, collecting and taking things home was popular; 'they remind me of all the fun I've had' (Child I, Y2). Child I had a special box and enjoyed collecting small items. She would often take the time to investigate and the rewards she felt from this process were demonstrated. When asked to choose an experience to remember she chose 'sharing a moment' with a moth she encountered and said 'I felt really happy, special' (Child I, Y2). She often documented with a camera, narrating her observations through questions and reflection.

Socially Confident Learners

The confidence of the children improved and was maintained within the sessions. Their knowledge and skills increased as they became more confident and mature, which in turn helped them to become more responsible, to self-regulate and to gain resilience. This was not without some exceptions, mainly where children had challenging life circumstances or peer-to-peer conflicts. The children became more adept at recognising their emotional processes and at constructively acting upon them.

Choice and Independence

During the project sessions, the children chose free play, continued where they had left off previously, or participated in offered activities. For example, digging was popular and acted as a springboard for many experiences. The child-centred aspect of the project led to a culture of self-directed learning and existence. Many children chose to persist with a certain activity or pursuit over several sessions until they reached a conclusion or new level of mastery, with some degree of satisfaction and autonomy.

Towards the end of Year 3, the lead practitioner minimised resources and stopped initiating activities, to see what would happen. The children were positive in their freedom of choice and if they became disinterested, they changed for themselves, and according to their reports, did not get bored. When consulted at the halfway evaluation, all the children stated clearly that they wished to continue the project and demonstrated signs to their parents and teachers of enthusiasm in their relationship to nature. This newfound independence also appeared to align with other outdoor play research findings (e.g. Ridgers et al., 2012).

In-School Themes

There was a significant and considerable culture change within the school, with outdoor learning embraced and championed. The project was the springboard for this burgeoning interest in outdoor learning and a widespread 'Wild' culture change took place in the school. There has been, in essence, a re-wilding of the school. So much so that the Head declared 2015–2016 a Wild Year, reinforcing the access he wished every child to have to learning outdoors. The strong theme of culture change meant that it became important to observe the effects on the wider school as well as the children.

From an interview with the headteacher at the halfway stage in March 2015, the distance the children had travelled over the first half of the project had started to become clear to him, through both observation and academic results. The headteacher said he knew the project was working for the children and the school. By the end of the project, he was still cautiously positive.

The parents were harder to reach but where they did make links with the project and their children's development, they were direct and positive. One trend identified was that the parents of the study children engaged more positively with the school, as noticed by staff.

Behaviour Perceptions

Within Years 2 and 3, some school staff were surprised by the different behaviour during the sessions as compared to behaviour at school. In other studies (Roe & Aspinall, 2011; Borradaile, 2006), being selected to go to a Forest School project for behavioural reasons has had a negative effect. Importantly, Borradaile (2006) cautions against Forest School as a tool for behavioural management and segregation within a mainstream school, as children may feel excluded. This was not the case within the current research. Roe and Aspinall's research (2011) highlights the rich potential of forest school when the drive for learner achievement is relaxed and the restorative relationship with the setting is explicit.

Teachers had a variety of viewpoints on whether any changes of behaviour were observable in class. The children perceived the two spaces very differently in terms of behaviour codes and acted accordingly. When asked, they were clear about the difference in settings between project and school time, and about the behaviour codes expected. Several of the study cohorts had an increase in challenging life circumstances at home in Year 3. There was a visible impact on behaviour and attendance, reported by school and session staff. It was in this year that some staff began to question whether 3 years was too long for the children to be involved. It is hard to say whether their home life challenges or the length of the project had more impact. Additionally, and similarly to the discussion around academic development, it is difficult to isolate parameters such as growing maturity over the time-period. However, what arose was a difference in behaviour expectation that became evident over the long term in that the children did not want to behave in the woods as they did in school.

TEACHING STAFF PERSPECTIVES

Each year staff involved with the study children attended two or more focus groups. The headteacher was interviewed once a year with regular informal contact throughout. The teachers and assistants with study children in their classes, along with session assistants, completed a questionnaire pre- and post- the project. As part of the entry questionnaire, staff were asked to describe the outcomes they hoped for. In the exit questionnaire, they were asked which of these outcomes they thought had transferred to the children in school. The most frequently observed outcomes were increased self-confidence, knowledge about the natural environment and improved social skills. Often observed outcomes were willingness to try new experiences, ability to apply skills learnt in class, improved self-image, self-esteem and increased independence. The least observed outcomes were an ability to learn creatively, working with others as a team and academic development through self-belief.

However, most recognised that the changes in wellbeing and academic development within the study cohort was through positive engagement and the championing of outdoor learning. The cohort was encouraged to demonstrate and share their new skills and knowledge with other pupils and was rewarded for doing so. The school was impressive in both its recognition and its adoption of outdoor play and learning across the whole school culture. These two factors were symbiotic, in that a positive approach enabled deeper involvement from both the study children and the whole school. The theme of 'behaviour perceptions' was a limiting factor. Being 'wild experts' encouraged integration by recognising and utilising the children's new skills in the school and classroom environment. This gave the children a feeling of distinction and being special, increasing their confidence. 'New perspectives' were limited to those who could attend the sessions, meaning that changes in wellbeing may not have been noticed so easily but 'whole school culture change' enabled the spread of outdoor pedagogy effectively, encouraging academic development based on the 'wild' experiences.

Conclusions

The findings of this study suggest a variety of ways in which positive changes relating to the children's wellbeing and academic development were demonstrated. In terms of wellbeing, notably their self-regulation and emotional resilience developed and was supported by project factors and in-school integration. The children increased in their physical and social wellbeing, confidence for learning and connection to the rest of nature. This was embodied in their increasing confidence outdoors and by being recognised as 'wild experts' at school. The children's academic development across the subjects compared favourably with their equivalent peers, with positive shifts in attainment and attendance. Given the wide range of potential parameters, it is difficult to claim causality, however, the children, their parents and the school team identified the project as having primary influence. Other positive correlations relating to the project were made but lacked direct reports to strengthen them, or in most cases, the influences could not be separated from the wider context of the children's lives.

Herein lies part of the challenge of demonstrating the positive effect that complex intervention such as long term systemic outdoor play and learning can have. With the three-year Natural Connections Demonstration Project complete in the UK and a strong body of international evidence to back up such assertions (Malone & Waite, 2016), the authors are confident that there is now sufficient rationale to institute policy changes that actively promote learning opportunities in outdoor settings given the recognisable positive and systemic change benefits to education and care. At this point, we encourage settings to trust in the process and develop understanding within their teams and the wider communities they inhabit.

There is a danger when outdoor play and learning is discussed, or variants of it such as Forest School, in assuming that all projects are the same in delivery, impact or outcomes. Such an assumption can be commonly found, yet no two complex interventions are the same. It is worth taking note of the specific form the project has taken. Several outstanding factors contributed to its success in helping the children to be well, grow and achieve. Highly skilled practitioners designed the project with wellbeing and self-regulation in mind and were able to support the children's experience and build on their relational inter-subjectivity. This includes respecting their autonomy, agency, providing nurture, emotional time and space away from school agendas. The focus has been not on what the children are doing or learning, but on their inhabiting a living space, regularly, over a substantial period, with the freedom to choose, time alone and in company. There were no fixed set activities. The living natural environments had great affordances for play, learning, growth and health, creating an opportunity for success through deep relationships with nature, each other and themselves. The children regularly visited one site, growing a sense of relationship with place. They also benefitted from exploring other sites, with whole day visits year-round. Finally, the project was integrated positively within the school.

This research tested the suggestion that, for disadvantaged children, wellbeing through outdoor learning is important in improving school-readiness and achievement (Dillon & Dickie, 2012). The present research had a small cohort, yet the influence is clear over time, as shown in the impact factors being better than those not participating in the project. The findings indicate that positive wellbeing outcomes and learning competencies may best be served through the 'long way round' of engaging children restoratively in inhabiting living environments.

Pastoral support can include many different elements and interventions. The project was part of the offer for disadvantaged children in the school, who also received one-to-one specialist help and other interventions. Therefore the project cannot be found to be solely responsible for any improvements in the children's wellbeing or academic development, but the research findings show that the project has helped, consolidated by school support. Partnership working with the practitioners and school leadership supported integration. Thus, the project had a greater positive impact on the children, e.g. praised for their involvement and regarded as 'wild experts' within the school. The school strongly upheld and championed the project's values, beginning a culture change in the school and local area to deliver similar projects in future and embed it sustainably as an everyday part of the school's offer, embracing an outdoor affective ethos with contagious enthusiasm. The school support demonstrated the essential role of values, school culture and senior leadership in creating sustainable, 'do-able' projects and lasting positive change.

The project was successful in supporting the children's wellbeing and socio-emotional development, which had a role in improving their academic development. Much like the folk story of the hare and the tortoise, the more effective approach can be seen as the long way round to achievement, one that takes longer, but it is no less effective. Pastoral support and affective learning are needed to help disadvantaged children succeed at school, with direct links between improving wellbeing and academic outcomes (Rose et al., 2012). The specific outdoor play and learning in living environments demonstrated by the project provided effective pastoral support and therefore is a helpful and recommended intervention for any school or children's setting to employ.

Through the children's participation in the project, a gap was closed between the study cohort's and the school's overall levels of attendance and academic development and that of the school's. 'Closing the gap' is a frequent debate in public education policy (e.g. Wilson, 2014), with various interventions and panaceas offered to enable disadvantaged children to have similar opportunities to succeed at school com-pared to better-off peers. Further, within the Wild Woods project, the school underwent a culture change whereby the outdoor offer for disadvantaged pupils was then extended to the whole school.

After three years of study and another of analyses and writing, perhaps the findings accord and are best concluded with the following view.

'[Children's} learning is an underground river, you can't see it, can't even feel it at times. Then suddenly they soar. You can't control it; you can't take credit for it. It's theirs. You have to be there, providing warmth and stability, providing tools and resources, answering questions, telling stories, having meaningful adult conversations and doing meaningful adult work in their presence. But when they soar, it's on their own wings'. (Black, 2016)

Acknowledgement This chapter is taken from a paper originally published by Taylor Francis in the journal Early Child Development and Care https://www.tandfonline.com. The final, definitive version of this paper has been published in the journal *Early Child Development and Care* in October 2017 by Taylor Francis Online.

REFERENCES

Austin, C., Knowles, Z., Richards, K., McCree, M., Sayer, J., & Ridgers, N. (2015). It's natural to play: Creating enabling environments for physically active play in the forest setting. In T. Skelton, K. Nairn, & P. Kraftl (Eds.), *Space, landscape, and environment* (Geographies of children and young people) (Vol. 2). Springer.

Black, C. (2016). A thousand rivers. Retrieved November 27, 2016 from http://carolblack.org/a-thousand-rivers [Google Scholar].

Borradaile, L. (2006). *Forest School Scotland: An evaluation.* Forestry Commission.

Bragg, R., Wood, C., Barton, J., & Pretty, J. (2013). *Measuring connection to nature in children aged 8–12: A robust methodology for the RSPB.* Unpublished report for RSPB, University of Essex.

Cheng, J. C.-H., & Monroe, M. C. (2012). Connection to nature: Children's affective attitude toward nature. *Environment and Behavior, 44*(1), 31–49.

Clark, A., & Moss, P. (2001). *Listening to young children: The mosaic approach.* National Children's Bureau Enterprises Ltd.

Dillon, J., & Dickie, I. (2012). *Learning in the natural environment: Review of social and economic benefits and barriers.* Natural England Commissioned Reports, Number 092, Natural England, London.

Gallacher, L. A., & Gallagher, M. (2008). Methodological immaturity in childhood research?: Thinking through 'participatory methods'. *Childhood, 15*(4), 499–516.

Laevers, F. (Ed.). (2005). *Well-being and involvement in care settings. A process-oriented self-evaluation Instrument (SiCs) (Research Centre for Experiential Education, Leuven University).* Kind & Gezin.

Malone, K., & Waite, S. (2016). *Student outcomes and natural schooling.* Plymouth University. http://www.plymouth.ac.uk/research/oelres-net

Ridgers, N. D., Knowles, Z. R., & Sayers, J. (2012). Encouraging play in the natural environment: A child-focused case study of Forest School. *Children's Geographies, 10*(1), 49–65.

Roe, J., & Aspinall, P. (2011). The restorative outcomes of Forest School and conventional school in young people with good and poor behavior. *Urban Forestry & Urban Greening, 10*(3), 153–256.

Rose, J., Gilbert, L., & Smith, H. (2012). Affective teaching and the affective dimensions of learning. In S. Ward (Ed.), *A student's guide to education studies* (3rd ed.). Routledge.

RSPB. (2013). *Connecting with nature: Finding out how connected to nature the UK's children are.* Unpublished report, Sandy, Bedfordshire. www.rspb.org.uk/connectionmeasure

Strauss, A., & Corbin, J. M. (1998). *Basics of qualitative research: Techniques and procedures for developing grounded theory* (2nd ed.). Sage.

Wilson, J. (2014). *Closing the gap with the new primary national curriculum.* Unpublished report for Dept for Education DFE-374, Carmel Education Trust / National College of Teaching and Leadership.

The Freedom to Have Fun, Play, Make Friends, and Be a Child: Findings from an Ethnographic Research Study of Learning Outside in Alternative Provision

Kelly Davis

INTRODUCTION

Schools reflect the society from which the children are drawn; schools mirror the social and economic inequalities of this society. This chapter addresses one particular inequality, primarily that of the year after year overrepresentation of particular groups of children in exclusion data. For example, simply being male increases a child's likelihood of being permanently excluded from mainstream education; male pupils are 3.1 times more likely to experience a permanent exclusion than their female counterparts (IntegratEd, 2020, p. 19). It is the social injustice of such a risk of exclusion that sparked my original interest in exploring the pedagogical approaches that are used with some of the most vulnerable children in our

K. Davis (✉)
University of Plymouth, Plymouth, UK
e-mail: kelly.davis@plymouth.ac.uk

© The Author(s), under exclusive license to Springer Nature
Switzerland AG 2022
R. Cutting, R. Passy (eds.), *Contemporary Approaches to Outdoor Learning*, Palgrave Studies in Alternative Education,
https://doi.org/10.1007/978-3-030-85095-1_10

society—those that are at risk of, or who have been excluded from, mainstream education. In this chapter I focus on pedagogy that supports excluded children's behaviour and relationship development by providing needs-led outdoor learning experiences.

Exclusions from schools occur for many reasons. The most common, for both permanent and fixed-term exclusions (FTEs) in England, 'is persistent disruptive behaviour, accounting for 35% and 31% of exclusions respectively' (IntegratEd, 2020, p. 15). When children are excluded from mainstream schools in England, they attend an alternative provision. The government definition of an alternative provision (AP) is that it is an alternative 'for children of compulsory school age who do not attend mainstream or special schools and who would not otherwise receive suitable education, for any reason' (DfE, 2018, p. 5). APs focus on developing positive learning experiences that reach far beyond core curriculum content, and they concentrate on the development of team-work, positive peer relationships, self-esteem and building learning behaviours where learning can take place.

Undoubtedly APs have a mountain to climb when it comes to building trust and rapport with new pupils. There is wide recognition that 'exclusion for disruptive behaviour is perhaps the most explicit form of rejection by a school of its pupils and for some pupils increases the likelihood of wider exclusion' (Munn & Lloyd 2005, p. 205). Social exclusion from the schools that they previously attended puts these children at even greater risk of social marginalisation in wider aspects of their lives and has a detrimental effect on their life chances (McCluskey et al., 2016, p. 529). It is indeed these negative, potentially life-shaping experiences, that APs need to work through with the attending children.

The very act of exclusion from school is a traumatic and confusing experience for many children. Losing contact with friends and exclusion from their original school settings as they transition to a new environment is often difficult for children to navigate. Practitioners are now embarking on trauma-informed teaching techniques to understand how to best work with children that have complex lives and require a different pedagogical approach. Trauma-informed teaching is recognised as an approach that 'reinforces the significance of developing authentic relationships with young people as a way of restoring their capacity for connection and learning' (Morgan et al., 2015, p. 1041).

There appears to be a significant correlation between those who are at high risk of exclusion and those who are at risk of developing a negative relationship with their teachers. Exclusion statistics highlight that there are particular 'groups' that are at higher risk of exclusion in comparison to their peers; being male; having a Special Educational Need or disability; having an education and health care plan; being a Gypsy/Roma or traveller from Irish heritage; being black Caribbean or white and black Caribbean; and being eligible for free school meals all put children at 'high risk' of exclusion (IntegratEd, 2020, p. 15). Some of these very same characteristics place children at greater risk of developing negative relationships with teachers (McGrath & Van Bergen, 2015, p. 4). These characteristics include gender; girls have higher quality and closer relationships with teachers than their male counterparts, while boys tend to have more conflictual relationships with their teachers (McGrath & Van Bergen, 2015, p. 5). Ethnicity has been identified as a risk factor for poor teacher-student relationships, as minority groups are said to experience 'less close' relationships than those of their non-minority peers (McGrath &Van Bergen, 2015, p. 5). Students from a low socioeconomic status are more likely to experience 'student-teacher relationships characterised by low closeness and high conflict', and there is a higher risk of these students participating in risky behaviours and their behaviours being deemed aggressive (McGrath & Van Bergen, 2015, p. 5). Students with disabilities and learning difficulties are also at greater risk of developing poor student-teacher relationships (McGrath & Van Bergen, 2015, p. 7). While there are other characteristics that increase a child's probability of such deleterious relationships, these specific risk factors are also found to increase a child's probability of exclusion from mainstream schooling. The very clear correlation between student-teacher relationships and exclusion that has been identified here needs to be recognised, and alternative pedagogies, such as learning outside, that develop positive student-teacher relationships, need to be acknowledged as integral to these children's future educational successes.

APs have utilised outdoor learning within their flexible curriculum coverage for many years; the outdoors provides a space away from the classroom and allows for the incorporation of 'relational learning and experiential learning of democratic processes' that are integral in helping to build more positive and thereby productive relationships (Morgan et al., 2015, p. 1041). Outdoor learning is also recognised to assist in a far wider range of benefits for children, beyond that of relationship development. The incorporation of outdoor learning into AP pedagogy is based on the perceived benefits to children's mental health and wellbeing. This, for APs, is at the heart of the restorative process, and there is much literature that supports the use of the outdoors in terms of this restorative impact. For instance, outdoor learning in natural environments has been described as having the ability to 'heighten healthy behaviours' (Zamani, 2016, p. 172). Improvements in social skills, confidence when interacting with the natural environment, understanding, interest, motor skills and leadership skills have all been cited as benefits of learning outside (Ridgers et al., 2012, p. 64). APs—and arguably all provisions—need to put the pastoral needs of the child first in order to restore and build a positive relationship with learning. Sharpe's (2014) research 'targeted children aged 10–11 who were assessed by teachers as at risk of social exclusion or underachieving at school' and explored the use of gardening as a restorative process (2014, p. 197). This 'needs-led' programme was focused around a flexible approach to developing the 'intellectual, social, emotional and physical needs' of the pupils, focusing on enabling 'pupils either at risk of exclusion or not reaching their full potential in school to take a break from their formal education and step out into a real-world setting and find solutions to everyday challenges' (Sharpe, 2014, p. 198). Sharpe found that learning outside exposed children to experiences that challenged their critical thinking and problem-solving abilities, while problem-solving and working together encouraged the development of trusting relationships and in turn the development of new peer friendships (2014, p. 205). Learning outside has been linked to authenticity whereby teachers and learners experience 'real' relationships that promote positive attitudes and behaviours (Humberstone & Stan, 2012, p. 184), and in which children take ownership of new relationships and are empowered to take their own initiative (Sharpe, 2014, p. 206).

An exploration of behaviours and interactions between participants in the different environments allows us to identify if the environment has a positive impact. If interactions between peers improve, the learning environment for those students and others becomes safer, calmer and more conducive to learning. Forming positive peer-to-peer relationships is even more important for the children that attend alternative provisions because these children have been socially excluded from their school community. Relationships are at the core of any learning, and relationships with peers and teachers have been identified as key factors that determine educational success for young people. In fact, teacher-student relationships are cited as being significantly associated with students' social functioning, behaviour problems, engagement in learning activities and academic achievement

(Roorda et al., 2011, p. 494). Rudasill et al. (2020, p. 2) found that 'teacher–child relationships are reliable predictors of children's academic achievement and social and behavioural competence'.

Researchers have also identified benefits of learning outside in relation to children's behaviours. Stan (2008) found the concept of 'empowerment' of the participants (children) to be integral to 'effective learning' (p. 1). This empowerment allowed children to feel as though they had a place in their own learning and indeed, could take ownership of the process, allowing them to have autonomy over their own learning outside, which in turn facilitated authentic and meaningful learning experiences. Waite and Davis's research also found that children had the opportunity to 'reconstruct (reposition) themselves as strong, competent children rather than as underachieving pupils' when learning outdoors in the natural environment (2007, p. 223). Corraliza et al. (2011) focused on children in the age range of 10–13, and concluded that children coped better with stressful events if they had access to natural environments. Specifically they found that low accessibility to the natural world 'negatively affects children's wellbeing and reduces their capacity to cope with adversity' (Corraliza et al., 2011, p. 37). Roe and Aspinall's (2011) study suggest that being outside in the natural environment can reduce anger and raise mood in young people, which in turn may well have positive implications for young people's long-term behaviour. The experience of learning outside provides a degree of freedom for children to take their own initiative and self-regulate their own behaviour and learning, which in turn has implications for their wellbeing and future prospects (Sharpe, 2014). These benefits form a compelling argument for the importance of taking children's learning outside, where children can find new spaces to reposition themselves and start to develop more positive relationships with learning, peers, teachers and with schooling in general.

Project Methodology

Throughout my teaching career I have found myself working with children who displayed what many in the teaching profession term 'challenging behaviour'. Challenging behaviours are complex in the sense that there is not one single type of behaviour expressed. However, schools, nurseries and others involved with teaching and caring for children use this broad umbrella term to describe many different behaviours which are not deemed to be 'normal' expressions of emotions or interactions with others (Nag et al., 2020, p. 1). In a school setting, these challenging behaviours often have a negative impact on children's academic performance and make the learning environment for others particularly difficult (Nag et al., 2020). In the English education system, if these challenging behaviours persist, children are at risk of being excluded from their mainstream school and being placed in an alternative provision school. When working with children displaying these behaviours, I certainly found that in most cases their behaviour appeared improved when they were taught outdoors in the natural environment. It was an exploration of these observed improvements in behaviour that shaped the aims of an initial pilot study as part of a doctoral research project. APs were selected over mainstream schools as sites for this research for the following reasons:

Behaviour: The focus of the study was on behaviour and children attending APs do so as their behaviours have been deemed to be too challenging by their mainstream schools. Furthermore, APs work with children to help them to learn the 'school behaviours' required by mainstream provision with the aim of reintegration into schooling.

Learning outside: The APs in the study incorporated outdoor learning as a curriculum offering.

Curriculum flexibility: APs have greater flexibility regarding curriculum construction and interpretation. This meant that outdoor learning had a high profile in the participating APs and was carried out regularly within their curriculum.

The focus of the research was to explore the learning outside provision delivered in one AP setting and the behaviours displayed by the children taking part in the outdoor education experiences. There was a particular focus on finding out more about:

- the variety of behaviours displayed by the children when learning outside.
- the interactions between peers in different environmental contexts.
- the interactions between teachers and students in different environmental contexts.

The Setting and Participants

The research was carried out in an inner city AP in the South West of England. There are approximately 290 students on roll, with children and young people ranging from 4–19 years old. The school forms part of a larger multi-academy trust (a wider group of schools all working together under the same board of trustees). The research was carried out at one of five potential sites, as the students in this setting were attending due to expressing emotional and behavioural issues which had led to their temporary or permanent exclusions. Research focused on the KS3/KS4 age range (11–16) because this age group of children would be able to give voluntary informed consent to taking part in the research. Confidentiality, anonymity, secure data management, data protection and voluntary informed consent were all aspects considered in the approved departmental ethics application.

A combination of researcher participatory observation, student semi-structured focus group interviews, informal conversations with students, teacher and mentor semi-structured interviews and researcher reflections formed the dataset. Researcher participatory observations were selected as the most appropriate form of observation after discussing this with teachers, as it was felt that the children would feel more comfortable with me being in their learning environment if I engaged with the sessions and helped where needed. Overall, the pilot study included approximately 18 hours of observations, four semi-structured interviews with teachers and students, and researcher reflections. After transcription of audio-recordings and the write-up of researcher field notes, the findings were manually thematically coded. All data was anonymised in order to protect the identity of participants throughout.

Environmental Context

The learning outside sessions took place at beaches where students could swim, climb and rock-pool, and on the bank of a river near a woodland where the students could swim in the river. The environments were natural and the students and teachers utilised the affordances within the environments throughout the outdoor sessions. The observation sessions consisted of three full days spanning across a number of weeks.

Environmental context one was a local beach. The key learning that the teacher wanted the students to engage with was skills-based and included developing teamwork, building relationships with peers, building self-confidence and self-regulating anger. Key outdoor skills included water safety, including getting in and out of the water safely. Additional learning took place around the identification of different organisms in the rock pools and safety when bouldering. Environmental context two was a different beach, and the key learning the teacher wanted the students to engage in focused around positive interactions with peers, following instructions and working as a team. Additional skills-based objectives included managing risks safely, improving swimming and developing confidence in the water. Environmental context three was at the side of a river within a woodland area. Key learning that the teacher planned was the development of peer-to-peer relationships and working as a team. New skills included teaching students to learn how to snorkel, and use a mask and snorkel safely.

RESEARCH THEMES

Individual Student Behaviour Is Better When They Are Learning Outside

My observations outside found that swearing was reduced significantly in comparison to when the students were observed inside the school environment or when travelling to the various locations on the minibus. Peer-to-peer negative interactions, low-level disruption incidents, and aggression towards peers were less frequent when students were learning outside the classroom. These findings support the concept of learning in the natural environment helping children to self-regulate behaviours (Sharpe, 2014) and Roe and Aspinall's (2011) research that found that the natural environment can reduce and raise mood in young people.

When one student was asked how they felt their behaviour was on one of the days, they responded *'Ten, the best, I haven't swore all day outside'*. Students seem to link 'good' or expected 'school behaviour' with a reduction in swearing. When teachers were asked about how they felt the student's behaviour had been throughout that day, one teacher commented that *'There was some swearing, but it could have been worse, they did really well. 8.5/9 out of 10 for behaviour'*. Swearing is something many of these students do and its frequency increases when they are angry or when they are disrupting lessons in the classroom. It may act as a barrier to learning because students are aware that they should not be swearing, and often the swearing of one student will disrupt the learning of others because they get involved with the language, viewing it as funny or in some cases telling the student responsible not to swear. This can lead to arguments and peer-to-peer conflict. In turn, this often diverts the teacher's focus from learning towards behaviour and de-escalating potentially volatile situations.

On a different day, another teacher stated that the behaviour in that session was good and that *'100% of them participated and one of the students at the end of the day said they had a nice day. They were very positive about it'*. This was a significant finding, because often these students were not engaging in the learning on the school site and were excluding themselves from involvement with peers. This comment signified that the students were all participating through their own free will and expressing gratitude to the teaching staff. This was a really positive outcome, as often these students are resistant to learning and they are very rarely positive about school experiences. One of the students commented that their behaviour must have been good because they have not been swearing whilst they have been outside and it is clear that they felt a degree of pride that they had not sworn. This can be related to the 'school behaviours' that English school systems ask students to conform to; swearing in an English school, specifically at a teacher, can mean that the student would be excluded from the setting. This is why both the student and the teacher place such significance on swearing.

Behaviour Between Peers Is More Positive When Learning Outside

Researcher observations across 18 hours, recorded as field notes, found that 'from an observational perspective the behaviour issues of the students seem to disappear [when outside] … children are respectful to each other and generally get along together quite well'. This is in contrast to the behaviours observed on site in the school grounds, which included peer-to-peer conflict and lack of any positive interaction between peers, and demonstrates that learning outdoors had a positive impact on the students' behaviours and peer-to-peer interactions.

Across the learning outside sessions, teachers stated that the students displayed kindness and helped each other throughout the sessions. Teachers felt some of the most positive aspects of the students' learning outside was the 'teamwork, they have bonded and relationship building', again reinforcing the peer-peer connections being forged in the outdoor environment.

My reflections highlighted that 'Students helped each other with learning new skills such as swimming, bouldering and snorkelling. When bouldering they pointed out where the others students' feet should go and guided them so that they were successful. They even started doing things like sharing food with each other and arranging to meet up with one another after school'. These acts of kindness towards each other were rare to observe and demonstrated that peer-to-peer relationships based on kindness and mutual respect were starting to form. Not only does this link to research that shows the importance of peer-peer relationships for effective learning, but it also highlights the positive aspects of students developing a sense of community through forming connections with peers (Morgan et al., 2015).

Students Work Together When Learning Outside

Teachers often commented that there was little teamwork displayed in the school environment, however, the learning outside experiences encouraged students to work together and demonstrate the kind and caring aspects of their personalities. In my reflections, I wrote: 'Then the teacher asks the students to swim around and support a less able swimmer in the group by saying …

> Teacher: If [name] swims around you need to swim around with him.
> Student 1: 'Yeah, we will'.
> Student 2: I'm proud of jumping off of things, proud of myself today' (whilst swimming with the other student, this student refers to the fact that he was able to pluck up the courage to jump into the water like his peers today, when previously he had been too scared to do so). My reflections found 'Teamwork and kindness are demonstrated here—the students work together and they support a member of the group that is nervous in the water. The students appear happy, calm and they are demonstrating mutual respect for one another'. The students are starting to form connections whereby they are displaying empathy and kindness towards their peers. These behaviours will be necessary for students to build new and meaningful peer relationships in their schools.

Teachers commented that the students worked well as a team together in the outdoor sessions. This correlated with researcher observations when students were playing, swimming, looking at wildlife in the rock pools, climbing rocks and bouldering, working well together and having fun. My reflections found that 'The students are working together, they are asking questions, they are laughing and playing, being kind to one another and sharing. There really seems to be very positive peer-peer interaction'. The students were able to spend time getting to know one another, developing and improving social skills, playing as children and working together.

These skills will be necessary in future social interactions and in the development and maintenance of positive relationships.

When teachers were asked about the positives of the learning outside sessions, one teacher described the development of new social interactions: 'Friendship development, the students arranged to meet after school'. Another teacher described 'Working together, positive relationships, participation. Trust and attitudes' as the positive outcomes of the outdoor sessions. Teachers had said that it takes time for many of the students attending the alternative provisions to build up trust and to develop positive relationships. These positive experiences demonstrate to the teachers and the students that they can develop positive, mutually respectful friendships and that they are capable and deserving of them. Children that have been excluded from mainstream provision often find it difficult to develop trust in others; they struggle to work together and these skills often need to be fostered and developed over time. Learning outside in this instance has provided the right context for healthy behaviours to occur and for important social skills to be developed (Zamani, 2016; Ridgers et al., 2012).

Students Enjoy Learning Outside

Across the 18 hours of observations and during the interviews it was very clear that the students enjoyed being outside in the natural environment. This was stated numerous times by students and teachers, and observations and researcher reflections confirmed this. 'One student comments that LOtC is MUCH better than being in school'. Another student commented that they enjoy LOtC because 'We learn different things that some other schools don't let us learn'. These comments demonstrate that the students feel that there is a difference between being within the school grounds and being in the natural environment and link this to their willingness to participate. When one student states that when learning outside they are able to learn different things that other schools do not let them learn, I wonder if is this about curriculum coverage or about the social and relational aspects that are nurtured when these children are learning outside?

In one of the interviews with the teacher and learning support mentor I asked 'How do you think the children felt in this session?'

> Teacher: 'They felt like they could be kids, laughing, messing around, and playing—they all join in'. This statement again focuses on the concept of

participation; when learning outside the students are willingly participating, they want to be involved and learn and play together. This is incredibly important for their social and emotional development.

Many students that attend APs have experienced adverse childhood experiences and at the very least they have experienced the adverse experience of exclusion. This section highlights the restorative impact that being in nature can have on children and highlights the need for time and space for children to be able to be children (Sharpe, 2014). This section also demonstrates the hopeful, joyous aspects of these students feeling free enough to play, laugh and participate with each other.

Student-Teacher Interactions Are More Positive Outside

Throughout all of the sessions I observed, each day started inside the school, prior to visiting the different locations to learn outside. The interactions between students and teachers were often limited and occasionally quite conflictive in nature. Peers would argue and be rude and disrespectful to one another (name-calling and being generally unpleasant), and students would talk over and often ignore the teacher. Conversations were procedural and often about rules or the fact that some students were not following the rules. There was one clear similarity across the three groups I observed. The students seemed to have a boundary, which was ensuring that they were not disrespectful enough to one another or to the teacher that they lost the opportunity to learn outside. It was always clear that this was something they wanted to do and that they would be able to moderate their own behaviour so that they did not lose this opportunity because it was important to them.

Through my observations, I found that when students and teachers are outside together, away from the school grounds and in nature, conversations seem to happen more freely. Both students and teachers displayed an interest in getting to know each other more, conversations lasted longer and did not necessarily have a specific objective. Students seemed to be more willing and open to chatting to the teachers. Moments of one to one conversations between students and teachers happened frequently. There were also glimmers of appreciation towards the teachers, where students thanked them. There were also opportunities for light-hearted interactions and I cannot help wondering if the classroom dynamics would allow for these interactions.

Student: 'First time I have ever jumped and I'm only 12! Thank you for today, sir'. This may seem like an insignificant comment to someone who does not work with these students, but this comment meant that the student was grateful and appreciated the learning experience. This student was so happy that they had achieved something that meant something to them, and they took the time to show their appreciation, building on positive social interactions and in particular demonstrating that they can have positive interactions with teachers. Being outside with students allowed both students and teachers to interact more readily; they laughed, wanted to find out more about one another and better rapports were building before my eyes. The student-teacher relationship is indeed fundamental to ensuring that children have good educational outcomes. Humberstone and Stan (2012) found that learning outside helped to facilitate an 'authenticity' in relationships between students and teachers, interpreted as the development of trusting, mutually respectful, real teacher-student relationships (2012, p. 184), which in turn will benefit future learning experiences. This is why repeated positive interactions with teachers and students are so important to successful learning.

Conclusions

APs have been utilising the benefits of learning outside when working with vulnerable children for some time. Their deep and complex understanding of the importance of a flexible curriculum that responds to the needs of the child allows for regular and continued inclusion of outdoor learning in their curriculum. At the heart of this pedagogical approach is clearly the concept of relational teaching strategies, whereby the importance of developing positive experiences between peers and between students and teachers is placed at the core of every experience. This pilot study afforded me the privilege of unpicking some of the reasons why learning outside pedagogies are so valuable in this context. Five specific themes were generated through thematic coding of the data obtained; individual student behaviour is improved, peer-to-peer interactions are improved, students work together when learning outside, students enjoy learning outside and student-teacher interactions are improved.

Participants clearly valued the time they spent outside (students and teachers alike) and the enthusiasm and desire for students to participate in outdoor learning was observed. Students introduced interesting levels of self-restraint in terms of self-regulating inappropriate behaviour that might prevent them from being involved in outdoor learning experiences.

Whilst this research took place as part of a wider research project, conclusions and recommendations for practice should be explored with the understanding that further research will need to be conducted. Learning outside in the natural environment, away from the school grounds, seems to offer students a space that they are able to shape in collaboration with peers and teaching staff. This space is one where behaviours can change and relationships can shift and develop into positive and mutually respectful ones. Students seem to slowly and temporarily reinvent themselves in these spaces outside. Clear recommendations for mainstream provisions are that they incorporate outdoor learning into the core curriculum for all students. However, this type of relational learning outside should be considered as an intervention for children that are at high risk of exclusion from mainstream schooling. This will offer opportunities for new and more positive peer-peer relationships to develop and for more positive student teacher relationships to emerge.

At times during this study, the restorative effects of learning outside appeared to shine through in extraordinarily special moments within the research where children felt free to play, chase each other, laugh and simply be children for short moments (Sharpe, 2014). APs certainly seem to be using a unique pedagogy when working with vulnerable children outside, or perhaps the pedagogical approach is not unique at all but has been lost in mainstream environments. Lost under the constraints of absolute behavioural conformity and the inflexibility of an education system that is currently unable to meet the complex needs of some of the most vulnerable, at risk, children; children that simply need and deserve a different approach.

References

Corraliza, J., Collado, S., & Bethelmy, L. (2011). Effects of nearby nature on urban children's stress. *Asian Journal of Environment and Behaviour Studies, 2*(4), 27–38. Retrieved January 15, 2021, from https://fspu.uitm.edu.my/cebs/images/stories/aj3josecorralizaetal.pdf

Department for Education. (2018). *Creating opportunity for all: Our vision for alternative provision.* Retrieved March 10, 2021, from https://assets.publishing.service.gov.uk/government/uploads/system/uploads/attachment_data/file/713665/Creating_opportunity_for_all_-_AP_roadmap.pdf

Humberstone, B., & Stan, I. (2012). 'Nature and well-being in outdoor learning: authenticity or performativity'. *Journal of Adventure Education and Outdoor*

Learning, 12(3), pp. 183–197, https://doi.org/10.1080/14729679. 2012.699803

IntegratEd. (2020). IntegratEd annual report 2020: Fewer exclusions. Better alternative provision. London. Retrieved January 1, 2021, from http://www.percipio.london/

McCluskey, G., Riddell, S., Weedon, E., & Fordyce, M. (2016). Exclusion from school and recognition of difference. Discourse: Studies in the Cultural Politics of Education, 37(4), 529–539. https://doi.org/10.1080/0159630 6.2015.1073015

McGrath, K., & F. and Van Bergen, P. (2015). Review Who, when, why and to what end? Students at risk of negative student–teacher relationships and their outcomes. Australia Educational Research Review, 14(2015), 1–17.

Morgan, A., Pendergast, D., Brown, R., & Heck, D. (2015). Relational ways of being an educator: Trauma-informed practice supporting disenfranchised young people. International Journal of Inclusive Education, 19(10), 1037–1051. https://doi.org/10.1080/13603116.2015.1035344

Munn, P., & Lloyd, G. (2005). Exclusion and excluded pupils. British Educational Research Journal, 31(2), 205–221. https://doi.org/10.1080/ 0141192052000340215

Nag, H., Overland, K., & Naerland, T. (2020). School staff's experiences and coping related to the challenging behaviour of children with Smith-Magenis syndrome in schools: A Q methodological study. International Journal of Disability, Development and Education. https://doi.org/10.1080/ 1034912X.2020.1780199

Ridgers, N., Knowles, Z., & Sayers, J. (2012). Encouraging play in the natural environment: A child-focused case study of Forest School. Children's Geographies, 10(1), 49–65. https://doi.org/10.1080/14733285.2011.638176

Roe, J., & Aspinall, P. (2011). The restorative outcomes of forest school and conventional school in young people with good and poor behaviour. Urban Forestry and Urban Greening, 10(3), 205–212.

Roorda, D. L., Koomen, H. M., Spilt, J. L., & Oort, F. J. (2011). The influence of affective teacher-student relationships on students' school engagement and achievement: A meta-analytic approach. Review of Educational Research, 81(4), 493–529.

Rudasill, K., Reichenberg, R., Eum, J., Stoneman Barrett, J., Joo, Y., Wilson, E., & Sealy, M. (2020). Promoting higher quality teacher–child relationships: The INSIGHTS intervention in rural schools. International Journal of Environmental Health and Public Health, 17(9371), 1–12. https://doi. org/10.3390/ijerph17249371

Sharpe, D. (2014). Independent thinkers and learners: A critical evaluation of the 'Growing Together Schools Programme'. Pastoral Care in Education, 32(3), 197–207. https://doi.org/10.1080/02643944.2014.940551

Stan, I. (2008). Group Interaction in the 'Outdoor Classroom': the Process of Learning in Outdoor Education. PhD thesis. Brunel University. Available at: https://www.researchgate.net/profile/Ina_Stan/publication/268301764_Group_Interaction_in_the_'Outdoor_Classroom'_the_Process_of_Learning_in_Outdoor_Education/links/55099c0b0cf27e990e0f4f12/Interaction-in-the-Outdoor-Classroom-the-Process-of-Learning-in-Outdoor-Education.pdf (Accessed: 10th of June).

Waite, S., & Davis, B. (2007). 'The contribution of free play and structured activities in forest school to learning and beyond cognition: and English case'. In Ravn, B. and Kryger, N. (ed.) *Learning beyond cognition* (pp. 257–274). The Danish University of Education: Copenhagen.

Zamani, Z. (2016). The woods is a more free space for children to be creative; their imagination kind of sparks out there': Exploring young children's cognitive play opportunities in natural, manufactured and mixed outdoor preschool zones. *Journal of Adventure Education and Outdoor Learning, 16*(2), 172–189. https://doi.org/10.1080/14729679.2015.1122538

All Aboard for Ocean Literacy: Marine Outdoor Environmental Learning in the South West of England

Alun Morgan and John Hepburn

INTRODUCTION

The ocean and seas are emerging as a new focus for environmental concern both globally and locally with issues such as rising sea temperatures, increasing levels of acidity and pollution alongside declining biodiversity and shifting baselines in fisheries (Rudd, 2014). This is now highlighted in terms of the international policy agenda: The United Nation's Sustainable Development Goals (SDGs) running from 2015–2030 include specifically the SDG Goal 14 to 'Conserve and sustainably use the oceans, seas and marine resources for sustainable development' (United Nations, 2015); and 2021 marks the start the UN Decade for Ocean Science (2021–2030;

A. Morgan (✉)
University of Plymouth, Plymouth, UK
e-mail: alun.morgan@plymouth.ac.uk

J. Hepburn
The Island Trust, Exeter, UK

© The Author(s), under exclusive license to Springer Nature
Switzerland AG 2022
R. Cutting, R. Passy (eds.), *Contemporary Approaches to Outdoor
Learning*, Palgrave Studies in Alternative Education,
https://doi.org/10.1007/978-3-030-85095-1_11

McLean, 2018). At the same time, research is focusing on the psychological and physical health benefits of human-environment engagements with water, with ideas such as Blue Mind (Nichols, 2015), Blue Gym (White et al., 2016) and 'healthy blue space' (Foley et al., 2019; Foley & Kistemann, 2015). The so-called 'Blue Planet' effect describes an enhanced environmental awareness of marine issues amongst the general public associated with viewing David Attenborough's 'Blue Planet 2' (Gell, 2019). In addition 'marine ecotourism' is a growing and increasingly lucrative sector of the leisure industry that is partly driven by a desire to engage with, and learn about, the marine environment and wildlife (Wilson & Garrod, 2003). Most recently, the impact of COVID-19 has highlighted society's appreciation of the solace provided by 'blue' environments as witnessed by the (sometimes reckless) dash to coastal locations as lockdown eased (Halliday, 2020).

This 'blue turn' arguably represents a more recent subset of a broader societal acknowledgement of the ecosystem services provided by the natural world (Millennium Ecosystem Assessment, 2003), and the value of going 'outdoors' (Twohig-Bennett & Jones, 2018). Within the education sector, such sensibilities are most clearly associated with the subfields of 'environmental education' (EE) and 'outdoor learning' (OL) (Rickinson et al., 2004). This chapter is situated at the interface of these fields as they relate specifically to marine contexts. Such a 'marine outdoor environmental learning' (MOEL) has the synergistic goals of enhancing: human-marine connectedness; human well-being (physical and mental); and 'Ocean Literacy' (OcLit) (NOAA, 2013). Educational strategies capable of connecting people with the marine environment will underpin MOEL, whether through cognitive, affective and/or embodied engagements. MOEL that combines adventurous learning (Beames & Brown, 2016), environmental awareness and nature connection would represent a particularly powerful vehicle. This chapter outlines one initiative that attempts to do this by adopting an inclusive approach—Ocean Discoverability, a programme combining sailing with marine science and awareness of maritime activities for young people with special needs. However, before focusing on this case study, it is important to explore the particular challenges, but also potential, of MOEL more broadly.

MARINE-BASED OUTDOOR ENVIRONMENTAL LEARNING: CHALLENGES AND OPPORTUNITIES

More so than for EE, OL and ecotourism in terrestrial contexts, MOEL is particularly challenging. First, despite the positive blue-turn trends noted above, there remains a significant disconnect between the general population and the marine environment, even in some coastal communities (Lindland & Volmert, 2017). This is perhaps unsurprising given that the marine environment represents, for most, an inaccessible 'hidden commons', at best perceived only at, or as, the 'surface' (ibid.); the vast majority remains 'out of sight and out of mind' for all but a small number of people with the combined motivation, technical equipment and expertise to access the undersea realm. This minority might include marine scientists (professional or amateur/'natural science enthusiasts'), commercial and/or recreational fishers, scuba-divers, kayakers and sailors (wind or motor-powered). Mainstream society seems generally unaware of the importance of, and their impacts on, the marine environment. Even 'specialists' might not fully appreciate the ocean environment in holistic terms, focusing narrowly on those aspects that affect their chosen pursuit. Thus, fishers might not fully understand the undersea ecological systems affecting their targeted catches, and crucially their impacts upon them. Arguably, therefore, most people are relatively Ocean Illiterate, particularly in relation to Principle 6: 'Ocean and Humans are inextricably connected' (NOAA, 2013) both in terms of environmental/ecological relations, and the significance and impact of the maritime sector and the 'blue economy'. This calls for learning opportunities to enhance 'Ocean Literacy' (OcLit) for all (Ibid.; Gough, 2017).

This general disconnect is perhaps not surprising when compared to terrestrial environments since the focus is on tide-affected and saline foreshore, offshore, and coast zones (Wilson & Garrod, 2003), which represent relatively inaccessible (for all but coastal residents), alien and potentially dangerous places. While it is a truism that nowhere is further than 70 miles from the sea in the British Isles, most people do not visit often. Indeed, some communities who live within a mile of the sea rarely visit. The reasons are complex, but often relate to socioeconomic factors and, therefore, represent an issue of inclusion. Whilst it is possible to learn about such environments vicariously via multimedia sources (as illustrated by the armchair impacts of 'Blue Planet 2'), it is far preferable to facilitate real-world experiential engagements with their associated multisensory affordances of sights, sounds, smells and bodily sensations (Leather, 2018; Nichols, 2015). However, this necessarily presents further significant challenges for MOEL in terms of overcoming barriers of access, perception, and safety.

The accessible coastal shore, so beloved of family holidays, presents relatively simple and safe opportunities, although engagement tends to be limited. Sandy or pebble beaches are relatively devoid of wildlife (without extensive searching and digging) and typically present only shallow off-shore waters to explore. Rocky shores might have the added bonus of rock-pools or tide-pools, but are not accessible to all given the nature of the terrain and still provide only superficial glimpses into the marine environment without informed guidance. It is preferable to have opportunities to engage with a water column extending vertically across different habitat zones providing the potential to access a wider variety of specimen sizes (microscopic to large) and types (i.e. species; pelagic or demersal lifestyles). Quaysides, harbour walls, jetties and piers provide accessible platforms to access such deeper waters. Snorkelling and SCUBA-diving represent perhaps the most 'immersive' opportunities since they take place *in* the water, although they are somewhat exclusive pursuits, depending to a greater or lesser extent on the ability of participants and availability of equipment and suitable support. Floating craft provide still greater flexibility as mobile platforms capable of conveying passengers off-shore to different locations and deeper waters.

However, any interaction is likely to be constrained by the level of awareness and motivation of participants. Too often, this is limited to ill-informed recreational fishing or 'crabbing', typified by a wanton extractive-accumulative logic of 'filling the bucket' rather than careful observation of single specimens. This often leads to distress and fatalities in the 'catch' due to overcrowding and oxygen depletion, and can result in significant biodiversity loss at the coast, particularly in tourist 'honeypots', without any particular learning benefit. This lack of sensitivity is perhaps unsurprising given the tourism and media-driven misperception that quality marine environments are only to be found in the crystal-clear waters of warmer climes. Consequently, most people in temperate locations such as the UK are not likely to appreciate the richness of the marine environment 'on their doorstep'. Similarly, the media and tourism industries reinforce the general human predilection towards 'charismatic megafauna' and/or relatable features such as fur and human-like faces (Myers & Saunders, 2002). This means that people are likely to value marine species such as cetaceans, pinnipeds, sharks, turtles and some large fish species that are seldom encountered in UK waters. Consequently, people feel less inclined to value the generally small, common, 'uncharismatic' or less-relatable species more typically encountered (such as 'faceless', 'plant-like', or non-cuddly invertebrates). Crabs, starfish, shrimps and fish are valued more as 'fodder for the bucket' than enchanting living organisms.

People's appreciation of, and fascination with, these underappreciated species and habitats can be enhanced through guided instruction.

Educationally-oriented marine citizen science projects have recently become popular as vehicles to promote such environmental awareness-raising, while also enhancing the efficacy of marine science (Cigliano & Ballard, 2018; Earp & Liconti, 2020; Fauville et al., 2019). Projects such as these promote an informed, limited collection of specimens for specific observational purposes in temporary containers, or better still, 'in situ'. They often employ technology that can magnify, highlight and record underwater to reveal greater detail. Furthermore, whilst social media and online-resources are often used to increase their reach, the best projects involve face-to-face encounters with suitably engaging, passionate, informed environmental mentors or *animateurs* equipped with technical and conceptual devices to reveal the wonder of the undersea world. However, it must be acknowledged that the reach of such initiatives is necessarily limited to self-selecting participants or organisations (such as schools).

'Capturing Our Coast' (CoCoast, n.d.) represents one such UK-based project which used simple, engaging and facilitated inquiry-based informal marine science activities such as 'Barnacle Bonanza', 'Like it or Limpet', 'Keep your Friends Close, and Anemones Closer', and 'Absolutely Crabulous' to engage and inform. Similarly, 'Crabwatch' (MBA, n.d.) sought to empower citizens to become environmental 'sentinels' in terms of identifying invasive species, especially the 'Chinese mitten crab (Sewell & Parr, 2018). Ocean Discoverability can be situated alongside such projects, employing the various good practices outlined above, including enhanced access to the marine environment by using both the static platform of marina boardwalks and the floating platform of a sailing ship; creative use of digital technology to enhance visualisations; and 'On Board Ocean Educators' as OcLit *animateurs*.

The final general barrier relates to health and safety considerations associated with potential hazards, including drowning and hypothermia from immersion in marine environments. This carries significant implications in terms of equipment and associated expertise and confidence on the part of learning facilitators. The field of OL is particularly exercised by these issues, given its use of 'water-based adventurous pursuits' with an emphasis on human- or non-motor-powered modes of travel such as canoeing, kayaking, surfing and sailing. Health and safety are therefore paramount concerns. However, the field tends to be oriented towards using the activity or experience and associated challenges for enskilment in the particular outdoor pursuit, and more generally, personal and social development. This traditional emphasis on risk and challenge as the driver for 'personal growth through adventure' (Hopkins & Putnam, 1993; Mortlock, 1984) has been critiqued for being somewhat 'heroic', 'masculinist', 'ableist' and 'ethnocentric' in orientation (Beames et al., 2017) with sometimes questionable environmental credentials. There have, therefore, been calls within the field for consideration of 'wider socio-cultural, ecological and geopolitical circumstances' (Ibid., p. 275), resulting in greater emphases on inclusion, environmental sustainability and 'place responsiveness' (Wattchow & Brown, 2011).

'Sail training' (McCulloch, 2016) represents a form of OL that is, by definition, an educational environment at sea in which the marine environment represents a crucial dimension, more so than for powered craft. Consequently, one might expect sail training and OcLit to be natural 'bedfellows'. However, whilst it is true that environmental themes related to the craft of sailing (tides, currents, weather and climate) represent a crucial and explicit dimension of marine environmental science, those dimensions related to the technical constraints and affordances of sailing are not generally foregrounded. Additionally, although safety at sea demands an awareness of other sea users, there is generally little attention paid to what these users are doing, why they are doing it and its wider significance. More usually, greater emphasis is placed on 'participants developing social and self-confidence, capacities such as cooperation with others, and attitudinal change in relation to, for example, tolerance of diversity' (McCulloch, 2016, p. 239). Therefore, inclusion represents a key dimension of the field, and there has been a long-standing emphasis on working with 'people with disabilities' (PWD; Crosbie, 2016). The Island Trust's Ocean Discoverability programme has emerged from such an emphasis but, crucially, places a more overt emphasis on marine environmental education. The beauty of the programme is that the main crew take responsibility for the technical demands of the sailing, arguably presenting a less onerous /more inclusive stable learning platform from which to engage in OcLit activities. As such, rather than 'sail training' as generally perceived, Ocean Discoverability (OD) represents a 'sailing-based' MOEL initiative that addresses many of the issues raised above.

CASE STUDY: OCEAN DISCOVERABILITY AND ON-BOARD OCEAN EDUCATORS

OD is a project within The Island Trust that supports disabled children from local special needs schools, schools with Special Educational Needs (SEN) streams, and community groups supporting disabled children. It is managed by John Hepburn who has been part of the project since it started in the Bristol Channel Pilot Cutter Trust (BCPCT) in 2010.

In 2010, Tony Winter, the trustee of BCPCT and owner of Cornubia, which he had recently restored, conceived the idea of taking disabled children day sailing in her. He invited John to sail as the mate and to develop fund-raising so that those taking part would not have to pay, at that point calling it 'Sailing for Disabled Children in the South West'. John persuaded the National Marine Aquarium to lend a mini Remote Operated Vehicle (ROV) to Cornubia to create a sense of 'Wow!' in the young people. He found young marine biologists to help the children understand what was going on, and to share their particular areas of expertise. The children could spot marine life, ships, boats and maritime infrastructure in the 'Cornubia Guide to Plymouth Sound and Estuaries,' which included snapshots of those working in the sector (Fig. 1).

In August 2010 four disabled young people and two carers sailed on Cornubia's first voyage of discovery. It was a mixed age, capacity and ability group whose specific conditions covered a range of needs including

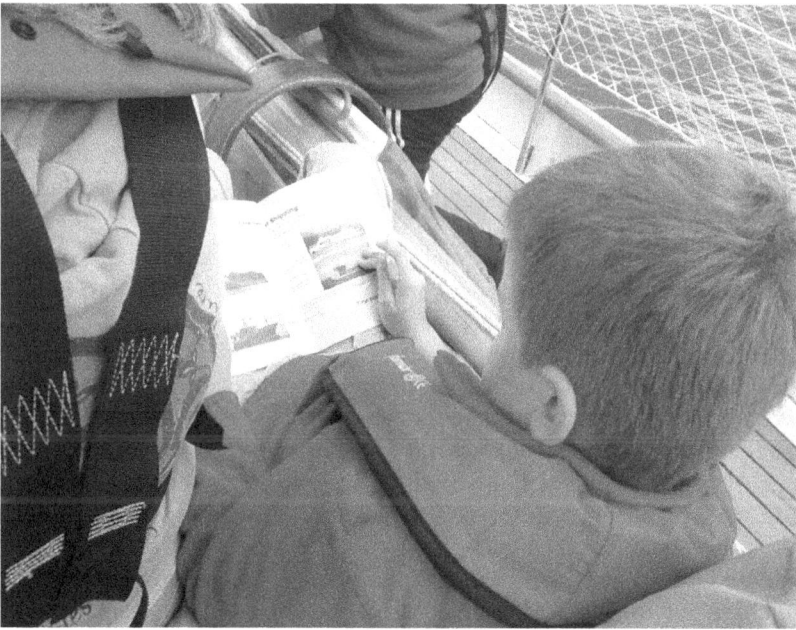

Fig. 1   Using the 'Cornubia Guide to Plymouth Sound and Estuaries'

Fig. 2 On board rope work—hoisting the sails

communication and learning difficulties, mobility for the wheelchair user and autistic issues. They sailed up the Tamar and back, allowing all to get used to the boat and its motion and to see maritime activities and their impacts on the landscape. The children who wished to do so helped hoist the sails (Fig. 2) and they spent some time sailing in Plymouth Sound where they gained an appreciation of the topography, marine life and other ships and boats, thereby developing a strong 'sense of place'. They all had a chance to steer. If they were sufficiently physically able, they worked in their watches to haul on the sheets as the boat manoeuvred. They collected samples of plankton for microscopic examination. Those unable to participate in these activities were made comfortable on deck (on large beanbags) and enjoyed the sights and sounds of being at sea— the sensory stimulation is particularly good for those with lower cognitive abilities. The voyage was well-received by all and its success led to three further trips in this year, two of which were funded by the Plymouth Public Dispensary.

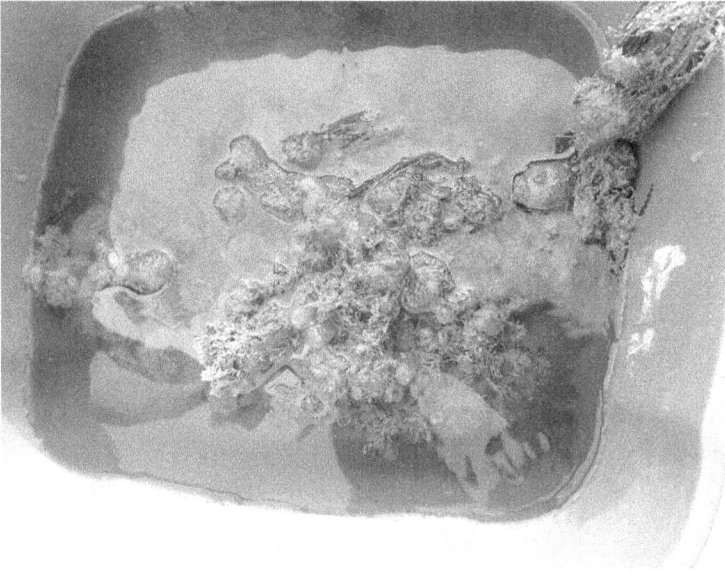

Fig. 3 Settlement Plate populated with samples from pontoon

Development of the OD programme continued as lessons were identified from that first year. The availability of the marine biologist volunteers was uncertain, so more crew were recruited to take the deckwork load off John, freeing him up to do the marine science. The project bought its own equipment. He started using the pontoon as platform for exploring marine life with settlement plates, six-inch squares of corrugated plastic hung beneath the pontoon, to be colonised by marine life. When drawn up, they go in observation trays for closer examination (see Fig. 3).

He designed a cheap alternative to the ROV, 'Crab Cam'—a Baited Recoverable Underwater Video incorporating a drop-down video (Fig. 4) that could be connected to the TV and deployed whilst in the marina to watch life on the seabed (Fig. 4). The children and their carers were riveted by the spectacle: watching netted dog whelks emerging from the benthic ooze, the occasional fish or a spiny spider crab, and a particular crowd-pleaser—hordes of crabs squabbling over the bait on the t.v. monitor (Fig. 5). Plastic pollution is often seen under the microscope in the plankton, and even being trapped by the filter feeders from the pontoon (Fig. 6).

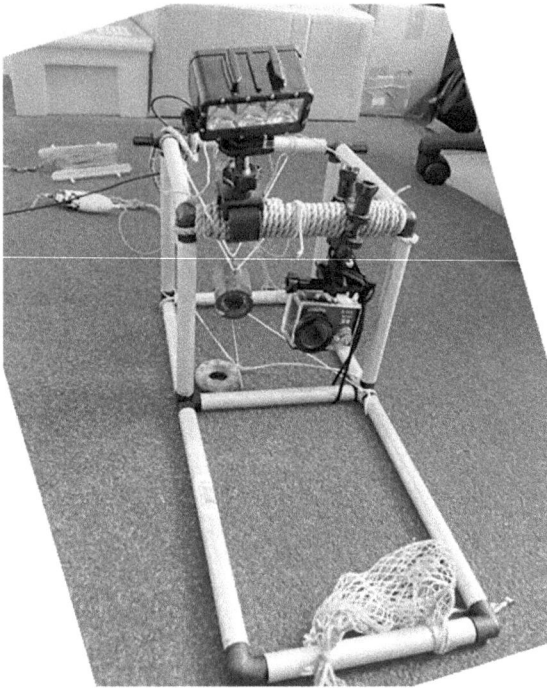

Fig. 4   The 'Do-it-Yourself' baited recoverable underwater video array, designed and assembled by John

The basic routine has not changed from the first trip. Project leaders have added other educational activities depending on the abilities of the children such as: counting objects on board, calculating the sail area of the boat and a word search. Depending on their ability, they look for obscure items on board, tie knots, steer the boat, help with the sails, make the tea and do the washing up (Fig. 7).

Plankton trawling took place, with the boat hove-to and moving as slowly as possible; the crew not only towed a net on the surface as before, but also trawled vertically which sampling deeper water and avoiding clogging the nets during phytoplankton blooms. As it is difficult to completely stop a large, traditionally rigged sailing vessel, one of the children drops the net near the bows, with a line leading outside of everything to the stern. As the pick-up point passed over the net, another of the young

Fig. 5 Crab attracted to BRUV—in situ natural behaviour on sea floor streamed to on board TV screen

people pulls it up as quickly as possible and passes it back to bows via all the others hand-to-hand for dropping again (Fig. 8). Once the dropper has dropped twice, the child at the bows goes to the stern and everyone else moves up a place. Whilst this is not the most effective way of collecting plankton, as school staff pointed out, it was good for mobility, communication, cooperation and team-working, and most found it great fun.

After 2016, due to changing circumstances, the project transferred from BCPCT and Cornubia to The Island Trust and Tectona, moored in Plymouth Yacht Haven. The Island Trust is a sail training organisation and a member of the Association of Sail Training Organisations, which saw sailing for children with disabilities in the South West as an opportunity to expand its term-time offer. The Trust scheduled two weeks in the Spring and Autumn terms for 'Cornubia Legacy' voyages. A key factor in the voyages' success was the enthusiastic, cheerful and thoughtful way that Tectona's professional crew relished this new challenge.

Fig. 6 John using microscope technology to share samples in Cornubia's saloon

Tectona is bigger than Cornubia, with an extra mast, much more deck space, a capacious saloon, and a permanent skipper and mate. This frees John up to focus on being the On Board Ocean Educator (OBOE) and to be in contact with the children and the school staff, able to discuss possible developments in the daily programme.

In 2018 the programme changed its name to Ocean Discoverability. Usually 'discoverability' refers to the ability of a website to be discovered. In this context it is the children (and their carers) who are being given the ability to discover, in this case, the ocean as well as their own capabilities. The programme expanded through 2019, and Tectona was replaced by Johanna Lucretia. John sailed in another boat Pegasus as OBOE for the first dedicated week long OcLit cruise, creating the programme from a suite of potential activities as the week progressed depending on weather and crew ability. Covid-19 prevented further progress, although there were two 'Life Beneath the Keel' events online drawing on the marine science elements of OD, with more planned for 2021.

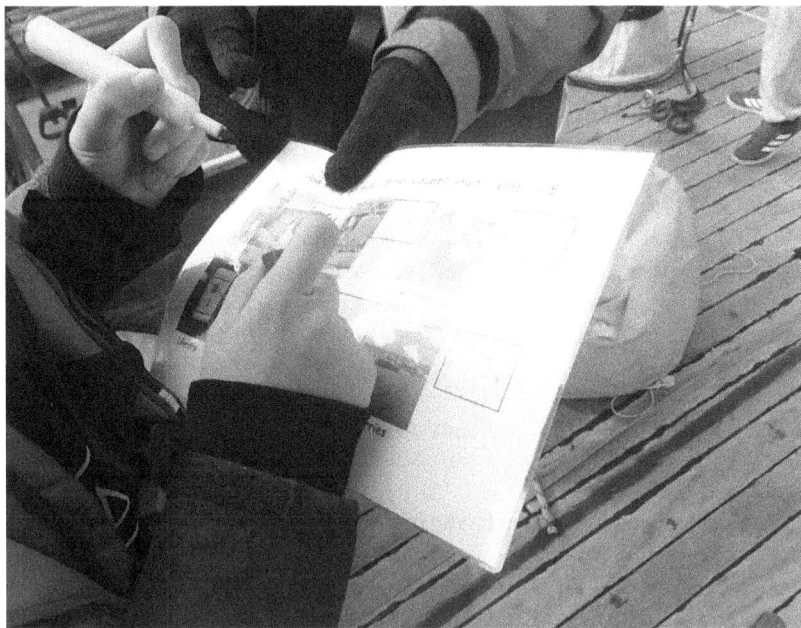

Fig. 7 On board activity sheet

Fig. 8 Collaborative plankton sampling on board Pegasus

EVALUATION

Initially there were no formal aims, and no performance measurement, but evidence of the project's achievements was needed if funders were to continue to fund it. Such evidence had to be provided by the beneficiaries, many of whom had serious learning difficulties, and the effort to collect it had to be proportionate to the scale of participation—one day, at the most six hours. Eventually, following guidance in the National Council for Voluntary Organisations' book, *True Colours*, the project found a simple system for measuring the four elements of 'Full Value (Eliot & Piper, 2008)':

Primary outcomes Secondary outcomes
　　Primary satisfaction   Secondary satisfaction

Levels of perceived knowledge in children (primary users) and carers (secondary users) were measured before and after the trip, asking them to rate on a scale of 1 to 9 how much they thought they know about the ocean and what lives in it, and what people do with and on it (see Figs. 9 and 10). The annual outcomes are the changes in average perceived knowledge. Since inception in 2013, scores indicated that both students and accompanying staff consistently felt they learnt during the day across both 'marine' and 'maritime' topics; satisfaction was measured using smiley, neutral and sad faces, scoring +1, 0 and -1 to achieve annual averages (Table 1). Although not so amenable to numerical measurement, narrative statements were also valuable in helping the team see what they are getting right, and in writing funding bids, press releases and reports (see Tables 2 and 3).

Other metrics could include the number of schools who have remained with the project, and of funders who have continued to support it especially across the change to The Island Trust. The only organisations to have stopped using it did so as a result of their own internal changes. Repeat funder support is more difficult to measure; some supported both charities before the transfer but did not increase their donations after, many have a policy of not making repeat donations, but 12 funders have made multiple grants, including Plymouth Public Dispensary, first to give a grant in 2010, and after the transfer in 2017 and all other years.

Ocean Discoverability—
Impact

What is your name?

Are you a child/carer/parent/
teaching assistant/teacher?
(Tick)

....

How much do you think you know about the ocean and
what lives in it?

Almost nothing	Just a bit	Enough to know how little I know			Quite a bit	Lots
1	2	3	4	5	6	7	8	9

How much do you think you know about what people
do with the ocean?

Almost nothing	Just a bit	Enough to know how little I know			Quite a bit	Lots
1	2	3	4	5	6	7	8	9

Figs. 9 and 10   Evaluation survey sheet, pages 1 and 2

Now that you have been sailing with us for a day ...

How much do you think you know about the ocean and what lives in it?

Almost nothing	Just a bit	Enough to know how little I know			Quite a bit		Lots
1	2	3	4	5	6	7	8	9

How much do you think you know about what people do with the ocean?

Almost nothing	Just a bit	Enough to know how little I know			Quite a bit		Lots
1	2	3	4	5	6	7	8	9

What do you think you got out of your day?

Did you enjoy your day?

If you can think of anything else we could do, or anything we could do better, please put it here.

Figs. 9 and 10 (continued)

Table 1 Outcomes—Averages of levels of knowledge and satisfaction

Season		Knowledge (1–9)				Satisfaction (%)
		Marine		Maritime		
		- pre	- post	- pre	- post	
2013	Children (n = 80)	4.84	6.49	4.69	6.25	100
	Adults (n = 55)	4.85	6.87	5.05	6.60	100
2014	Children (n = 62)	4.02	6.13	3.90	6.07	97
	Adults (n = 39)	4.72	6.85	4.95	6.72	100
2015	Children (n = 97)	4.37	6.29	3.24	6.31	96
	Adults (n = 47)	5.14	7.05	5.38	7.13	100
2016	Children (n = 119)	4.31	6.24	4.28	6.44	97
	Adults (n = 54)	4.73	6.77	4.92	6.88	100
2017	Children (n = 100)	4.74	6.78	4.50	6.67	93
	Adults (n = 38)	4.67	7.20	5.23	7.00	100
2018	Children (n = 128)	4.05	5.78	4.11	5.93	93
	Adults (n = 50)	4.76	6.63	4.78	6.67	100
2019	Children (n = 120)	4.40	6.14	4.42	6.07	98
	Adults (n = 5)	4.91	6.70	5.08	6.74	*100*

Table 2 Children's narrative responses

'I really enjoyed steering the boat, being part of the crew and fishing with the net to investigate ocean life. I learnt a lot!' (2013, male)

'—helped to tie a knot and learnt about different knots. He threw the net into the sea and looked at the tiny animals that were caught.—loved his trip on the boat.' (2014, male [represented by support worker])

'My favourite bit of the day was spotting the things in my book.' (2015, female)

'I enjoyed helping—do the teas and wash up. I loved steering.' (2016, girl)

'I was very worried about coming and so was my mum. I now know I can do these things and enjoy joining in.' (2018, male)

'Loved waves, steering, pulling up the sail.' (2018, girl)

'It was best day in my life and I learnt everything I need to know. Good stuff.' (2019, female)

Conclusion

This chapter aimed to present a cogent argument for promoting positive and informed engagements with the marine environment and its creatures upon which we all depend. We have advocated for MOEL as an educational subfield simultaneously promoting the therapeutic benefits of 'blue

Table 3   Adult (staff or carer) narrative responses

'Great to be able to facilitate independence skills in a different context. Out of classroom learning is a fantastic way to build more positive relationships with pupils.' (2013, female)
'Watching our boys work as a team was great and seeing the wildlife that is in just a drop of sea water was really fascinating.' (2013, female)
'The power of outdoor education. The pupils learn lots of information but more importantly they learn about: working as a team, communication, self confidence, the enjoyment of being on the sea, interaction, social skills. Spending time with the pupils in a relaxed and informal setting. Thank you very much. The boat is perfect for this experience.' (2015, female)
'Really good day for staff and students. Really liked the camera downstairs.' (2015, male)
'Excellent for both sensory and national curriculum approach, using YouTube technology, clear, simple sailing explanations and local knowledge.' (2016, female)
'I feel privileged to be part of a team that with the help of the crew can allow complex physical and medical needing learners the opportunity to experience sailing on a beautiful pilot cutter. Thank you.' (2016, female)
'It was so good to see—steering the boat and being so confident on deck and afloat. He has a fear of water and I didn't think he would turn up let alone be so at ease. It will be a day he remembers for a very long time and something we can use to boost his confidence in other ways.' (2018, male)
'—had never managed a school trip due to emotional and violent behavioural difficulties. Her needs have been isolating for her. Whilst sailing she started to see that she could work with another member of my class and this friendship has continued on our return to school. Having achieved this success has undoubtedly improved her confidence and belief in herself that she can try and be successful at new things. She told me the following day how pleased she was that she now she can go on school trips.' (2018, female)

space', personal and social development and Ocean Literacy. The Ocean Discoverability programme has been presented as a specific 'place-responsive' initiative that demonstrates 'exemplary practice' in MOEL, and as such joins a range of emerging initiatives around the world (see e.g. contributions in Cigliano & Ballard, 2018; Fauville et al., 2019).

In particular, the affordances of 'sailing' as an environmentally benign and immersive activity represent a powerful 'vehicle', both literally and metaphorically, to promote human-marine connectedness and well-being through cognitive, affective and embodied engagements (Brown, 2019). Independently of the work undertaken by BCPCT and The Island Trust recounted in this chapter, other organisations have also been exploring the potential for sailing vessels to provide a platform for both OcLit and personal and social development. For example, 'Adventure under Sail' based in Gloucestershire, UK has developed OcLit programmes for their tall ship, the three-masted, square-rigged, 'Pelican of London'. Similar 'Ocean

Literacy in Sail Training' (OLiST) initiatives are underway in other parts of the World, for example, 'Tall Ships America', USA and 'ABraVela', Portugal (Oceanie Ltd., 2020).

The challenge will be to realise the potential of MOEL, and specifically, 'Sail-based MOEL' or OLiST in as broad and inclusive a manner as possible, given the costs involved. This will necessarily present some significant challenges in terms of access and provision for *all*, regardless of ability, socioeconomic background, cultural capital and, fundamentally, proximity to coastal locations. Fortunately, Plymouth and the wider South West peninsula, with their exemplary marine ecology, strong maritime heritage and identity, and contemporary maritime sector (maritime business, tourism and leisure), represent fantastic 'place-based learning laboratories' to explore how to achieve these goals for locals and visitors alike. 2020 added considerable impetus with the designation of the 'Plymouth Sound National Marine Park', the first of its kind in the UK, which is intended to 'encourage greater prosperity and enhanced engagement with our marine environment'" (PSNMP, n.d., n.p.). With associated multi-stakeholder support, Ocean Discoverability and OBOEs will continue to make an important and increasing contribution to realising these goals within the city, region and wider world.

References

Beames, S., & Brown, M. (2016). *Adventurous learning: A pedagogy for a changing world*. Routledge.

Beames, S., Humberstone, B., & Allin, L. (2017). Adventure revisited: Critically examining the concept of adventure and its relations with contemporary outdoor education and learning. *Journal of Adventure Education and Outdoor Learning, 17*(4), 275–279. https://doi.org/10.1080/14729679.2017.1370278

Brown, M. (2019). Sailing, health and wellbeing. In R. Foley, R. Kearns, T. Kistemann, & B. Wheeler (Eds.), *Blue space, health and wellbeing: Hydrophilia unbounded* (pp. 52–64). Routledge.

Cigliano, J. A., & Ballard, H. L. (Eds.). (2018). *Citizen science for coastal and marine conservation*. Routledge.

CoCoast. (n.d.). Capturing our Coast: An innovation in marine citizen science. https://www.capturingourcoast.co.uk/

Crosbie, J. (2016). Disabilities and the outdoors: Some considerations for inclusion. In B. Humberstone, H. Prince, & K. A. Henderson (Eds.), *Routledge international handbook of outdoor studies* (pp. 378–387). Routledge.

Earp, H. S., & Liconti, A. (2020). Science for the future: The use of citizen science in marine research and conservation. In *YOUMARES 9-The Oceans: Our research, our future* (pp. 1–19). Springer.

Eliot, J., & Piper, R. (2008). *Full value. Public services and the third sector.* Performance Hub.

Fauville, G., Payne, D. L., Marrero, M. E., Lantz-Anderson, A., & Crouch, F. (Eds.). (2019). *Exemplary practices in marine science education.* Springer.

Foley, R., Kearns, R., Kistemann, T., & Wheeler, B. (Eds.). (2019). *Blue space, health and wellbeing: Hydrophilia unbounded.* Routledge.

Foley, R., & Kistemann, T. (2015). Blue space geographies: Enabling health in place. *Health & Place, 35,* 157–165.

Gell, F. (2019). The Blue Planet effect: The plastics revolution is just the start. *The Guardian.* https://www.theguardian.com/commentisfree/2019/mar/25/plastics-revolution-marine-life

Gough, A. (2017). Educating for the marine environment: Challenges for schools and scientists. *Marine Pollution Bulletin, 124*(2), 633–638. https://doi.org/10.1016/j.marpolbul.2017.06.069

Halliday, J. (2020). Coastal towns tell visitors to stay away as lockdown eases in England. *The Guardian.* https://www.theguardian.com/uk-news/2020/may/13/coastal-towns-visitors-stay-away-lockdown-eases-england-blackpool-covid-19-seaside-resorts

Hopkins, D., & Putnam, R. (1993). *Personal growth through adventure.* David Fulton.

Leather, M. (2018). Water environments and informal education. In T. Jeffs & J. Ord (Eds.), *Rethinking outdoor, experiential and informal education* (pp. 124–138). Routledge.

Lindland, E., & Volmert, A. (2017). Getting below the surface: Mapping the gaps between expert and the public's understanding of marine conservation in the UK. *FrameWorks Institute.*

MBA. (n.d.). Crabwatch. https://www.mba.ac.uk/crabwatch/

McCulloch, K. (2016). Sail training. In B. Humberstone, H. Prince, & K. A. Henderson (Eds.), *Routledge international handbook of outdoor studies* (pp. 236–243). Routledge.

McLean, C. N. (2018). United Nations decade of ocean science for sustainable development. *AGUFM, 2018,* PA54B-10.

Millennium Ecosystem Assessment. (2003). *Ecosystems and human well-being: A framework for assessment: A report of the conceptual framework working group of the millennium ecosystem assessment.* Island Press.

Mortlock, C. (1984). *The adventure alternative.* Cicerone Press.

Myers, O. E., Jr., & Saunders, C. D. (2002). Animals as links toward developing caring relationships with the natural world. In P. H. Kahn Jr. & S. R. Kellert (Eds.), *Children and nature: Psychological, sociocultural and evolutionary investigations* (pp. 153–178). The MIT Press.

Nichols, W. J. (2015). *Blue mind: The surprising science that shows how being near, in, on, or under water can make you happier, healthier, more connected, and better at what you do* (Paperback ed.). Back Bay Books.

NOAA. (2013). *Ocean Literacy: The Essential Principles and Fundamental Concepts of Ocean Sciences for Learners of All Ages Version 2* (NOAA Ed., 2nd ed.). NOAA.

Oceanie Ltd. (2020). *OLIST: Ocean Literacy in Sail Training: Progress report: 16 January 2020.* https://oceanconference.un.org/commitments/?id=27955#:~:text=The%20Ocean%20Conference%20%7C%20OLIST%3A%20Ocean%20Literacy%20in%20Sail%20Training&text=The%20principal%20objective%20is%20to,to%20their%20alternative%20education%20space

PSNMP. (n.d.). Plymouth Sound National Mark Park: Statement of Intent. https://plymouthsoundnationalmarinepark.com/wp-content/uploads/2019/09/NMP-declaration-of-intent-A4.pdf

Rickinson, M., Dillon, J., Teamey, K., Morris, M., Choi, M. Y., Sanders, D., & Benefield, P. (2004). *A review of research on outdoor learning.* Field Studies Council.

Rudd, M. A. (2014). Scientists' perspectives on global ocean research priorities. *Frontiers in Marine Science, 1*, 36.

Sewell, J., & Parr, J. (2018). Citizen sentinels: The role of citizen scientists in reporting and monitoring invasive non-native species. In J. A. Cigliano & H. L. Ballard (Eds.), *Citizen science for coastal and marine conservation* (pp. 59–76). Routledge.

Twohig-Bennett, C., & Jones, A. (2018). The health benefits of the great outdoors: A systematic review and meta-analysis of greenspace exposure and health outcomes. *Environmental Research, 166*, 628–637.

United Nations. (2015). *Transforming our world: The 2030 agenda for sustainable development.*

Wattchow, B., & Brown, M. (2011). *Pedagogy of place: Outdoor education for a changing world.* Monash University Publishing.

White, M., Pahl, S., Wheeler, B., Fleming, L., & Depledge, M. (2016). The 'Blue Gym': What can blue space do for you and what can you do for blue space? *Journal of the Marine Biological Association of the United Kingdom, 96*(1), 5–12.

Wilson, J. C., & Garrod, B. (2003). Introduction. In B. Garrod & J. C. Wilson (Eds.), *Marine ecotourism: Issues and experiences* (pp. 1–11). Channel View Publications.

Uncomfortable Learning and Ethical Tensions: Animal Butchery and Environmental Education

Lewis Winks

INTRODUCTION

Against a backdrop of increasing isolation from nature and a so-called 'extinction of experience' (Soga & Gaston, 2016), environmental educators are being prompted to find ways to renew their approaches and to increase learner sensitivity to the world (Selby & Kagawa, 2015). Environmental education programmes which bring young people into close contact with more-than-human aspects of the environment now often do so under the charge of developing nature connection—with the dual associated outcomes of developing pro-environmental behaviours and enhancing wellbeing (Lumber et al., 2017). However, developing sensitivity and closeness to the natural world through direct experience often entails discomfort on the part of the learners through which new

L. Winks (✉)
University of Exeter, Exeter, UK
e-mail: l.winks@exeter.ac.uk

environmental narratives and understandings may be unearthed. Stepping into, or orchestrating situations which deliberately disquiet, decentre and unsettle learners is both powerful, and ethically problematic (Rust, 2014; Harvey, 2005; Zembylas, 2015).

A 'pedagogy of discomfort' has been forwarded by Megan Boler (1999) as a conceptual mechanism for understanding how encounters, conversations and experiences which unsettle might be better developed and utilised for transformative learning within social justice education (Boler, 1999; Zembylas & Mcglynn, 2012). This chapter draws upon a specific set of circumstances and reflections surrounding the experiences of students taking part in the skinning and butchery of a wild deer as part of an extra-curricular residential learning programme in South Devon, UK, and explores them through the lens of a pedagogy of discomfort. For the purposes of this chapter, these experiences and reflections are taken out of the context of the programme but serve as a useful opportunity to consider and critique the ways in which these approaches work in practice and how a pedagogy of discomfort might be applied to environmental experiential education.

CHALLENGE AND DISCOMFORT IN ENVIRONMENTAL EDUCATION

Discomfort as a deliberative pedagogical approach has been proposed by Megan Boler (2004, 1999) through a 'Pedagogy of Discomfort', and has since been developed by others (see: Zembylas & Mcglynn, 2012; Zembylas & Chubbuck, 2009; Jacobson, 2003). The Pedagogy of Discomfort asserts that injustices are socially and culturally manifested and as such are carried as implicit aspects of the self. The process of simply learning *about* injustice does not ensure a challenge to these often deeply embedded norms. Instead, a decentring and discomforting of the self creates opportunities to reflexively examine the social and cultural narratives which give rise to injustice.

Unsurprisingly, such a process has been shown to be unsettling and upsetting for students confronted with their own values, assumptions, beliefs and practices in light of their implications upon others (Boler, 2004; Zembylas & Mcglynn, 2012), but is also argued to be fundamental to engaging with the emotional association between socially normalised practices and reproductions or disruptions of injustice (Zembylas &

Chubbuck, 2009). To avoid reproducing modes of injustice, a pedagogy of discomfort 'invite[s] students and educators to examine how our modes of seeing have been shaped specifically by the dominant culture of the historical moment' (Boler, 1999, p. 179) and urges us to 'willingly inhabit a more ambiguous and flexible sense of self [and to engage with a] critical enquiry regarding values and cherished beliefs' (Boler, 1999, p. 176). Thus, it is the work of the educator to enable critical enquiry to take place, while supporting the emotional engagement of the learning community as it uncovers socially and culturally held values and beliefs, many of which will generate discomfort and uncertainty.

Much of this work is carried out through critical enquiry and what is sometimes termed 'emancipatory learning' (Wals et al., 2008), which aims to 'promote an intentional and conscious shift from dualistic, categorical, and entrenched positionality to a more ambiguous engagement with social reality' (Wolgemuth & Donohue, 2006, p. 1024). Emancipatory learning in turn is allied to the broader concept of transformative learning approaches which also concern themselves with critical enquiry through learning. Mezirow (1997) comments that transformative learning entails the challenging of culturally manifested points of view, eventually to the degree of altering what he calls 'habits of mind'. Writing about the importance of challenging our perspectives and cherished beliefs in this process, Mezirow (1997) remarks; 'We do not make transformative changes in the way we learn as long as what we learn fits comfortably in our existing frames of reference' (p. 7). This sentiment is given further clarity by Cranton and Taylor (2012) who, in review of recent developments in understandings of transformative learning theory, follow on from Mezirow (1991) to explain that transformative learning occurs at the juncture of normal experience and challenge to dominant discourses, at which point understandings are examined and revised.

Application and theorisation of discomfort as part of an explicit educational approach have centred on issues of race, gender, class, poverty and political conflict and have been applied in fields of teacher education (Cutri & Whiting, 2015), social work training (Coulter et al., 2013; Redmond, 2010; Nadan & Stark, 2016), and medical education (Aultman, 2005; Wear & Kuczewski, 2008), amongst others. Deeply held prejudices and preconceptions are routinely challenged in the literature relating to discomfort.

The power of challenge and discomfort in learning and personal development has also been picked up on by educators and therapists working in particular in outdoor environments, in connection with more-than-human entities, where plants, animals and non-sentient beings are available to provoke transformative experiences at a 'mind-body-world' intersection (Buzzell & Chalquist, 2010). Here, in the fields of ecopsychology and ecotherapy, this transformation entails the natural world 'performing' and helping participants to critically examine personal and societal narratives, feelings and attributed behaviours (e.g. Jordan, 2014; Greenleaf et al., 2014; Buzzell & Chalquist, 2010; Clinebell, 2013). Writing about encounters with other ecologies, Conradson (2005) comments that 'environmental encounters are in part appreciated for their capacity to move us to think and feel differently… [and] in coming close to other ecologies and rhythms of life we may [find] different perspectives upon our circumstances'. This echoes and agrees with Boler's assertion that being confronted with contrary and unsettling patterns of experience and interrelations can help us to 'explore how our identities are precariously constructed in relation to one another' (Boler, 1999, p. 198).

Mary-Jayne Rust (2014) explores the notion of reconciliation with discomfort in order to reconnect ourselves with the rest of nature, making use of what she terms 'dissolving into boundlessness'—an act which Rust suggests is essential if we are to address the extinction of experience:

> …*gradual withdrawal from an intimacy with the earth has had many consequences: an unfamiliarity with our own wild animal nature, a less embodied life, and a loss of loving exchange and communion with the non-human world which has provided such a great source of nourishment for human body and soul.* (Rust, 2014, p. 40)

Many educators and therapists are now working on the thresholds of discomfort, and are explicitly attempting to use their work to bring humans into communion with the non-human world (Harper et al., 2011; Rust, 2004; Davis & Atkins, 2004; McGeeney, 2016). Elsewhere, nature connection and ecotherapy approaches are used to engender pro-environmental behaviour and to promote health and wellbeing (Wilson et al., 2009; Burls, 2007), although, wellness in association with time spent outdoors has also been said to encourage a more innate connection to the natural world (Brymer et al., 2010).

LEARNING WITH THE LAND

Embercombe ran residential land based learning programmes for 11–18 year olds for over a decade.[1] Situated in the Teign Valley near Exeter in South Devon, Embercombe occupies a valley consisting of a large area of woodland, orchards, a market garden, two 'yurt villages' which provide accommodation during residential visits and other infrastructure providing kitchen and workshop spaces. Programmes running at Embercombe last between 4–10 days. The days revolve around 'meaningful work', which includes a variety of tasks such as chopping fire wood, working in the gardens or preparing food. Other tasks are arranged as needed by the community. The programmes are infused with principles of personal development and aimed to 'inspire and empower young people, connecting them to a world where they feel able to make positive change' (Embercombe, 2016). Often the themes, which provide the basis for both the physical work to be done, and the personal development of students are oriented around simple aspects of living, such as food, shelter and warmth. In particular, food plays a pivotal role in most of the programmes with connections being forged between planting, tending and harvesting in the gardens, and the cooking and eating in the kitchen. The food at Embercombe is vegetarian with very little dairy used on site, except for when an animal is brought in for a butchering or skinning activity during a programme as this chapter elaborates.

Empirical work presented here is the result of ethnographic fieldwork carried out in the setting over 10 months in 2016. This study focuses in particular on two separate occasions at Embercombe, one from February and the other from October 2016 with groups of 14–15 year olds. Methodological approaches included participant observation, reflective journaling, focus groups and interviewing. Participant observation was recorded using detailed field notes and written up at two separate intervals each day. These notes were then 'written out' more extensively at the end of each programme. This process has been shown to be effective at maximising detail while retaining a large degree of direct participation (Madden, 2010; Angrosino, 2007). Toward the end of each programme (normally on the second to last day), participants were invited to take part in a semi-structured focus group. Participant numbers were between 4–6, and focus

---

[1] These experiential education programmes no longer run at Embercombe and are now hosted at a nearby farm with the organisation 'On The Hill': https://onthehill.camp.

groups lasted approximately 45 minutes. The purpose of the focus groups was to allow participants to discuss their experiences with each other. The facilitators role in these groups was to guide the discussion using open ended prompts to focus upon the experience of the residential – in general terms, or particular aspects of it. In particular, focus groups were chosen to uncover the relational aspects of participant experiences as part of residential learning. These discussions were recorded and later transcribed. The authors own personal reflections were recorded during the course of each programme in written and audio-recorded form each evening.

A Deer and a Deliberate Disquiet

On some of the longer (7–10 day) programmes with older groups (15–18 year olds) a locally hunted wild animal—rabbits or deer—would be brought into the courtyard. This would occur during the second half of the programme and was often cited as a 'pivotal' moment for the group. The hunter would talk the group through the foraging habits and life of the animal before talking about the process of skinning and butchering—which the young people were invited to take part in. There were always alternative activities on offer such as baking or other food preparation, and the invitation was positioned well in advance of the activity—often the previous day. However, as will become apparent—the situation which unfolds can create deep anxiety and discomfort amongst the group.

Told through notes from participant observation, transcripts from focus groups and author reflections this section provides an account of one such occasion. A recently shot Roe deer arrived at Embercombe, provided by Bill—the local hunter. The students gathered around the table where the deer was placed in an open-sided barn. I witnessed the activity which then took place and made notes:

> *Whether to take part in, watch, or step away from the preparation of the deer was left open to the students to decide. Those who decided they would not be involved went straight to the kitchen to help prepare lunch, while the rest of us went down to the deer which was laid out on a table.*

The facilitators holding the process with the young people would often invoke imagery of the life of the deer. Depending on the time of the year, the students could sometimes hear wild deer rutting in the woods around Embercombe, and it was rare for a group to attend a residential programme without encountering a live deer whilst on a night walk. On this occasion, one of the facilitators—Jim—spoke some words which conjured the wider environment and the life of the deer:

> *This deer has felt the wind and the rain, it felt the thunder the other night, it knew the paths and tracks around here—some of which you will have walked, it knew the beauty of the flowers and the trees, it will have played with and known others of its kind, and of its own age—just like you. This deer is now passing from the deer's world into the human's world—and whether you take part in this, whether you eat this animal or not, this deer will always be a part of your world—and it will be returned to the world for a new story to begin.*

After Jim's words, Bill began to talk to the students about his profession. They were gathered closely around as he spoke. Once Bill had finished talking, he shifted his attention toward the body of the deer:

> *I watched the student's reactions—some were fascinated by the animal, others were more cautious and kept their distance. They all kept their eyes on the deer and on what Bill was doing. Bill worked quickly and without hesitation. He showed where the bullet had gone in and come out of the neck. He also showed where he had bled the deer once it had been killed. There was some disturbance in the group at the sight of blood.*

At this point, the tension had built and I could see and sense the unease in the group. Often this was manifested in conversation but sometimes a person would remove themselves from the group and walk away. Often they would come back, but not always. Facilitators would always ensure that there was something for them to be involved with away from the butchery (which in the following excerpt becomes very graphic in its description):

> *Next, [Bill] quickly severed the tendons on the lower legs before snapping them off at the joint. This surprised the students and some stepped back abruptly at the sound of snapping tissue and bone. One by one the legs were removed and laid on the table—each with the same snapping sound and the same reaction. I felt uneasy at this point and even from a little distance, found the sound of the snapping legs difficult.*

This, for me, was a deeply difficult and disturbing experience. I have been graphic in my descriptions because I wanted to capture the fullest essence of the occasion possible. However, I cannot help but be challenged myself by this experience—arguably orchestrated to shock, challenge and even upset. This chapter will later return to question the pedagogical approach utilised. However, what follows is an account of the reactions and reflections of the young people for whom this situation was 'planned'.

> *Many of the students were upset and some retreated to the kitchen at this point—one girl visibly shaken and upset. The rib cage was sawn open. Two more boys walked away. Some of the students who had left earlier returned, curious about what was happening. The internal organs were removed—the heart, the spleen and the lungs. Bill removed the air way and pointed out the food still trapped in the throat.*
>
> *Following the removal of the last of the organs, the limbless, headless body was hung from a rope from the apex of the roof where it was skinned by the children. The hide was peeled off from the top to the bottom using knives to free it from the flesh beneath. Once skinned, the butchering began, with joints removed one by one and then processed further on the tables before being sent to the kitchen to be made into the evening's dinner.*

The activity was orchestrated in such a way that uncertainty, discomfort, choice and challenge played important roles to ask questions of participant beliefs and values relating to food choices, hunting as a cultural practice and the treatment of animals. Through a predetermined, yet highly subjective set of experiences, social and cultural narratives were brought into question. In total the process lasted no more than three hours—with some young people working longer in the kitchen. A reflection then followed which the next section discusses.

Participant Reflections

In the Moment

In the activity, challenge presented itself in a number of ways; as a challenge to food choices, to the relationship between animals and humans, the way in which death presents itself as a part or apart from life, as well as to the relationship (and transition) between animal and meat. Combinations of these in various degrees which were experienced by individuals in differing ways. For many of those who worked at Embercombe the concept of food choice and responsible consumption was held in high regard—the notion that if you eat meat you should be in some way connected with it was commonplace. This provided a strong basis for a cultural perspective which placed hunting and gathering of wild meat as a component of responsible living. It was a clear objective of the activity to provide a stark contrast to factory farming and the challenging of consumption of meat as a right and reframing it as a privilege. Many of the facilitators brought their own values and experiences to bear on programmes—this was indeed encouraged. As such young people experienced the activity as guided by facilitators whom themselves had strong ideas and ideals regarding the consumption of meat.

For example students such as Ollie noted the importance of being directly involved with the process, which he linked back to a talk one of the facilitators had given about working in a refugee camp:

> *I think it's kind of like, you know how Corrie* [a staff member who had spoken about refugees in Europe on the previous day] *was talking about the refugees and how you can see it on the news and you can see what's going on and you can think that's awful, but it's a very different feeling to actually being there in the moment while it's happening.* (Ollie—student)

The notion of direct participation was strong however, and for most was not something that they associated with the preparation of meat. The challenging of narratives pertaining to meat production and consumption became a clear theme throughout these encounters. Here, Karis makes a distinction between being directly involved and being remote from such events, and teases out some particular dimensions of direct participation:

> *There's a level of separation. It's like seeing it in a movie, when you know it's fake. When you do see one of those videos from warehouses when you know it's not fake but there is still a level of, it's behind the screen. When you're actually there, it's happening, and in a sense it's my fault because I'm going to eat meat. So like, it's just different and essential and I think everyone that eats meat, and even if they don't, at some point in their life needs to see that.* (Karis—student)

While a pedagogy of discomfort offers us a reference point and potential justification for unsettling participants by demonstrating the 'reality' of meat consumption, challenging these worldviews in such a forceful way is also ethically problematic. As noted above already by Karis—some young people felt guilty about the deer's death. Others were simply shocked by the gore. Rhian speaks directly to the notion of shock associated with witnessing a dead body:

> *I found it really hard when the legs were snapped—the sound was just so gross. Also, when the head was sawn off and when the body was moved… it was just so much like a body. It was really heavy and blood was coming out of it.* (Rhian—student)

Can challenge in this sense be said to have revealed something new to the participants? Clearly the activity provided an indisputable novel and 'memorable' experience for the young people—yet multiple questions remain regarding the utilisation of the deer for such outcomes; the pluralistic and subjective outcomes themselves, and the degree to which the participants can be said to have consented to such an experience. For the facilitators themselves these were not resolved questions and there remained differences between ideas of how and whether this activity should be brought into the programme.

Opening Pandora's Box

During the initial stages of butchery, most of the students stayed—some to take part, but most simply watched. As time went by, a small number went away, with some coming back later on to take part, like Daniel:

> *I went away because I didn't want to see it, but then I came back and thought— oh it's alright now—I'm glad I came back. I just needed time away to think.* (Daniel—Student)

The choice to willingly and intentionally engage with the activity seemed important in order to enable emancipatory learning to emerge from the experience (Wolgemuth & Donohue, 2006; Boler, 1999). There was no doubt that this was an uncomfortable experience for many, but there remained the freedom to choose to place oneself into a position of discomfort, nonetheless.

Discussing the obvious ethical concerns of making use of discomfort as a purposeful part of education, Zembylas and McGlynn (2012) suggest that because a pedagogy of discomfort entails pushing both students and educators outside of their comfort zones, there is a requirement for understanding the ways in which discomfort might be experienced and expressed.

In the example of the deer, the support and nurturing of choice as part of the activity may be seen in this light. This may have enabled students to confront their beliefs and assumptions on their own terms and in line with established ideals of dialogic empowerment rather than oppression. The programme conveners themselves later commented that the process could be unsettling for participants and care should be taken when facilitating confrontation:

> *[What are] the implications of opening this Pandora's Box—we need to consider certain things and the ways in which we approach them… how deep is the experience?* (Embercombe programme facilitator)

This so-called Pandora's Box of experiencing the butchery of the deer might be read as an ethical warning, but it also recognises the uncontrollability and wildness of the experience. The multiplicities of meaning which emerge from this activity are portrayed by the rich and varied reactions of students. Emancipatory learning might be important in facilitating the potential for transformative learning and behaviour change (Mezirow, 1990), but we are also made aware of the pluralistic nature of experiencing such an activity. The facilitator's remarks can be interpreted as a desire for control and certainty regarding the meaning of the activity, yet the concept at play here is that individuals experiencing the butchery and skinning become agents of their own experience, making choices regarding the nature and extent of their involvement.

How and when is it appropriate to bring such an experience in to a programme of learning—and importantly, is it necessary for a deer to die in order for these experiences to be gained within the group? The butchered deer was carefully prepared for freezing and consumption as the only meat which was eaten at Embercombe; yet there remain serious ethical tensions here—involving the life of an animal; the positioning of meat consumption and that of hunting (seen in some instances as a spiritual pursuit (Kheel, 1991), and a way of reconnecting to a forgotten Neolithic past (Parry, 2009)—each of these aspects were voiced at various times by facilitation staff at Embercombe whilst I was there); alongside the degree to which young people can be said to have consented to taking part in this process. For consent-based education expert Sophie Christophy, consent in a learning environment looks and feels like this:

it needs to offer freedom of movement, it needs to genuinely listen to and respect the people within it, to offer space and time, and access to things of interest and value, as perceived by the participants as well as the providers—and those can be flexible roles. It needs to be an attractive and comfortable space that people want to be in, where people are free to meet their own needs, and can reach out for support if needed. (Christophy, 2016)

How does the skinning and butchery of the deer compare to Christophy's assertions of 'freedom of movement', 'respect, and comfort? Indeed how does this interrelate with a pedagogy where the intention is to discomfort? One potential opportunity is to look back to the strong presence and holding of choice at the centre of this activity—the freedom to choose to move away, or to step in, and to do this with prior knowledge and agreement. Indeed, my own observations in the days leading up to the activity itself gave me reason to believe that participants to some extent understood what was to happen—yet in many ways could not prepare themselves for what would actually occur because for so many this was about far more than a practical activity, it was also about metamorphosis and transformation.

Transformation

Much of what took place during the activity—from the initial introduction to the deer, the butchery, skinning and eventual cooking of the meat spoke to conceptions of continuousness between humans and animals, animism, and the challenging of conceptual boundaries in an effort to learn from one another (Harvey, 2005). Such challenging experiences might be understood in ways that Abrams (1996) has put it, as a 'rejuvenation of our carnal, sensorial empathy with the living land that sustains us' (p. 69). The notion that the metaphysical transformation of the deer speaks to aspects of human empathy and understanding about life and death was articulated by the students following the encounter:

I think it was quite … emotive to think that there's this animal that's been born has had a life and lived, you know- a being that has had ups and downs, whether as a deer or anything. I just see it as an animal that has had a whole life—seeing it as a full being and then just seeing it as a slab of meat which is for consumption. (Izzie—student)

Here, the 'animal which has had a whole life' is juxtaposed with the notion of 'meat which is for consumption' in an unsettling yet perceptive way of relating the discomfort felt by many of the students which is difficult to prepare for.

The physical transformation of the deer was also of interest to students, who also noted the difference in how they felt between seeing the deer as 'animal' and 'meat':

There was a transformation... it was like an animal—then the legs came off, then the head and you could see it was meat and less like a deer. (Connor—student)

When I saw it as a block of meat, I felt disconnected from it—there was no emotional connection. That was interesting. (Daniel—student)

Lula comments on how the group responded initially to the body of the deer, and later how this changed—discomfort giving way to familiarity:

I think one of the most important moments for me was how quickly all of us became accustomed to it. I'll never forget that. All of us seeing the deer being brought out... [There were] squeals, and all of our faces were pale and stricken with disgust, and then... After the head, the legs, the opening of the stomach... I feel like, suddenly, within a matter of minutes... fifteen minutes, twenty minutes, whatever—we all became accustomed, and we were all okay with it... I think that was really interesting, because suddenly when we saw the meat it became, familiar because I think most of us have seen meat before. (Lula—student)

For many of the Embercombe education staff this was the goal of the activity—to illuminate the link between the animal and the meat which we consume. Related to this, conceptions of hunting and wild meat were also at the fore and notions of responsible consumption and stewardship were strong guiding ethics for this activity. Metaphysical and physical transformations were observed by participants, and certainly discomfort was encountered with all of its ethical pitfalls. Returning to the Pandora's Box question posed by one of the facilitators earlier—to what extent can the use of a deer in such a way be justified? On the one hand the encounter with the deer was made possible through exploitation of the more-than-human world and violence against an animal in order that learning may take place—with outcomes which are unpredictable and subjective.

Hunting is framed in this context as a 'management tool' for dealing with 'overpopulation' which further the narrative of human dominance and control; and as a way of connecting to a holistic ecological way of being—somehow spiritually connected to the process. However, as Keel (Kheel, 1996) outlines, each of these typologies remains an act of violence, albeit situated differently within cultures.

On the other hand, for many participants this was an effective way of uncovering previously unexplored ways of seeing dietary choices, for exploring the treatment of animals and their own relationship with the natural world, in turn opening the potential for significant transformative learning. So too, it should be noted that Embercombe was a vegetarian site—and only ate meat in exceptional circumstances. The same cannot be said for many education centres which source their meat in potentially unquestioned ways.

From one perspective this approach may be seen as speciesist and anthropocentric, favouring the learning of human participants on an education programme at the expense of the more-than-human world which could not consent; from another perspective it is a rare opportunity to encounter, discover and challenge narratives and cultural identities relating to food, hunting and nature connection. Either way, the encounter entailed discomfort, challenge and brought to the surface questions and considerations which are not often developed to such an extent.

CLOSING REFLECTIONS

This chapter tells a story of discomfort operating within a programme of environmental education. Discomfort can be seen here to have acted as a powerful force to uncover hidden and accepted modes of seeing animals and non-human nature as part of a programme broadly oriented toward environmental education. Sentiments of Boler's pedagogy of discomfort can be seen to be operationalised here (Boler, 1999), albeit with a focus on ecological justice: the bringing to attention of socially and culturally normalised traditions acted to challenge and disquiet inherited narratives pertaining to socio-environmental relations.

Providing opportunities to step away from and toward the locale of discomfort appeared to enable students to make choices in terms of where to position themselves in accordance with their personalised thresholds. This then placed the learner into the position of making an 'intentional and conscious' decision concerning engagement with the subject matter

(Wolgemuth & Donohue, 2006), providing a basis for emancipatory learning to occur in terms of learner choice and consent. Equally, space for discussion, reflection, and consideration of the events told in this chapter offered opportunities to articulate these perspectives thus becoming a central part of the learning experience.

It is suggested here that discomfort as part of emancipatory learning operates alongside learner choice and subsequent reflection in order to create a personalised and accepted confrontation emerging from the circumstance. Retuning to Rust's consideration of communion with the natural world, we might instead observe that a 'dissolving into boundlessness' was enabled in which dualisms and otherness became secondary to the experience of becoming and transformation commented on by the participants (Rust, 2014).

Yet it is necessary to consider the contradiction between the conceptualisation of discomfort in this setting as a means of 'dissolving into boundlessness', and the instrumental regard for more-than-human life. There is a distinct and recognised difference in the way in which we come to respect and then utilise (or not) the bodies of animals as compared to humans (Taylor, 2013). Joy (2020) has documented the psychological mechanisms we use to normalise such behaviour and distance us from our actions toward other animals, yet for many of us the choices we make go unchallenged to the extent that we barely consider the ethics of meat consumption. For myself, witnessing this challenged my own sense of educational ethics and ecological justice. I remain unconvinced by the utilisation of the body of the deer for such educational purposes from a moral standpoint; yet cannot turn away from the power of these uncomfortable experiences to challenge perceptions and bring to the surface conversations and reflections which would be difficult to elicit in other circumstances.

Acknowledgement The author wishes to thank participants and education staff on programmes at Embercombe during 2016. Thanks too to Sophie Christophy for reading an early excerpt of this chapter and for guiding my thinking on consent in education. The names of participants and staff have been changed for the purpose of anonymity.

References

Abrams, D. (1996). *The spell of the sensuous.* Pantheon.

Angrosino, M. (2007). *Doing ethnographic and observational research.* Sage.

Aultman, J. M. (2005). Uncovering the hidden medical curriculum through a pedagogy of discomfort. *Advances in Health Sciences Education, 10,* 263–273.

Boler, M. (1999). *Feeling power: Emotions and education*. Psychology Press.

Boler, M. (2004). Teaching for hope. In J. Garrison & D. Liston (Eds.), *Teaching, learning, and loving: Reclaiming passion in educational practice*. Routledge.

Brymer, E., Cuddihy, T. F., & Sharma-Brymer, V. (2010). The role of nature-based experiences in the development and maintenance of wellness. *Asia-Pacific Journal of Health, Sport and Physical Education, 1*, 21–27.

Burls, A. (2007). People and green spaces: Promoting public health and mental well-being through ecotherapy. *Journal of Public Mental Health, 6*, 24–39.

Buzzell, L., & Chalquist, C. (2010). *Ecotherapy: Healing with nature in mind*. Counterpoint.

Christophy, S. (2016). Consent based education: What can a flock of Spanish geese tell us about schooling? Retrieved November 21, 2020, from https://sophiechristophy.wordpress.com/2016/11/21/consent-based-education-what-can-a-flock-of-spanish-geese-tell-us-about-schooling/

Clinebell, H. (2013). *Ecotherapy: Healing ourselves, healing the earth*. Routledge.

Conradson, D. (2005). Freedom, space and perspective: Moving encounters with other ecologies. In *Emotional Geographies* (pp. 103–116). Routledge.

Coulter, S., Campbell, J., Duffy, J., & Reilly, I. (2013). Enabling social work students to deal with the consequences of political conflict: Engaging with victim/survivor service users and a 'pedagogy of discomfort'. *Social Work Education, 32*, 439–452.

Cranton, P., & Taylor, E. W. (2012). Transformative learning theory: Seeking a more unified theory. In *The handbook of transformative learning: Theory, research, and practice* (pp. 3–20). Jossey-Bass.

Cutri, R. M., & Whiting, E. F. (2015). The emotional work of discomfort and vulnerability in multicultural teacher education. *Teachers and Teaching, 21*, 1010–1025.

Davis, K. M., & Atkins, S. S. (2004). Creating and teaching a course in ecotherapy: We went to the woods. *The Journal of Humanistic Counseling, 43*, 211.

Embercombe. (2016). *Vision and mission* [Online]. http://embercombe.org/what-we-do/vision-mission/

Greenleaf, A. T., Bryant, R. M., & Pollock, J. B. (2014). Nature-based counseling: Integrating the healing benefits of nature into practice. *International Journal for the Advancement of Counselling, 36*, 162–174.

Harper, N. J., Carpenter, C., & Segal, D. (2011). Self and place: Journeys in the land. *Ecopsychology, 4*, 319–325.

Harvey, G. (2005). *Animism: Respecting the living world*. Wakefield Press.

Jacobson, T. (2003). *Confronting our discomfort: Clearing the way for anti-bias in early childhood*. ERIC.

Jordan, M. (2014). Moving beyond counselling and psychotherapy as it currently is–taking therapy outside. *European Journal of Psychotherapy & Counselling, 16*, 361–375.

Joy, M. (2020). *Why we love dogs, eat pigs, and wear cows: An introduction to carnism.* Red Wheel.

Kheel, M. (1991). Ecofeminism and deep ecology: Reflections on identity and difference. *The Trumpeter, 8,* 62–72.

Kheel, M. (1996). The killing game: An ecofeminist critique of hunting. *Journal of the Philosophy of Sport, 23,* 30–44.

Lumber, R., Richardson, M., & Sheffield, D. (2017). Beyond knowing nature: Contact, emotion, compassion, meaning, and beauty are pathways to nature connection. *PLoS One, 12,* e0177186.

Madden, R. (2010). *Being ethnographic: A guide to the theory and practice of ethnography.* Sage Publications.

Mcgeeney, A. (2016). *With nature in mind: The ecotherapy manual for mental health professionals.* Jessica Kingsley Publishers.

Mezirow, J. (1990). Conclusion: Toward transformative learning and emancipatory education. In *Fostering critical reflection in adulthood: A guide to transformative and emancipatory learning* (pp. 354–376). Jossey-Bass.

Mezirow, J. (1991). *Transformative dimensions of adult learning.* ERIC.

Mezirow, J. (1997). Transformative learning: Theory to practice. *New Directions for Adult and Continuing Education, 74,* 5–12.

Nadan, Y., & Stark, M. (2016). The pedagogy of discomfort: Enhancing reflectivity on stereotypes and bias. *British Journal of Social Work, 47,* bcw023.

Parry, J. (2009). Oryx and Crake and the new nostalgia for meat. *Society and Animals, 17,* 241–256.

Redmond, M. (2010). Safe space oddity: Revisiting critical pedagogy. *Journal of Teaching in Social Work, 30,* 1–14.

Rust, M. J. (2004). Creating psychotherapy for a sustainable future. *Psychotherapy and Politics International, 2,* 50–63.

Rust, M.-J. (2014). Eros, animal and earth. *Self & Society, 41,* 38–43.

Selby, D., & Kagawa, F. (2015). Drawing threads together: A critical and transformative agenda for sustainability education. In D. Selby & F. Kagawa (Eds.), *Sustainability frontiers.* Barbara Budrich.

Soga, M., & Gaston, K. J. (2016). Extinction of experience: The loss of human–nature interactions. *Frontiers in Ecology and the Environment, 14,* 94–101.

Taylor, C. (2013). *Respect for the (animal) dead.* Sydney University Press.

Wals, A. E., Geerling-Eijff, F., Hubeek, F., Van Der Kroon, S., & Vader, J. (2008). All mixed up? Instrumental and emancipatory learning toward a more sustainable world: Considerations for EE policymakers. *Applied Environmental Education and Communication, 7,* 55–65.

Wear, D., & Kuczewski, M. G. (2008). Perspective: Medical students' perceptions of the poor: What impact can medical education have? *Academic Medicine, 83,* 639–645.

Wilson, N., Ross, M., Lafferty, K., & Jones, R. (2009). A review of ecotherapy as an adjunct form of treatment for those who use mental health services. *Journal of Public Mental Health, 7*, 23–35.

Wolgemuth, J. R., & Donohue, R. (2006). Toward an inquiry of discomfort guiding transformation in "emancipatory" narrative research. *Qualitative Inquiry, 12*, 1012–1021.

Zembylas, M. (2015). 'Pedagogy of discomfort' and its ethical implications: The tensions of ethical violence in social justice education. *Ethics and Education, 10*, 163–174.

Zembylas, M., & Chubbuck, S. (2009). Emotions and social inequalities: Mobilizing emotions for social justice education. In *Advances in teacher emotion research*. Springer.

Zembylas, M., & Mcglynn, C. (2012). Discomforting pedagogies: Emotional tensions, ethical dilemmas and transformative possibilities. *British Educational Research Journal, 38*, 41–59.

Outdoor Learning and Student Teacher Identity

Orla Kelly

Introduction

Place-based pedagogies are teaching and learning approaches that are intertwined with place, bringing together the locality, the community and the learners. Place-based learning sits within the wider context of outdoor learning, which is conceptualised as learning that takes place not just outside the classroom but outdoors, under the open sky. Importantly, such outdoor learning promotes a change of location rather than a change of curriculum (Lloyd, 2018). In the context of primary education, outdoor learning, at its basic level, can be described as teaching and learning which could take place in the classroom but is taught outdoors with little or no connection to the environment or place. At another level, it can be described as teaching and learning which supports the development of children's knowledge and understanding of their environment through direct engagement. This would reflect traditional outdoor learning within

O. Kelly (✉)
Dublin City University, Dublin, Ireland
e-mail: orla.kelly@dcu.ie

© The Author(s), under exclusive license to Springer Nature Switzerland AG 2022
R. Cutting, R. Passy (eds.), *Contemporary Approaches to Outdoor Learning*, Palgrave Studies in Alternative Education,
https://doi.org/10.1007/978-3-030-85095-1_13

science and geography contexts. At a deeper level, it can be described as a pedagogy which supports children's learning and development across a range of domains, with the outdoors providing the context, resources, setting and/or space for rich experiential and authentic learning. Such pedagogy has strong connections with the Sustainable Development Goals (United Nations, 2015).

Research has shown that regular visits to the same environments promote knowledge, attachment, and connection to place, with children appearing more connected to the local landscapes and no longer estranged from their local environments (Lloyd, 2018). Higgins (2009) argues that this 'allows for further developmental outcomes, such as understanding the consequences of one's actions and an ethics of citizenship and care' (p. 48). Furthermore, Hales (2018) argues for personal and community history to be at the heart of the history curriculum, supporting children to begin to consider not only who they are, but their backgrounds and how they are contributing to the wider environment.

Beames et al. (2012, p. 6) argue that:

> school grounds are often rich in ecological and cultural stories with tremendous relevance to the lives of the children and advocate for outdoor learning that takes place within the school grounds and in local places before moving to places further afield.

Furthermore, Beames et al. (2017) stress the importance of an integrated approach to teaching, which promotes 'a coherent meshing of indoor and outdoor sites for learning' (p. 82) and equally argue for cross-curricular approaches, combining elements of the formal curriculum to provide students with more life-like and relevant learning experiences. Christensen and Wistoft (2019) also note the importance of connecting the indoor learning environment with the outdoor one for effective integration.

The Irish curriculum (DES/NCCA, 1999a), which is undergoing review, aims to provide a broad learning experience and is designed to nurture the child in all dimensions of her or his life. Geography, history and science subjects are explored under Social, Environmental and Scientific Education (SESE), which provides opportunities for the child to explore, investigate and develop an understanding of the natural, human, social and cultural dimensions of local and wider environments; to learn and practise a wide range of skills; and to acquire open, critical and responsible attitudes (DES/NCCA, 1999b). There are ample opportunities for place-based learning and outdoor learning in the SESE curriculum and it is explicitly supported in the curriculum and guidelines for teachers. This is also the case for Physical Education and Visual Arts. However, as is often the case in the face of the various conflicting demands of policies, practice and societal expectations, the enactment of the curriculum can look a little different. Usher (2019) raises the issue of the narrowing of the Irish primary curriculum within the context of new numeracy and literacy curricula, as well as a focus on science, technology, engineering and maths (STEM), to the detriment of geography. This no doubt would be argued by other subject area teachers. This has a knock-on impact on student teachers when they engage in a school placement, as they get less opportunity to observe and practise the full breadth of the curriculum. Additionally, teachers who try to adopt alternative pedagogies, such as outdoor and place-based learning, which are not part of the usual school culture, may struggle to make this part of their normal practice. However, Pike (2011) suggests that attempts to make children's geographies in their local environments central to primary geography through content and activities like many of those outlined in the Primary School Curriculum would be successful.

Within the context of initial teacher education (ITE) programmes in Ireland, there is a focus on supporting outdoor learning and place-based pedagogies across a range of subject areas. However, this can be largely subject driven which may lessen the potential for authentic place-based pedagogies as described above. Furthermore, in the context of high stakes school placement assessment, student teachers may choose to adopt safer lessons than potentially 'risky' outdoor lessons for fear of lessons going wrong when being assessed. Anecdotally, few student teachers recall observing outdoor lessons during school placement. Therefore, they get little opportunity to develop their confidence and competence with such an alternative pedagogy. The perceived risks centre around the commonly identified challenges to outdoor learning such as weather, classroom management, and health and safety. Without opportunities to put into practice the theory and experience from their ITE programmes, alternative pedagogies can fall by the way-side in light of pressures on newly qualified teachers.

ITE programmes, as professional degrees, are typically all-consuming as students strive to achieve not just degree level objectives across a range of subject areas but also, professional knowledge, understanding and skills gained through regular school placement opportunities to be able to effectively move straight in to a teaching career on completion of their degree. Therefore, to provide time and space for such opportunities to explore outdoor learning as a pedagogy, a professional development programme was developed as described in the following case study.

Case Study: Dublin City University

A professional development programme was designed and offered to students across the Bachelor in Primary Education (BEd) and Bachelor in Early Childhood Education (BECE) in Dublin City University. The main aim of this programme was to develop student teachers' confidence and competence to teach the primary curriculum through a pedagogy of outdoor learning. A transformative model of professional development was planned with four key elements; two days of workshops, mentoring by outdoor learning experts, application in a primary school setting and ongoing reflection. Nine student teachers took part and were from both BEd and BECE programmes and included 1st, 2nd and 4th year students. This was a voluntary programme and students gave up their time outside of term time to take part. There was a close relationship with the partner school for this professional development programme. The two teachers, whose 2nd classes would be experiencing the outdoor learning lessons, also attended the workshops and observed or participated in the outdoor learning lessons.

The workshops were largely delivered outdoors to model different pedagogies. They aimed to explore the 'why' of outdoor learning, highlighting key research, the potential for outdoor learning within the Irish curriculum, outdoor pedagogies, how to manage and organise learning outdoors, and planning for outdoor learning including use of technology as well as assessment and evaluation. Mid way through the second day the students were put into three groups, with a mix of students in each group allowing for peer support. Each group was assigned a mentor. The role of the mentor was to support the group with their planning both for and during the school sessions as well as supporting reflective practice. The mentors were outdoor learning experts, highly experienced practitioners in

(continued)

(continued)
various outdoor learning contexts, who were not part of the formal education system and so could provide alternative perspectives and experiences. Each group of three student teachers was responsible for a group of twenty 2nd class children from a local primary school and committed to planning and teaching four outdoor lessons over four weeks. They were encouraged to link with the children's ongoing work or make connections to prior learning where possible with the support of the class teachers. Additionally, in line with Beames and Ross' (2010) Outdoor Journeys model, the student teachers were encouraged to start off in the school grounds before potentially moving beyond the school gates and to support child led enquiries.

Reflection was a key part of the programme and this involved each student teacher and mentor keeping a reflective diary. At the end of each day of the workshops as well as after each session in school they were encouraged to write a reflection. They were prompted to use Gibb's model (1988) to guide their reflections but did not have to use this. At the end of each session in school, there was also a group reflection and the students were encouraged to share their thoughts on how it went, with the mentors filling the role of critical friend. Finally, a few weeks after the culmination of the school sessions, both mentors and student teachers were invited to take part in a focus group.

This case study was designed and delivered by Dr Orla Kelly, Dublin City University; Tomás Aylward, Munster Technological University; Dr Janet McKennedy, Technological University Dublin and Dr Yesim Tunali Flynn, Project Manager with support from the Higher Education Authority.

IMPACT OF THE PROFESSIONAL DEVELOPMENT PROGRAMME

Overall, the student teachers were very positive about the programme and all reported development of their confidence in taking learning outside the classroom. The programme was successful in demonstrating how an integrated curriculum could be supported through outdoor learning and in challenging the notion around class management being a barrier to outdoor learning. These will be briefly discussed in the following paragraphs. Other perceived barriers such as weather and resources were also challenged during this programme as highlighted in one of the reflective diaries:

> *Not limiting outdoors to sunny weather—which I have done in the past. Use clothes and resources to allow you to work in any weather.* (Student Teacher 6)

CURRICULAR CONNECTIONS

Dolan (2016) makes a strong case for the synergies between geography and outdoor learning, particularly in the context of education for sustainability. Cutting and Kelly (2015) highlight the learning opportunities afforded for science in outdoor settings, in particular the unbounded observations and context for ecological thinking. This was evident throughout this case study and given the strong potential for outdoor learning in science and geography in the Irish National Curriculum, not surprising. Indeed two groups reported integrating science into the outdoor sessions in school *often*, and one group reported integrating it *all the time*. Similarly, two groups reported integrating geography *often*, with one group reporting only *some of the time*. Physical Education was the other subject area integrated most often. English, Visual Arts, Social, Personal and Health Education (SPHE) and Maths were also integrated, though less frequently. Over the four outdoor learning sessions in school, History, Gaeilge, Music and Drama were rarely integrated, if at all. However, thematic analysis of the focus groups and reflective diaries highlighted the potential for curriculum learning and integration and the depth and range of learning that can emerge.

> *There were some amazing examples of cross curricular learning that happened today. Today's lesson allowed for a perfect demonstration of how explicit, implicit and null curriculum can intermingle to create a rich outdoor learning environment. The unexpected learning outcomes which were achieved throughout today's lesson were hugely beneficial and noted by the teachers as surprising and highly valuable.* (Outdoor Learning Mentor 1)

However, the student teachers equally noted that they would have liked more input from the workshops on the subjects that were perhaps less easy/obvious to take outdoors, specifically mentioning Gaeilge, Maths and History.

...if somebody said to me about doing Irish (Gaeilge) outside I would be kind of like, I wouldn't know where to start and so I think something like that would be very useful as well in CPD days, how to use Irish outside. I know we discussed it but even just to see it practically being put in use it would be really good. And history as well, kind of in my head it would be one that would be kind of difficult even though it probably isn't. (Student teacher 7)

This has direct relevance for initial teacher education courses where outdoor learning is often promoted through particular subjects. It also reinforces the point that for authentic place-based learning an integrated approach needs to be adopted.

Class Management

It was clear from the responses in the focus groups and the reflective diaries beforehand that the student teachers had concerns over managing the group outside and this was somewhat experienced, particularly in the earlier sessions. However, over the course of the four school sessions, and with modelling and support from the mentors, the student-teachers developed particular strategies, which were relevant for outdoor learning as well as using strategies which they would traditionally use in the classroom. In terms of managing the open space, some of the strategies included using trees to make a natural boundary, having 'hard' and 'soft' boundaries, walking the boundary with the children, and using a game to establish the boundaries. They also had a period of quiet on entering a new space, had active games to begin the lesson, carefully considered groupings once they got to know the children more, had a designated place to gather, fewer teacher-led activities, and clear instructions.

We used the trees as natural boundaries which were self-enforcing. When we entered the trees we facilitated a period of quiet so that the students could explore/imagine who lived in this area. (Outdoor Learning Mentor 1)

When we first go outside next time we will ask the children to sit in a circle. (Student teacher 2)

The student teachers acknowledged the high teacher/pupil ratio and high level of support that they were experiencing and expressed some concern over class management with more typical teacher/pupil ratio in Irish primary classrooms. However, by the end of the programme they felt confident that they were better able to support and manage learning outside.

I feel I have built confidence in working in the outdoors and taking children to the outside classroom with useful and practised management strategies. (Student teacher 5)

Yeah, I think before starting this my own knowledge (was a barrier), *I'm kind of wary about being able to control their behaviour but now it's more about the other factors or other people that affect it.* (Student teacher 4)

TEACHER IDENTITY

The above are more tangible outcomes in terms of developing the student teachers' confidence in planning for and managing learning outdoors as well as competence to meet curriculum objectives. However, when considering the impact on teacher identity and the student teachers' professional practice, the multifaceted nature of this needs to be explored, in particular, the role of collaboration and classroom cultures.

COLLABORATION

Izadinia (2018) states how the process of teacher identity formation, from a social constructivist perspective (Vygotsky, 1986), is believed to occur not in individual isolation but rather in a social-community context. Loughran (2006) suggests that teaching about teaching requires teacher educators to provide their students with access to 'the thoughts and actions that shape such practice; they need to be able to see and hear the pedagogical reasoning that underpins the teaching they are experiencing' (p. 5). This supports the key decision to have outdoor learning mentors, not just to support the social community aspect but also to share their practice and thoughts which offered an alternative lens to their traditional classroom-based experience with school-based mentors.

Izadinia (2018) identified principles which mentor teachers can apply into their practices to contribute to the development of robust teacher identity, including building and maintaining strong relationships, offering support and encouragement, providing ongoing feedback, making time for reflective activities and creating a positive environment. The mentors were successful in achieving this and the student teachers reported on the valuable role they played in shaping their practice.

> *I think by doing it and like doing it with you guys and having that confidence if anything does go wrong we can always ask you, that really helped.* (Student teacher 1)

Equally the students, who were from different degree programmes and different years, provided peer-to-peer support. This collaboration, particularly in small group settings, supported the student teachers to develop their practice in a safe and supportive manner. This is in line with findings from the study by Ní Chróinín et al. (2013) who reported that 'pair and group work activities that did not expose or isolate an individual or require them to perform alone were preferred as they provided a "safe" peer environment for their performances' in relation to developing pre-service teachers' professional practice in practical subject areas (p. 263). The student teachers were more readily able to explore their practice with support from others, in a non-assessed capacity.

CLASSROOM CULTURE

Alsup (2006) describes how developing a professional identity involves being able to 'build bridges' between the many different sets of ideas, assumptions or discourses that explain what it means to be a teacher. This is particularly pertinent when trying to develop a teacher identity that is perhaps a little left field, a teacher identity which values outdoor and place-based learning as part and parcel of their teaching toolkit.

Generally, when used effectively outdoor learning shifts the teacher's role to one of facilitator and observer, which offers opportunities for different relationships and dynamics to emerge. Outdoor contexts in cultures that generally favour more teacher-directed learning appear to disrupt the usual cultural expectations of adults and children, such that children experience more freedom to initiate their own learning experiences, to play for longer periods without interruptions and to show independence of thinking and action (Waite & Davis, 2007). This links with Waite and Pratt's work (2017) on the cultural density of places. These ambiguous outdoor spaces and places that are unfamiliar to staff and students are culturally light as they bring fewer rules and/or routines, allowing for more playful child-initiated learning and egalitarian management of how time is spent (Waite et al., 2013).

This cultural density of the outdoor classroom certainly played a key part in developing the student-teachers' outdoor learning practice. From both the focus groups and the reflective diaries, it was clear that the sessions in school were effective in challenging notions around teacher role and how time is spent.

> *We are beginning to really see student led learning emerge and the teachers are creating space and time within their lesson plans to allow this to happen.* (Outdoor Learning Mentor 1)

> *I learned today that it was better to go with the flow according to the children's learning and interests and not be strict on time management to a certain extent of trying to fit everything in.* (Student teacher 5)

> *Comparing this week to last week, I feel that there was less teacher input/instruction and more time given to engage in exploration and discovery.* (Student teacher 2)

The next quote suggests a shift in the mindset of one of the student teachers. As student teachers they felt constrained by the cultural norms of time management, with many reflections alluding to *not getting all the plan done* and *running out of time*. However, this student recognises that this issue was not one for the children and was certainly not holding back their learning.

> *I feel time was against us a lot today... On reflection, the time constraint was not an issue to the children as there was opportunity for child-led exploration and learning. The issue of time lies within the teacher and not the children. The relaxed time was highly beneficial in this lesson and can be to a certain extent in other lessons.* (Student teacher 5)

Another student teacher referred to the tension with the cultural norms of children's behaviour in a classroom setting and questioned whether the often active nature of lessons outdoors would be questioned by a supervisor (when on school placement). Clearly this student teacher is experiencing conflict between the social and cultural norms of the classroom and the more ambiguous outdoor space.

I feel that an art lesson or English lesson that takes place outside shouldn't need to have the children running around. I understand that it will help the children settle but as a student teacher I still question the relevancy of it to the learning of the lesson, as I feel if this were a teaching practice the inspector would question it too. (Student teacher 8)

Conclusion

Initial teacher education programmes are excellent at supporting pre-service teachers' professional development in the context of traditional classroom-based teaching and learning, with some opportunities for exploring opportunities for outdoor learning. This case study offers a brief snapshot into the complexities of developing student teachers' professional identity to include outdoor and place-based learning as a staple of their teaching toolkit. Through this case study, the development of teacher identity is recognised as both a process and product.

Overall, the student teachers who took part in this project were confident to embrace outdoor learning in their future teaching, though recognised school and policy factors that may be a barrier to this. This highlights the evolving nature of their professional understanding; whereas weather, resources, management, and health and safety were originally recognised as barriers, by the end of the programme they had developed their awareness of wider cultural issues that might prevent them being able to adopt these new practices. Furthermore, the case study highlights the importance of outdoor learning being promoted not just within specific subject areas but as a pedagogy for learning across the curriculum, as encapsulated by one of the outdoor learning mentors

…it can become the norm in the classroom then that the children are brought outside…and it is not seen as a treat, it is just part of another way of education and another way of learning for them. (Outdoor Learning Mentor 3)

Ultimately, a key factor in the success of this programme was the integral role of the mentors and peer-to-peer support. The outdoor learning mentors could offer alternative perspectives and experiences which at times challenged the cultural norms and practices of traditional classroom-based teaching and learning, and this allowed for formative development of the student teachers' professional knowledge and understanding in outdoor learning. Furthermore, the opportunity to plan together and co-teach offered peer-to-peer support which is generally not experienced during school placement, which tend to value individual placements. Equally, their confidence grew as they got to know the children and developed strategies for managing outdoor learning. This recognises the importance of sustained engagement with and opportunities to practice novel teaching and learning pedagogies.

> *I will take everything I have learned and done during these six sessions with me in my future teaching and I feel I have built confidence in working in the outdoors and taking children to the outside classroom with useful and practised management strategies.* (Student teacher 5)

REFERENCES

Alsup, J. (2006). *Teacher identity discourses: Negotiating personal and professional spaces.* Routledge.

Beames, S., & Ross, H. (2010). Journeys outside the classroom. *Journal of Adventure Education & Outdoor Learning, 10*(2), 95–109. https://doi.org/1 0.1080/14729679.2010.505708

Beames, S., Higgins, P., & Nicol, R. (2012). *Learning outside the classroom. Theory and guidelines for practice.* Routledge.

Beames, S., Christie, B., & Blackwell, I. (2017). Developing whole school approaches to integrated indoor/outdoor teaching. In S. Waite (Ed.), *Children learning outside the classroom from birth to eleven* (2nd ed.). Sage.

Christensen, J. H., & Wistoft, K. (2019). Investigating the effectiveness of subject-integrated school garden teaching. *Journal of Outdoor and Experiential Education, 22*, 237–251.

Cutting, R., & Kelly, O. (2015). *Creative teaching in primary science.* Sage.

Department of Education and Science/National Council for Curriculum and Assessment. (1999a). *Primary school curriculum.* https://www.curriculumonline.ie/Primary/

Department of Education and Science/National Council for Curriculum and Assessment. (1999b). *Primary school curriculum – Science.* https://www.curriculumonline.ie/getmedia/346522bd-f9f6-49ce-9676-49b59fdb5505/PSEC03c_Science_Curriculum.pdf

Dolan, A. M. (2016). Place-based curriculum making: Devising a synthesis between primary geography and outdoor learning. *Journal of Adventure Education and Outdoor Learning, 16*(1), 49–62. https://doi.org/10.1080/14729679.2015.1051563

Gibbs, G. (1988). *Learning by doing: A guide to teaching and learning methods.* Oxford Further Education Unit.

Hales, A. (2018). The local in history: Personal and community history and its impact on identity. *Education 3-13, 46*(6), 671–684. https://doi.org/10.108 0/03004279.2018.1483802

Higgins, P. (2009). Into the big wide world: Sustainable experiential education for the 21st century. *Journal of Experiential Education, 32*(1), 44–60.

Izadinia, M. (2018). Mentor teachers. Contributions to the development of pre-service teachers' identity. In P. Schutz, J. Hong, & D. Cross Francis (Eds.), *Research on teacher identity.* Springer. https://doi.org/10.1007/ 978-3-319-93836-3_10

Lloyd, A. (2018). Outdoor learning in primary schools: Predominantly female ground. In T. Gray & D. Mitten (Eds.), *The Palgrave international handbook of women and outdoor learning* (Palgrave Studies in Gender and Education) (pp. 637–648). https://doi.org/10.1007/978-3-319-53550-0_43

Loughran, J. J. (2006). *Developing a pedagogy of teacher education.* Routledge.

Ní Chróinín, D., Mitchell, E., Kenny, A., Murtagh, E., & Vaughan, E. (2013). How can pre-service primary teachers' perspectives contribute to a pedagogy that problematises the 'practical' in teacher education? *Irish Educational Studies, 32*(2), 251–267. https://doi.org/10.1080/03323315.2013.798524

Pike, S. (2011). "If you went out it would stick": Irish children's learning in their local environments. *International Research in Geographical and Environmental Education, 20*(2), 139–159. https://doi.org/10.1080/10382046.2011. 564787

United Nations (2015). *Sustainable Development Goals.* https://sdgs. un.org/goals

Usher, J. (2019). Is geography lost? Curriculum policy analysis: Finding a place for geography within a changing primary school curriculum in the Republic of Ireland. *Irish Educational Studies.* https://doi.org/10.1080/0332331 5.2019.1697945

Vygotsky, L. (1986). *Thought and Language.* Edited by A. Kozulin. MIT Press.

Waite, S., & Davis, B. (2007). The contribution of free play and structured activities in Forest School to learning beyond cognition: An English case. In B. Ravn & N. Kryger (Eds.), *Learning beyond cognition* (pp. 257–274). The Danish University of Education.

Waite, S., & Pratt, N. (2017). Theoretical perspectives on learning outside the classroom – Relationships between learning and place. In S. Waite (Ed.), *Children learning outside the classroom from birth to eleven* (2nd ed.). Sage.

Waite, S., Rogers, S., & Evans, J. (2013). Freedom, flow and fairness: Exploring how children develop socially at school through outdoor play. *Journal of Adventure Education & Outdoor Learning, 13*(3), 255–276. https://doi. org/10.1080/14729679.2013.798590

Ecological Identity Work

Rosamonde Birch

...the story of Earth is at stake as we participate in it....
—Donna Haraway: Storytelling for Earthly Survival (2017)

INTRODUCTION

The international *Youth Strike 4 Climate, Fridays for Future* and *Extinction Rebellion* movements have considerably and irreversibly raised the profile of planetary scale crisis (IPCC, 2018; IPBES, 2019), placing the urgency for eco-socially just (Gruenewald, 2003) learning alternatives directly in the path of the neo-liberal capitalist growth model (Latour, 2018). The planetary scale activism and the encountering of crisis narratives means some young people have *nascent (eco)identities* that are already engaging with the transdisciplinary 'head, heart and hands' (Orr, 1992) of transformative learning and ecological literacy (Goleman et al., 2012; Mezirow, 2002; Sterling, 2003, 2011a). This engagement, as teachers of Education for Sustainability (ESD) subjects and specialisms know, is immeasurably and presciently imperative because the 'well-being of the biosphere hinges

R. Birch (✉)
University of Dundee, Dundee, UK
e-mail: roz@rosamondebirch.space

R. Cutting, R. Passy (eds.), *Contemporary Approaches to Outdoor Learning*, Palgrave Studies in Alternative Education,
https://doi.org/10.1007/978-3-030-85095-1_14

on our ability to establish relationships with our surrounding ecologies which are not purely utilitarian from a human perspective' (Scott & Fraser, 2010, p. 136). Consequently, this chapter intends to explore, through contemporary approaches and methods, the practice of *ecological identity work* (EIW) from Mitchell Thomashow (1995).

Through EIW, Thomashow (ibid.) suggests that relating to nature and understanding our ecological interdependence will use 'the direct experience of nature as a framework for personal decisions, professional choices, political actions and spiritual inquiry' (p. xiii). With this in mind, the contemporary EIW approaches and methods being proposed through this chapter adopt an 'ethic of becomings' (De Freites et al., 2018; Deleuze & Guattari, 1987) where *becoming* is awareness of relational interconnectedness and learning is perceived as generative not transmissive. Additionally, with a Global Citizenship 'ethics of care' (Bowden, 1997; Held, 2006) and posthumanist framing throughout this chapter there is an emphasis on 'world-making' (Barad, 2007; Haraway, 2016) and caring co-creative practices of learning. Barad (2007) states 'we are part of the nature we seek to understand' (p. 26) and that through the entanglement of dialogue, place and relational knowledges we encounter our agency as part of dynamic systems. Thus, the discussion will suggest that through outdoor learning with *place, dialogue* and *narrative* the EIW focus of reflective participation, relational communities of inquiry and the vital role 'nature' has in affecting *ecological identity* will be realised. Firstly, this chapter examines identity in relation to social theory and then establishes a definition of *(eco)identities*, which extends on Thomashow's (1995) original EIW. Lastly, the three key themes of the chapter, *place, dialogue and narrative* will link to EIW and how 'learning about who we are as we dwell in the world may save our ecosphere' (Morris, 2002, p. 572).

Identity and (Eco)Identities

From contemporary literature and discourse on *(eco)identities* (Hayes-Conroy & Vanderbeck, 2005; Light, 2000; Scott & Fraser, 2010; Thomashow, 1995) there are two important clarifications to be made before proceeding. Firstly, focusing on the process by which identity is constructed: this chapter is defining identity as a socially formed, 'contestable, always up for dispute' (Appiah, 2018, p. 12) sense of 'self', where 'identities' are multifaceted and relationally responsive to the social (ecosystems) environments (Stets & Biga, 2003). Through the subjective and intersubjective exploration of values, norms, ethics and 'self', identity is 'constructed and reconstructed in relation to socio-cultural contexts' (Hayes-Conroy & Vanderbeck, 2005, p. 313). Therefore, *(eco)identities* are part of the multifaceted presence of 'self', also dynamic and relationally constructed, hence *place, dialogue* and *narratives* as praxis (Freire, 1970) are profound in forming *(eco)identity.* The positioning of *(eco)identities* as *becoming*—generative knowledges—alongside being 'material-discursive' intra-actions (Barad, 2007) frames intersubjective 'world-making' as relational and entangled with subjective meaning-making. Thus, this chapter intentionally moves away from measurable quantitative approaches of defining 'values' or 'identity', such as the 'Environmental World View' (Blaikie, 1992), or the 'New Ecological Paradigm' (Dunlop & Van Liere, 2008) due to the reductionist dimensions of these models not being applicable to EIW. The focus of the chapter additionally detaches the concept of *(eco)identities* from identity politics (Light, 2000), not to unpoliticise them entirely, but to hold space for identity to be explored free from stereotyping or political spectrum positioning (Latour, 2018; Light, 2000). To participate in community means being political with a small 'p', and this is emphasised by Thomashow (1995) as vital to EIW, especially when learning about relational and place-based political infrastructures alongside the local to global political landscapes.

Secondly, the term *(eco)*identity needs to be further defined. Thomashow (1995) establishes his definition as 'all the different ways people construe themselves in relationship to the earth … how we extend our sense of self in relationship to nature' (Thomashow, 1995, p. 3). Through EIW, one is invited to be open to change and self-transformation through nature and ecological awareness, which distinctly situates his method within the *deep ecology* ethos (Curry, 2011; Næss, 2008) and the 'self-realisation' focus of Arne Næss's (2008) *Ecosophy.* Scott and Fraser (2010), by also mentioning the global 'web of relationships' in their EIW work, conceive of 'ecological identity as this ontological sense of identification with surrounding ecologies, up to and including the global commons, as one's own, as one's home' (Scott & Fraser, 2010, p. 136), which adds learning about complex systems thinking (Goleman et al., 2012; Sterling, 2003, 2011a) as vital to EIW.

Nascent and Affective (Eco)Identities

Nascent (eco)identities are defined as *becoming* with emergent and unmapped *eco* lifestyle choices and *eco* purchasing habits that have occurred in response to mainstream campaigns alongside youth activism promoting more ethical and environmentally friendly choices. Students will already be making these *nascent* choices and lifestyle decisions (Hayes-Conroy & Vanderbeck, 2005) based on prior learning, existing awareness of ecological crisis and exposure to mainstream media climate warnings. Some students may have existing *affective (eco)identities* and be involved with activism, grassroots action and lifestyle changes, whilst others may not align to predefined and preconceived conceptualisations of (*eco)identities* (Hayes-Conroy & Vanderbeck, 2005).

In research, using Thomashow's (1995) EIW, Hayes-Conroy and Vanderbeck (2005) evidenced that because of *nascent (eco)identities* students do intentionally select ESD subjects and modules or programmes of study. They concluded that this additionally demonstrated students' desire for ESD topics not only due to the subject, content or knowledge but because the 'learning' is different to other subjects. The study found that students preferred the pedagogies of an ESD module as they had space for exploring 'real life' issues about one's role in local and global ecologies. 'For many students, choosing to study the environment is a step towards identifying themselves as part of a community of like-minded, ecologically concerned individuals' (Hayes-Conroy & Vanderbeck, 2005, p. 319), thus beginning EIW.

The students also identified limitations to the learning, where some rejected experiences when a particular ethos or morality about environmental concerns was being imposed, especially so when expected to work within the confines of a singular worldview and compelled to align with the responses of their peers or lecturer. The 'classroom' was unfortunately identified as a muted place due to it 'policing the boundary of an established ecological identity' (Hayes-Conroy & Vanderbeck, 2005, p. 323) rather than a receptive place for exploration. To form *affective (eco)identities* students individually and collectively (Schwalbe and Mason-Schrock, 1996 in Dunn & Creek, 2015) must explore their own boundaries of subjective and intersubjective values, ethics and agency, doing their own identity 'policing' to decide who they are and who they are not (Hadden and Lester, 1978 in Hayes-Conroy & Vanderbeck, 2005). These conclusions of the study informed the contemporary methods being proposed through this chapter, where *place, dialogue* and *narrative* enable discourse that embodies 'openness' for exploration.

Terminology was likewise raised by the students as problematic, where ecocentric and anthropocentric were used opposingly and students 'worried that this kind of binary opposition failed to represent the interconnections of real world experiences and events' (Hayes-Conroy & Vanderbeck, 2005, p. 324). Jones (2017) argues for knowledge to be 'un-dividing the world' (p. 161) and that we need to *reassemble dualities* in ESD work whilst also conceding that established dualist thinking makes this an inherently challenging paradox. By experiencing non-binary thinking and 'exploding entrenched ideas' (Barad, 2007, p. 3) students can choose to interpret the world differently and not perpetuate the same cycles of knowledge that maintain eco-social injustice. However, it is important to note that the methods and approaches of an ESD module today would also expose discernible differences in student responses due to being influenced by the *Sustainable Development Goals* (SDG, n.d.) and the *United Nations Decade of Education for Sustainable Development* (UNESCO, 2014). Both of these global programmes have significantly raised the profile of ESD, and especially the use of different pedagogies for learning with nature, place and other sustainability specialisms.

Place and (Eco)Identities

The current global educational priorities of preparing students for work mobility and the neo-liberal capitalist agenda has created an emphasis on 'transcending place' (Biesta, 2006) and there is an on-going 'place-corrosive process' (Næss, 2008) fragmenting community solidarity and undermining access to knowledge through the *self-nature-place* relationship. Gruenewald (2003) states neo-liberalism is privatising space and Payne and Wattchow (2009) additionally argue that the 'fast' of neo-liberalism impacts community as it creates a 'disembodiment, displacement, disembedding and decontextualizing' (Payne & Wattchow, 2009, p. 17) of our relationships to each other and our ecologies.

In response to these concerns and fears, Place-Based Education (PBE) has been creating a counter-movement by intentionally using place as the focal point of outdoor, ecological, cultural and socio-political learning; (re)synthesising knowledge and 'viewing place as process' (Sun et al., 2016, p. 576). Place can be defined as the geographical, temporal, spatial, cultural, narrative ecological sphere one inhabits, or dwells with, especially linked to how one identifies with place as an experience of belonging. Gruenewald (2003), in exploring place exposes it as *paradoxical* and *mercurial*, yet concludes that 'place is where the world manifests itself to human beings … places can also be said to hold our culture and even our identity' (p. 625). Through place one encounters new inquiries of anthropology, sociology, geography, architecture and design (Dovey, 2009), and place—the outdoor places—is now being perceived as vital to ESD learning. Gruenewald (2003) further adds 'that places are what people make of them—that people are place makers and that places are a primary artifact of human culture—suggests a more active role for schools in the study, care, and creation of places' (p. 627).

The work of Gruenewald (2003) has influenced the landscape of understanding place and the important role PBE plays, and his variance to PBE, 'place-conscious education' is an approach that stimulates a receptively engaged and meaningful way of facilitating learning of and with place necessary for EIW. It is also important to mention his proposal of 'critical place-based pedagogy' (Gruenewald, 2008) due to the next discussion on dialogue with the work of Andreotti (2006) and her arguments for *'soft'* *learning* rather than 'critical' learning. Both Gruenewald (2008) and Andreotti (2006) are requesting practitioners to be *place-people* and *past-present-future* sensitive, allowing students to explore identity, as well as opportunities to explore historical, systemic and structural hegemony. For EIW, experience of *place* needs perhaps to be *'soft-critical'* and ethically situated (Curry, 2011) to meaningfully consider local to global scale nuances and ambiguities of eco-social justice. 'Local ethics connect up to become effectively global' (p. 174), and through experiencing local systems students begin forming their own 'ecological citizenship' (Curry, 2011) using knowledge of social justice alongside ecological justice. Through Payne and Wattchow's (2009) research they additionally argued for 'slow pedagogy' to be embedded in PBE, which ensures learners have *time* and *space* to understand complex identities with *place* and build relationships that will be new and challenging for them.

By going outside for PBE and through dialogue, learners access a *depth* and *width* of knowledge not achievable through traditional 'classroom' approaches, where they can uncover 'difference' and plurality with inclusivity (Hayes-Conroy & Vanderbeck, 2005; Morris, 2002; Scott & Fraser, 2010; Tooth & Renshaw, 2009). Sun et al. (2016) discuss how educational settings using PBE are more representative of 'real-world' plurality, which makes PBE integral to *becoming* global citizens. PBE facilitates cognisance of difference and diversity whilst creating belonging for students to apply environmental and place-based knowledge in authentic and relevant ways. It could be additionally argued that PBE as a method of EIW equips students with *affective (eco)identities* that are fluid and transformative for adaption to any ecosystem (community), perhaps even equipping students to be more globally 'mobile' than the neo-liberalised 'transcending place' system of education (Biesta, 2006).

Two approaches that could be adopted for EIW and PBE would be Service-Learning (Ward, 1999) and Productive Pedagogy (Ballantyne & Packer, 2008), where the former is more widely used in educational settings. The Productive Pedagogy model includes 'inner work' through five key layers of learning, where 'classroom' knowledge and practice are linked with real-life learning, outdoor sensory engagement with nature, learning by doing and ensuring students have a local context of learning (Tooth & Renshaw, 2009). It can be concluded that PBE is vital to the EIW for students, especially where place becomes the catalyst and co-creator for *becoming* and *affective (eco)identities*. PBE guarantees exploration into the outdoors; into the complexities of geography, climate, history, culture and society, philosophising about self and 'the other', and in many ways learning about humankind, community and what being human means. Students can be place-entangled, developing awareness of their own narrative and knowledge in relationship with others and the ecological community, 'experientially empowered as agents of social change through undertaking enquiry, problem-solving and critical reflection in real-world or community situations of real relevance to learners and their communities' (Morgan, 2012, p. 633).

Dialogue and (Eco)Identities

Light (2000), Hayes-Conroy and Vanderbeck (2005) and Scott and Fraser (2010) all emphasise identity is culturally, environmentally and temporally situated and when there is EIW taking place there is opportunity and possibility of ontological shift through transformative learning (Mezirow, 2002; Sterling, 2003, 2011a). Therefore, communities of students authentically and meaningfully exploring worldviews in complex ways to expand on 'levels of knowing' (Sterling, 2003) and acting competently in response to planetary scale issues (Næss, 2008; Sterling, 2011a) is needed for EIW.

Throughout the Hayes-Conroy and Vanderbeck (2005) study, students highlighted their interest in interdisciplinary learning with a focus on problem-solving and social-learning, which would enable them to relationally and collaboratively explore their ontologies, beliefs, perspectives and existing knowledge through ESD. Scott and Fraser (2010) argue that this is a process of *empathic inclusion*, where diversity, inclusivity, empathy and safe spaces for entering dialogue ensure students can engage with the complexity of planetary crisis and community hegemony. Additionally, outdoor spaces are fundamental to dialogical processes, where dwelling with place means new knowledges and transformations of *(eco)identities* come into *affective* being. 'According to agential realism, knowing, thinking, measuring, theorizing, and observing are material practices of intra-acting within and as part of the word' (Barad, 2007, p. 90), thus, dwelling with our surroundings as we materialise 'new worlds' and 'new knowledges' is an embodied practice for imagining eco-socially just futures.

Entering dialogue for EIW does require practices that can be used outdoors and also exemplify a head, hearts and hands process with the possibility of creating different and new 'world-making' and meaning making. Open Space for Dialogue (OSD) exemplifies a material-discursive (Barad, 2007) method of *'soft-critical'* global citizenship education and has been widely promoted by Vanessa Andreotti (2006). Andreotti (2006) argues that rather than continuing the 'critical' focus of some ESD approaches, practitioners should be 'creating spaces where they [students] are safe to analyse and experiment with other forms of seeing/thinking and being/relating to one another' (p. 49). The use of OSD and other group inquiry or dialogue methods, such as Philosophy for Children (P4C) (Lipman et al., 1980), are key to achieving this aim of changing how we co-construct knowledge and meaning, especially related to simply taking these methods outdoors and into place settings of our immediate surroundings or natural environments.

EIW incorporates the *soft-critical* learning approach, but also what Andreotti and Dowling (2004) call *unfinishedness* in their work on World Social Forum, where the uncertain and incomplete is embraced as revealing difference and self-reflexivity is a conduit to knowing another world is possible. The *unfinishedness* is part of sustaining 'openness' for exploration and also connects to Barad's (2007) material-discursive spaces being boundary-less, disrupting assumptions and binary-thinking, and that knowledge is emergent and (re)configuring as we engage with dialogue and place. OSD and P4C as 'community of inquiry' models create *place-dialogue* for student *becoming* through reflection, questioning assumptions, empathic listening and dwelling with community. 'Community of inquiry' methods can be incorporated into ESD and across outdoor learning practice as part of the elaborate, embodied and profound EIW students undertake.

NARRATIVE AND (ECO)IDENTITIES

Through the dialogical and PBE outdoor learning approaches reflective and autobiographical practice has been mentioned as an additional process that students can undertake as part of their learning portfolio. In the research by Payne and Wattchow (2009) students were required to complete an autobiographical exploration of early childhood outdoor and cultural experiences, reflecting on significant moments that shape who they are in the present. The *memory-work* (ibid.) meant students could 'understand what they bring, assume, or presuppose about learning and, therefore, about their sense of self, or identity, including previous environmental experiences and encounters' (Payne & Wattchow, 2009, p. 19). The use of storytelling, community narratives (Deininger, 2018) and personal narratives enhances awareness of singular and shared values, morals, choices and actions through ecological and ethical uncertainties. However, rather than simply focusing on storytelling and creating environmental narratives, EIW requires reflective and *soft-critical* autobiographical narratives of *self-nature-place* as a process of material, metaphysical and ontological *wayfinding* (O'Connor, 2019).

Rifà-Valls (2011) explores the use of 'visual storytelling' through trainee art teacher autobiographical portfolios where a range of methods and methodologies were used. The research identifies how autobiographical storytelling can be a form of 'subjective narrative inquiry' across a range of mediums and illustrates how 'the use of visual storytelling in visual pedagogy and narratives research generates the emergence of spaces in-between allowing us to produce *différence* and resistance' (p. 304). The 'spaces in-between', as relational entanglements (Barad, 2007) and connections across complex systems (Goleman et al., 2012; Sterling, 2003) in EIW could be used to analyse how stories are 'told, received and remembered (reconstructed)' (Rifà-Valls, 2011, p. 294) and always *becoming* as 'world-making' practices. The visual storytelling method could be adapted further as part of existing autobiographic and reflective practice in EIW and would be a creative extension of written journals that are often utilised as learning tools (Bloom, 2017). Unique visual autobiographical storytelling could be explored through filming walks and ways of interacting with place and nature. The essence of Rifà-Valls' (2011) proposal focuses on storytelling, narratives, autobiographical content and creativity as entanglements of artistic practice and being human. Therefore, students could additionally explore 'self' and 'community' through photographic journalling and sharing online or offline portfolios. Natural items can be collaged as art installations for abstract and co-creative storytelling of meta-narratives, subjective *wayfinding* or emerging eco-social community journeys. The visual storytelling can exemplify plurality, *unfinishedness* and the potential of heterogenous co-creative 'world-making'.

CONCLUSION

Through EIW, students can explore, discuss and examine other world-views, their personal narratives being exposed to dissonance, resonance and transformation, and where they can reflect on their own *(eco)identity* through relating in/with/as nature and place. Through these practices students can engage in deeper learning praxis (Freire, 1970), where meaning-making, new knowledges, new ideas and concepts will not remain abstract in a classroom but embodied as part of their singular *becoming* with the world. According to Thomashow (1995) EIW 'does not only occur through grand epiphanies and dramatic incidents. It is a lens through which the experiences of everyday life take on new meaning' (p. 17). Everyday personal narratives with reflective praxis based on our journeys with and of *nature-place* are instrumental in students accessing future sustainability competencies, skills and knowledge, while developing confidence as agents and custodians of *self-nature-place*.

Approaching EIW with an 'ethics of care' (Bowden, 1997; Held, 2006) means the *wayfinding* of students will be through *care* and with an ethical and profound sense of responsibility for generative 'world-making'. Orientating EIW with an 'ethic of becomings' the neo-liberal imposition of a 'passive' and 'banking model' of learning (De Freites et al., 2018; Freire, 1970) is resisted. Adopting these two ethics through EIW and outdoor learning with *place, dialogue* and *narrative* methods embodies Thomashow's aim that EIW can nurture our love of nature, alongside 'epistemic shifts' (Scott & Fraser, 2010), emerging 'ecological consciousness' (Hayes-Conroy & Vanderbeck, 2005) and ecological citizenship

(Curry, 2011). Additionally, it would create an *Ecosophy* for potential eco-socially just futures.

> *...you have to be here not everywhere. You have to be attached to some things no everything...* (*Donna Haraway: Storytelling for Earthly Survival*, 2017)

REFERENCES

Andreotti, V. (2006). Soft versus critical global citizenship education. *Policy and Practice: A Development Education Review, 3*, 40–51.

Andreotti, V., & Dowling, E. (2004). WSF, ethics and pedagogy. *International Science Journal, 56*(4), 605–613.

Appiah, K. A. (2018). *The lies that bind: Rethinking identity.* Profile Books.

Ballantyne, R., & Packer, J. (2008). *Learning for sustainability: The role and impact of outdoor and environmental education centre.* A Joint Initiative of The University of Queensland and Education Queensland. Retrieved May 5, 2019, from https://www.researchgate.net/publication/43521827_Learning_for_sustainability_The_role_and_impact_of_outdoor_and_environmental_education_centres

Barad, K. (2007). *Meeting the universe halfway.* Duke University Press.

Biesta, G. J. J. (2006). *Beyond learning: Democratic education for a human future.* Routledge.

Blaikie, N. (1992). The nature and origins of ecological world views: And Australian study. *Social Science Quarterly, 73*(1), 144–166.

Bloom, L. Z. (2017). Coming to life: Teaching undergraduates to write autobiography. *a/b: Auto/Biography Studies, 32*(1), 75–86.

Bowden, P. (1997). *Caring: Gender sensitive ethics.* Routledge.

Curry, P. (2011). *Ecological ethics: An introduction.* Polity Press.

De Freites, E., Seller, S., & Jensen, L. B. (2018). Thinking with Spinoza about education. *Educational Philosophy and Theory, 50*(9), 508–808.

Deininger, M. (2018). Pylons, playgrounds, and power stations: Ecofeminism and landscape in women's short fiction from Wales. In D. A. Vakoch & S. Mickey (Eds.), *Ecofeminism in dialogue.* Lexington Books.

Deleuze, G., & Guattari, F. (1987). *A thousand plateaus: Capitalism and schizophrenia.* Athlone Press.

Donna Haraway: Storytelling for Earthly Survival. (2017). Directed by L. Terranove [DVD]. Icarus Films.

Dovey, K. (2009). *Becoming places: Urbanism/architecture/identity/power.* Routledge.

Dunlop, R., & Van Liere, K. (2008). The 'new environmental paradigm'. *The Journal of Environmental Education, 40*(1), 19–28. (original 1978 re-release).

Dunn, J. L., & Creek, S. J. (2015). Identity dilemmas: Toward a more situated understanding. *Symbolic Interaction, 38*(2), 261–284.

Freire, P. (1970). *Pedagogy of the oppressed.* Penguin Random House. (2017 reprint).

Goleman, D., Bennett, L., & Barlow, Z. (2012). *Eco literate.* Jossey-Bass.

Gruenewald, D. (2003). Foundations of place: A multidisciplinary framework for place-conscious education. *American Educational Research Journal, 40*(3), 619–654.

Gruenewald, D. (2008). The best of both worlds: A critical pedagogy of place. *Environmental Education Research, 14*(3), 308–324.

Haraway, D. (2016). *Manifestly Haraway.* University of Minnesota Press.

Hayes-Conroy, J. S., & Vanderbeck, R. M. (2005). Ecological identity work in higher education: Theoretical perspectives and a case study. *Ethics, Place and Environment, 8*(3), 309–329.

Held, V. (2006). *The ethics of care: Personal, political, and global.* Oxford University Press.

Intergovernmental Panel on Climate Change. (2018). *Global warming of 1.5C: Summary for policymakers.* IPCC.

Intergovernmental Science-Policy Platform on Biodiversity and Ecosystem Service. (2019). *UN report: Nature's dangerous decline 'unprecedented'; Species extinction rates 'accelerating'.* Retrieved May 7, 2019, from https://www.un.org/sustainabledevelopment/blog/2019/05/nature-decline-unprecedented-report/

Jones, D. (2017). Embodied cognitive Ecosophy: The relationship of mind, body, meaning and ecology. *Geografiska Annaler: Series B, Human Geography, 99*(2), 156–171.

Latour, B. (2018). *Down to earth: Politics in the new climate regime.* Polity Press.

Light, A. (2000). What is an ecological identity? *Environmental Politics, 9*(4), 59–81.

Lipman, M., Sharp, A. M., & Oscanyan, F. S. (1980). *Philosophy in the classroom* (2nd ed.). Temple University Press.

Mezirow, J. (2002). Transformative learning: Theory to practice. *New Directions for Adult and Community Education, 74,* 5–12.

Morgan, A. (2012). Inclusive place-based education for 'just sustainability'. *International Journal of Inclusive Education, 16*(5), 627–642.

Morris, M. (2002). Ecological consciousness and curriculum. *Journal of Curriculum Studies, 34*(5), 571–587.

Næss, A. (2008). Ecology of wisdom (translated chapters). In A. Drengson & B. Devall (Eds.), *Arne Næss: Ecology of wisdom.* Penguin Random House.

O'Connor, M. R. (2019). *Wayfinding.* St. Martin's Press.

Orr, D. (1992). *Ecological literacy.* State University of New York Press.

Payne, P., & Wattchow, B. (2009). Phenomenological deconstruction, slow peda-gogy, and the corporeal turn in wild environmental/outdoor education. *Canadian Journal of Environmental Education, 14*, 15–32.

Rifà-Valls, M. (2011). Experimenting with visual storytelling in students' portfo-lios: Narratives of visual pedagogy for pre-service teacher education. *International Journal of Art & Design Education, 30*(2), 293–306.

Scott, C., & Fraser, S. (2010). Ecological identity through dialogue. *Canadian Journal of Environmental Education, 15*, 135–149.

SDG. (n.d.). *Sustainable development goals.* Retrieved May 5, 2019, from https://sustainabledevelopment.un.org/about

Sterling, S. (2003). *Whole systems thinking as a basis for paradigm change in educa-tion: Explorations in the context of sustainability* (PhD Thesis). Centre for Research in Education and the Environment, University of Bath.

Sterling, S. (2011a). Transformative learning and sustainability: Sketching the conceptual ground. *Learning and Teaching in Higher Education, 5*, 17–33.

Sterling, S. (2011b). Transformative learning and sustainability: Sketching the conceptual ground. *Learning and Teaching in Higher Education, 5*, 17–33.

Stets, J. E., & Biga, C. F. (2003). Bringing identity into environmental sociology. *Sociological Theory, 21*(4), 398–423.

Sun, Y., Chan, R., & Chen, H. (2016). Learning with geographical sensitivity: Place-based education and its praxis. *The Professional Geographer, 68*(4), 574–583.

Thomashow, M. (1995). *Ecological identity: Becoming a reflective environmental-ist.* The MIT Press.

Tooth, R., & Renshaw, P. (2009). Reflections on pedagogy of place: A journey into learning for sustainability through environmental narrative and deep atten-tive reflection. *Australian Journal of Environmental Education, 25*, 95–104.

UNESCO. (2014). *Shaping the future we want: UN decade of education for sus-tainability (2005–2014) final report.* United Nation Educational, Scientific and Cultural Organization.

Ward, H. (1999). Introduction: Why is service-learning so pervasive in environ-mental studies programs? In H. Ward (Ed.), *Acting locally: Concepts and models for service-learning in environmental studies.* American Association for Higher Education. Retrieved May 5, 2019, from https://files.eric.ed.gov/fulltext/ED449731.pdf

Gone Rogue: Re-wilding Education in Alternative Outdoor Learning Environments

Tonia Gray and Peter Bailey

INTRODUCTION

Boyd Varty poignantly remarked in his TedTalk (2013) and repeated in his subsequent monograph (Varty, 2014) '*In the cathedral of the wild we get to see the most beautiful parts of ourselves reflected back at us*'. However, imperceptibly and under the radar of most contemporary educators, our connection to 'wild spaces' has been insidiously erased from the student's educational experience (Gray, 2018). This observation has arisen from both authors' longstanding and deep involvement with Outdoor and Experiential Education (OEE) spanning multiple

T. Gray (✉)
Centre for Educational Research, School of Education,
Western Sydney University, Sydney, NSW, Australia
e-mail: T.Gray@westernsydney.edu.au

P. Bailey
Outdoor Education Advocate, Nowra, NSW, Australia

215
R. Cutting, R. Passy (eds.), *Contemporary Approaches to Outdoor
Learning*, Palgrave Studies in Alternative Education,
https://doi.org/10.1007/978-3-030-85095-1_15

decades (Gray, 1997; Bailey, 2003; Gray & Martin, 2012; Gray, 2018). As practitioner-researchers and teacher-educators, the authors have developed a sense of unease with the heightening disengagement with the natural world (Gray, 2018). Only recently, however, has the risk-averse nature of society, become critically apparent (O'Gorman, 2019). The ramification of bubble wrapping our students finds contemporary education at a crossroads. This begs the question: should we reset our pedagogical compasses? If so, we need transformational and visionary leaders who can chart these territories with heart and conviction.

Humans have always relied on an intimate relationship with nature for their growth, development (Selhub & Logan, 2012) and ongoing survival (Kahn & Kellert, 2002). E.O. Wilson, the Harvard biologist (Wilson, 1984), popularised what's called the biophilia hypothesis, the idea that we're biologically drawn to natural landscapes. With the increasing trend towards urban densification and biodiversity loss, we need our natural environments for optimal health and wellbeing (Bates, 2018; Passy et al., 2019; Fjørtoft, 2001; Mayer et al., 2009). For children and adolescents living in highly urbanised and industrialised settings, re-wilding education can offer a myriad of psycho-social, emotional, intellectual and physical benefits (Donnelly & MacIntyre, 2019; Dowdell et al., 2011). This chapter outlines ways in which unconventional outdoor teaching methods offer a potent vehicle for personal growth, transformation and learning.

Nature-Immersed Eclipsing Traditional Educational Methods

Akin to human nature, our educational system also contains the good, the bad and the ugly in terms of reality—what *is*—and in terms of possibility—what *could be*. This chapter is as both an interpretive reflection and existential exercise which is both ontological and philosophical in nature. We begin by locating our stories.

Tonia

During the late 1960s and 1970s Tonia enjoyed unbridled freedom in the natural world, riding her horses over farms and mountain ranges. She stumbled on the field of wilderness studies and outdoor education in a school setting nearly 40 years ago, purely by default and serendipity. Outdoor learning offered a fertile educational platform for transformational personal growth for her adolescent students in terms of augmenting positive behaviour change. This spawned her interest in pursuing a PhD to empirically explore the residual impact of outdoor education on adolescent participants in the 1990s (Gray, 1997). As a consequence, Tonia has facilitated numerous outdoor expeditions for secondary and tertiary students and witnessed the potency of this teaching medium.

Peter

During the late 1950s and 1960s Peter and the other children in the town enjoyed the magical playgrounds of the surrounding environment. The adventure of following the creeks as they wound their way through temperate rainforest, huge sandstone overhangs and dense heathland were all that was needed to create a fun-filled life in which to play, imagine and explore. The subliminal learning that occurred during these formative years still guides Peter's reflections on Outdoor Education as it has developed and grown in understanding how the environment influences our Social, Emotional, Physical and Spiritual wellbeing. Peter can still recall the many interesting stories he experienced all that time ago, with clarity and amazement, simply by visualising an aspect of that childhood playground.

In 1974, he and another colleague were teaching in the Blue Mountains area of NSW, Australia and decided to take a group of students to the Blue Gum Forest to introduce them to the adventure of hiking into new locations and to witness the feeling of wilderness. This school excursion was very different and would require the students to carry their food, clothing and sleeping gear at a time before light-weight hiking gear was freely available. The immediate benefits for these students were not fully understood by him and his colleague, but the impact of the wilderness experience became obvious as his career unfolded whilst doing a doctorate in outdoor education (Bailey, 2003).

The consistent thread for both authors is the enchantment with Nature-immersive education. Today, they continue to shape pre-service teacher educator programs in tertiary settings with Nature-enriched educational activities.

THE THROUGH LINE WITHIN OUR STORIES: NATURE AS A SUPERFOOD

Look deep into Nature and you will understand everything better. Albert Einstein (Du Plessis & Broeckhoven, 2019)

Historically, the potency of 'nature as a superfood' in the educative process can be witnessed in nature-enriched outdoor learning environments (Carson, 1956; Horwood, 1993; Ransbury, 1982; Wells & Lekies, 2006). However, set against the litigious backdrop of contemporary society, hazard mitigation and risk-averse classrooms have rendered outdoor adventurous activities being slowly erased from the Australian school curriculum in the last few decades (Gray, 2017). Yet as parents and veteran educators, we promote risk, uncertainty and adventure as the cornerstones of personal growth and development. Over the decades of teaching and learning, we have consistently found 'Nature is a superfood'. Re-wilding education not only enhances the pedagogical experience with visceral and embodied learning (Myers, 2019), but more importantly, has an indelible impact and life-long impact (Gray & Pigott, 2018).

The holistic development of students can be harnessed by alternative methods and '*going rogue to re-wilding education*'. In 2020, we find ourselves in a professional quandary, do we *toe-the-line* with conventional educational thought, or do we continue to do what we innately know is the right thing? Whilst education is arguably imbued with neoliberal and capitalist nuances, with alternative modalities and ubiquitous pedagogical activities such as Outdoor and Experiential Education (OEE), embracing their merits needs to be taken into consideration. In essence, the fabric of this chapter is a renewed call to arms for twenty-first century educators to interrogate and critique the modus operandi of our work and move from classrooms being hermetically sealed indoor environments, to ones which are authentic, embodied and taught from the heart of Nature (Charles, 2018).

Twenty-First Century Education: A Snapshot

Contemporary education is a confluence of complexity, paradox and ambiguity (Palmer, 2017; Hufford, 2013). The deep and enduring philosophical veins of education include such things as developing a sense of belonging, purpose, mastery, fostering personal fulfilment, resilience and positive self-concept (Gray, 2019). However, recently these pedagogical goals appear to be diluted in a contemporary educational debate and diluted in pedagogical practice (Sahlberg & Doyle, 2019).

With an increased focus on standardised national testing, curriculum compliance, unbridled competition between schools, and disconnect from natural settings (Gray & Pigott, 2018), many humanistic educators would argue education has lost its way (Sahlberg & Doyle, 2019). In turn, we have become increasingly disassociated from the natural world (Gray & Martin, 2012). Correspondingly, educators profess nature immersion is a precursor to instilling environmental appreciation and stewardship (Wells & Lekies, 2006; Breunig & Russell, 2020; Hinds & Sparks, 2008; Liefländer et al., 2013; Palmberg & Kuru, 2000). By leveraging practitioner-researcher experience alongside empirical research to 'Go Rogue' or in other words, rebel against convention, we discuss how education can benefit from re-wilding our students.

An Endangered Species: Children in Nature-Based Experiences

As educators with a rich history, both authors have devoted the majority of their careers to investigating the relation of humans and nature (Gray, 2017). Our most notable conclusion is that humanity remains the product of our interrelationship with the natural world (Kellert, 1993). Pedagogues have long known that various skills are fundamental for student learning and development—and particularly for executive function. These psycho-social, socio-emotional and physical skills include mental concentration, critical and creative thinking, problem-solving, coping, competitiveness, agility, balance, coordination, independence, self-confidence, self-esteem, and adventurous risk-taking among others (Gray, 2018; Hattie et al., 1997; Bezold et al., 2018). This begs the question, how can these qualities be imbued into a twenty-first century educational system? Especially place-based learning that occurs in the natural world (Lloyd et al., 2018; Lloyd & Gray, 2014) and embraces an increased appreciation for nature (Martin, 2005; Mannion & Lynch, 2016).

Letting Nature In

School students should explore Nature unhindered by fear, propelled by curiosity and motivated by a sense of self-discovery and exploration (Kahn & Kellert, 2002; Henley, 2010). Child and youth development is heavily influenced by both individual and social factors, however, the natural environment is increasingly seen as a crucial determinant that, in its absence, may have adverse effects (Margalit & Ben-Ari, 2014; Bezold et al., 2018). Evidence-based research convincingly shows that immersive nature-based experiences positively influence and afforded a myriad of cognitive, psychosocial, and physical factors (Holland et al., 2018; Louv, 2016).

Transformative Education

At a recent graduation speech one of our outdoor education students addressed the room and delivered her valedictory speech: She began:

> *Everyone thinks brain surgeons have the most important job in the world. I disagree. They only work on one brain at a time.*
> *We as teachers, are constantly working on 30 brains at any given time in our classrooms—never lose sight of the importance of your work.*

The essence of her comments crystallised, in that one split second, the influence educators have in transforming and shaping the learning of their students (Mezirow, 2000). Nurturing critical thinking, creativity, interpersonal skills, developing empathy and acquiring diverse worldviews come from the teachers' facilitation skills blended with the content delivered and student readiness.

Data Collection: Students' Blog Reflections

Recent qualitative research for this piece was collected in 2019 with tertiary students who provided blog entries of their reflections throughout their OEE course. Students were invited to write blogs focusing on three key ingredients: self, others and the environment. The OEE university students were from countries across the globe and their blog reflections illustrate the transcultural and universal influence of Nature upon them.

As part of the assessment process and following several field trips in National Parks, students reflected on their experiences using the structure known as the funnelling technique: *What, So What, Now What?* Participants whose narratives appear in this paper provided approval for quotes to be published as a means to help future and practising teachers better understand how OEE has a residual and enduring impact.

Findings and Discussion

Five themes emerged within the qualitative data we gathered in the blogs: (1) Holistic Self-Development, Health and Wellbeing; (2) Fostering Earth Stewardship; (3) Self-Awareness; (4) Transformations through Nature; and (5) Transcendence and Grace. Each will be discussed in detail in the following sections.

1. Holistic Self-Development, Health and Wellbeing

Nature has an inherent healing quality and there is much scientific evidence is attest to this claim (Selhub & Logan, 2012). Skills and attributes cultivated are transferrable to many different encounters throughout life, such as resilience, reflection, sense of belonging and relationship building. During a 3-day expedition, students develop enduring friendships and a better understanding of each another. The following blog entries articulate their varied perspectives about the influence on holistic self-development.

Student 13
Learning through the outdoors has given me a new outlook in life regarding myself, others and the environment. It enhances our self–awareness and responsibility; an ability to value and work with others; an environmental appreciation; a capacity to embrace challenge; and a tenacious spirit. I have reaped these benefits during my experiences and believe I am a better person.

Student 6
Nothing seems to bring people together like nature does. When people are taken away from the centres of civilisation, out into the wilderness and beauty of nature, their willingness to connect to other people rises dramatically. They soon find out that relationships with other people can grow rapidly, and enriched as human beings.

Student 21
Hiking for three days is not only physically healthy but mentally healthy as well. My mind after the trip was clear from the stress and discomfort that school in a big city can bring with it. I could fill up my water bottle in the 'fountain of youth'. This experience of standing under the waterfall was remarkable. I had never felt so refreshed and young. I grew up in the mountains ... I missed being away from the wilderness, the city is loud and busy with no place to gather your thoughts peacefully. On the hikes, I felt at home again. I learned that you can be looking at different landscapes of nature half way across the world yet feel the same calmness you feel when you are in the woods at home.

Student 18

In terms of essential life skills, I learned the importance of group work, communication and trust in others. I experienced cultural awareness during the hike as I mingled with students and learned a lot about their culture and life at school. I also found that the outdoor learning aids in self-reflection by talking about experiences with the people you are with. It benefitted me mentally, physically and socially. All important aspects of a good and happy life.

Student 16

When I was hiking I wasn't thinking as much about what I was saying, so it was more open and honest and helped bond our group as we shared stories with people like they were best friends.

Student 24

The fire draws us closer as we gather round to receive the warmth of the flames against the cold darkness of the night. No clearer was this evident than around the fire at night as dozens of chats hummed to the tune of the crackling flames. I was reminded on how easy it is to be kind—to tell a story and laugh, to ask and care about the lives of others.

Student 12

I was able to see first-hand the outcomes of experiential learning in Outdoor Education. I believe that it is in the best interests of students around the globe to participate because it allows them to better understand and explore themselves and their self-concept. The relationships with others is enhanced and to see the importance of nature and the natural environment.

Often students would remark that the outdoor experience helped them understand themselves and were content or comfortable in their own 'skin'. Outdoor Learning is empowering and students invariably, feel comfortable to express their inner feelings and thoughts without fear of judgement. Teamwork is strengthened, introspection and reflection skills heightened, and group bonding through shared lived experiences emerge. Galvanising relationships with newfound friends are created alongside learning about diverse cultures, traditions and individuals, rather than stereotypes. Collectively, these include physiological, psychological, sociological and cognitive gains that are immeasurable. The outdoors and Nature-based learning is a unique and holistic vehicle for developing self-concept, inter-intrapersonal skills, relationship building and self-development.

2. Fostering Earth Stewardship

Whilst reigniting students' connection with the natural world, many are reminded of their innate affinity with Nature. Nature-rich experiences for students help rediscover or reawaken our ancestral connection to Mother Earth (Capra, 2005) and in turn, this newfound love, affinity and bond with Nature instils in students a deep appreciation and commitment to Earth stewardship (Michael, 2005). These insights are conveyed in the following reflections where students gain a newfound respect for Mother Earth. They speak at length of their reawakened respect for the environment.

Student 3
I recall my childhood moments. I still miss drinking from sweet well water and breathing air with the scent of manure. After school, I usually ride a bike uphill to see the village shining in gold. However, these moments only exist in my memories. In recent years, the Government has been working to develop my hometown, but at the expense of the natural environment. My Grandparents' cornfield was destroyed to build a highway. A new recently built aluminium plant has seriously polluted to the soil and groundwater. This encourages me to explore the untarnished nature, to protect her, and my commitment grows stronger.

Student 8
While I was hiking I was constantly saying, 'wow'. The hike was pristine and protected and it made me feel a huge sense of responsibility to look after these places. I felt very connected to these landscapes and want to get a better awareness of how to protect them.

Student 26
Together with my group we did a ritual with one of the rocks in the park. One of my group mates used to do it with her dad and sisters when they visited the National Parks when they were younger. After a lot of searching for the rock in the magical place, then we noticed the perfect rock. After approaching the rock and acknowledging the rock has been around for many years and has seen much more than all of us together. **We asked the rock to share its story.** *This story we will of course, keep to ourselves and remember forever. Finally, we thanked the rock for sharing its wisdom and story, and for being there to guide us.*

Wilderness experiences are transformational and acknowledging Nature's power is greater than all of us is vividly displayed in the above-mentioned quotes. The natural world combined with outdoor pedagogies help create a tangible, visceral and emotional reaction. Albeit, all our senses are enlivened during the educative process. Consequently, developing an attunement to the natural rhythms and cycles invariably occurs through outdoor embodied learning.

3. Self-Awareness

Through the reflective process embedded in OEE, students gain the skills of self-awareness and clarity. A student expressing the disconnection from the modern world whilst being in Nature and not having access to the internet or social media remarked:

Student 28

I think I can best sum it up like this.
The Mountains gave you space.
Space to walk on your own and take in nature.
Space to find friends who feel like family,
and who feel like you have known them forever within the space of just a day.
Space to laugh and learn, and a space to reflect.

Students articulate the disconnection from the modern world whilst being in Nature and not having access to the internet or social media remarked:

Student 4

...the roaring waves towering above the sea and smashing into immovable cliffs. A true display of nature's raw uncontrollable power. It also displays the contrast between cultures. In the way that the waves and the rocks both offer two different scenic views, the combination of the two creates an even more outstanding and unique picture. In the same way does the merge of Australian, Danish and other cultures create something unique. We develop a true understanding of each other, which will bring unity into this diverse and multicultural world.

Student 24

To experience the beauty in a new terrain, even though the trails reminded me of hikes I took in Tennessee. There were many notable differences that make the experience both novel and inspiring. I felt these nuances in the sights, the sounds and smells of being in the bush. It is this transportation from the known to the mysterious that induced the experience of learning in the outdoors.

4. Transformations Through Nature

There are countless student quotes and testimonials both authors could provide over their decades of teaching in the natural world. However, the 2019 cohort's reflections reveal the common through-line of the outdoors as a vehicle for personal transformation and holistic development.

> **Student 11**
> *The environment just keeps impressing me. The sounds of water running over rocks and the sights of huge waterfalls were simply stunning. The whole experience was so calming, cathartic and peaceful.*

> **Student 20**
> *It was okay to feel vulnerable about showing your true colours when in Nature. However, let the usual never stop you from exploring new sides of yourself.*

> **Student 26**
> *I lost five kgs but gained five lifetimes of wisdom.*

> **Student 27**
> *Out here I am alive, back in suburbia I am just existing.*

As seasoned educators, we are cognisant of using alternative learning environments, such as nature's inherent beauty and awe, to activate untapped reservoirs of inspiration within our students. Although carefully facilitating outdoor learning experiences can heighten an appreciation of the natural environment, in most instances, we simply *get out of the way and let Nature weave her magic.*

5. Transcendence and Grace

Many times, students experience newfound clarity, a state of perfection and complete wholeness whilst in Nature. Some educational philosophers may call this transcendence or a state of grace, but whatever the terminology assigned, students invariably discover the same questions that we have all been searching answers for throughout life. The reflection below is of one small but significant experience for the student that resonated with the thoughts that Peter (the author) had once asked himself many years earlier.

Student 1

I plunged one foot into hard pebbles, another into soft sand. My next step landed on a smooth rock surface. I felt my feet slipping and steadied my balance, moving cautiously, deliberately onwards. I made it to the cave and peered ahead to a wall of darkened dirt. I paused, I felt, I listened. I turned back and looked out at the bright white light filling the star shaped gap between me and the watering hole. In a small way, the person returning back to the shore was different, changed from the person who had just crossed over. But different in which way? What had I just learnt and how might I express that learning?

This profound and somewhat ineffable question was created by a simple experience in the natural environment. Imagine what daily or repeated encounters with the natural world can offer students in terms of health and wellbeing. Other examples include:

Student 2

It was during a part of the hike where the track opened out from the beach onto a rocky cliff overlooking the ocean. I got this sense of infinity that was only one part of this endless environment. While one may think this impression would make me feel insignificant, it actually seemed to give me confidence.

In essence, however, we had to swim upstream against a normative driven school culture and 'go rogue', to bear witness to the transformative learning and holistic development achieved through an outdoor classroom environment. We call on like-minded educators to honour their convictions and follow their teaching instincts.

DISCUSSION

Both authors have concluded that performative-driven school culture, based on metrics and standardised testing signals the death knell of contemporary education. Locked within four walls of a classroom, rote learning and memorising meaningless information does little to prepare a child for life nor little to preserve our Mother Earth during these precarious times.

Like pioneering educator Winifred West from the early 1900s (Kennedy, 1976), throughout this chapter we have questioned: '*what is education for?*'. With a great interest in succession building in the teaching profession, we are becoming increasingly critical of the contemporary curriculum as it is unadventurous, conventional and stereotyped by standardised testing. More importantly, we urge transformative teachers to move from the dominant normative-driven culture of rote learning facts, regurgitating dead knowledge and encountering endless assessments along the way. In short, we need to pivot the systemic failures and provide learnings that are authentic, indelible and enduring.

If we deeply care about our student's socioemotional function, mental health and lowering stress levels, nature-immersive experiences are part of the panacea (Bezold et al., 2018). Alternative learning environments that embrace the transformative power of Nature, can indeed unlock this medium as a 'superfood' in the educative process. As Varty (2013) eloquently recounted in his TED Talk in the cathedral of the wild, 'we get to see the best parts of ourselves reflected back to us', and we need to engage wild spaces for this to occur. However, risk-averse classrooms shackled by risk mitigation, have resulted in adventurous activities being suppressed in the school curriculum. Circling back to where we started with the graduation speech of a fledgling teacher, we leave you to ponder this question:

If we as teachers are constantly influencing the brains of our students, what are you doing to re-wild education?

TEACHING AND LEARNING IN A POST-COVID-19 WORLD

Ghosh et al. (2020) recently researched the impact of COVID-19 on children and focused on psychosocial aspects. Lack of physical outdoor activity, school closures, irregular dietary patterns and poor sleeping habits severely disrupted their lifestyle and promoted distress, annoyance and varied neuropsychiatric manifestations. Teenage suicide rates have been escalating in turn. Given this bleak picture, never lose sight of the importance and gravitas of your educational work especially given the rising eminence of Outdoor Learning in a post-COVID-19 world. Countries who handled the COVID-19 crisis in 2020 with prowess had one unifying factor in common; they 'demanded a response that was swift, rational, and collective' (Parker, 2020). Internationally, we have witnessed an upsurge in demand for outdoor learning in many countries due to lowered risk of infection or contagion whilst outdoors. Epidemiologists are cognisant the virus does not last outside for extended periods of time (Department of Health, 2020). Further, in April 2020, Danish schools returned after lockdown and their guidelines include a recommendation to 'hold classes outside so that children can be outdoors as much as possible' (Mulvahill, 2020). In the same vein, Fife (2020) remarks the pandemic in Scotland may 'push parents and teachers to embrace the benefits of education in the outdoors'. All indicators point to one common unifying theme, the overwhelming need for more outdoor learning in 2020 and beyond.

Conclusion

Transformational education gives students both agency and voice in their development. These affordances when nurtured in nature-based settings, allow students to experiment, problem-solve, explore in wild places, fail, and bolster resilience by repeatedly trying again. This chapter has drawn on practitioner-researcher experience alongside empirical research to 'Go Rogue' and discussed the importance of educators to re-wild their educative practices. Time and time again, the potency of 'nature as a superfood' has been witnessed in the provision of alternative outdoor learning environments. Yet risk mitigation and risk-averse classrooms have rendered outdoor adventure being whitewashed from the school curriculum. The authors conclude by renewing the urgent call for the holistic development of students which can be harnessed by 'going rogue and re-wilding education'.

References

Bailey, P. L. (2003). *Rekindling the spirit of adventure: Through participation in the expedition component of the Duke of Edinburgh's Award: The value of this challenge for the participant.* University of Wollongong. Unpublished PhD thesis.

Bates, K. (2018). Bringing the inside out and the outside in: Place-based learning rendering classroom walls invisible. In *The Palgrave international handbook of women and outdoor learning.* Springer.

Bezold, C. P., Banay, R. F., Coull, B. A., Hart, J. E., James, P., Kubzansky, L. D., Missmer, S. A., & Laden, F. (2018). The association between natural environments and depressive symptoms in adolescents living in the United States. *Journal of Adolescent Health, 62*, 488–495.

Breunig, M., & Russell, C. (2020). Long-term impacts of two secondary school environmental studies programs on environmental behaviour: The shadows of patriarchy and neoliberalism. *Environmental Education Research, 26*(23), 1–15.

Capra, F. (2005). Speaking nature's language: Principles for sustainability. In *Ecological literacy: Educating our children for a sustainable world* (pp. 18–29). Sierra Club Books.

Carson, R. (1956). *The sense of wonder*. The Nature Company.

Charles, C. (2018). Leading from the heart of nature. In T. Gray & D. Mitten (Eds.), *The Palgrave international handbook of women and outdoor learning*. Springer.

Department of Health. (2020). *COVID-19 support*. Retrieved April 26, 2020, from https://headtohealth.gov.au/covid-19-support/covid-19

Donnelly, A. A., & MacIntyre, T. E. (2019). *Physical activity in natural settings: Green and blue exercise*. Routledge.

Dowdell, K., Gray, T., & Malone, K. (2011). Nature and its influence on children's outdoor play. *Journal of Outdoor and Environmental Education, 15*, 24–35.

Du Plessis, A., & Broeckhoven, C. (2019). Looking deep into nature: A review of micro-computed tomography in biomimicry. *Acta biomaterialia, 85*, 27–40.

Fife, L. (2020). Scotland eyes outdoor learning as model for reopening of schools. *The Guardian*. Retrieved May 30, 2020, from https://www.theguardian.com/uk-news/2020/may/10/scotland-eyes-outdoor-learning-as-model-for-reopening-of-schools?CMP=share_btn_tw

Fjørtoft, I. (2001). The natural environment as a playground for children: The impact of outdoor play activities in pre-primary school children. *Early Childhood Education Journal, 29*, 111–117.

Ghosh, R., Dubey, M. J., Chatterjee, S., & Dubey, S. (2020). Impact of COVID-19 on children: Special focus on the psychosocial aspect. *Minerva Pediatrics, 72*(3), 226–235. https://doi.org/10.23736/S0026-4946.20.05887-9

Gray, T. (1997). *The impact of an extended stay outdoor education school program upon adolescent participants*. PhD thesis, University of Wollongong. http://ro.uow.edu.au/cgi/viewcontent.cgi?article=2799&context=theses

Gray, T. (2017). A 30-year retrospective study of the impact of outdoor education upon adolescent participants: Salient lessons from the field. *Pathways: The Ontario Journal of Outdoor Education, 29*(3), 4–15.

Gray, T. (2018). Outdoor learning: Not new, just newly important. *Curriculum Perspectives, 38*, 145–149.

Gray, T. (2019). Outdoor Learning and psychological resilience: Making today's students better prepared for tomorrow's world. *Curriculum Perspectives, 39*, 67–72.

Gray, T., & Martin, P. (2012). The role and place of outdoor education in the Australian National Curriculum. *Journal of Outdoor and Environmental Education, 16*, 39–50.

Gray, T., & Pigott, F. (2018). Lasting lessons in outdoor learning: A facilitation model emerging from 30 years of reflective practice. *Ecopsychology, 10*, 195–204.

Hattie, J., Marsh, H. W., Neill, J. T., & Richards, G. E. (1997). Adventure education and outward bound: Out-of-class experiences that make a lasting difference. *Review of Educational Research, 67*, 43–87.

Henley, J. (2010). Why our children need to get outside and engage with nature. *The Guardian*, 16.

Hinds, J., & Sparks, P. (2008). Engaging with the natural environment: The role of affective connection and identity. *Journal of Environmental Psychology, 28*, 109–120.

Holland, W. H., Powell, R. B., Thomsen, J. M., & Monz, C. A. (2018). A systematic review of the psychological, social, and educational outcomes associated with participation in wildland recreational activities. *Journal of Outdoor Recreation, Education, and Leadership, 10*, 197–225.

Horwood, B. (1993). Excerpts from the Kurt Hahn address at the October 1992 AEE International Conference. *The Journal of Experimental Education, 16*, 46–49.

Hufford, D. (2013). Teaching to transcend: A personal educational philosophy. *Journal of Philosophy & History of Education, 63*, 169–180.

Kahn, P. H., Jr., & Kellert, S. R. (2002). *Children and nature: Psychological, sociocultural, and evolutionary investigations*. MIT Press.

Kellert, S. R. (1993). The biological basis for human values of nature. In S. R. Kellert & E. O. Wilson (Eds.), *The biophilia hypothesis* (pp. 42–69). Island Press.

Kennedy, P. W. H. (1976). *Portrait of Winifred West*. Fine Arts Press.

Liefländer, A. K., Fröhlich, G., Bogner, F. X., & Schultz, P. W. (2013). Promoting connectedness with nature through environmental education. *Environmental Education Research, 19*, 370–384.

Lloyd, A., & Gray, T. (2014). Place-based outdoor learning and environmental sustainability within Australian primary schools. *Journal of Sustainability Education, 1*(September). http://www.jsedimensions.org/wordpress/wp-content/uploads/2014/10/AmandaLloydToniaGrayPDFReady.pdf

Lloyd, A., Truong, S., & Gray, T. (2018). Take the class outside! A call for place-based outdoor learning in the Australian primary school curriculum. *Curriculum Perspectives, 38*, 163–167.

Louv, R. (2016). *Vitamin N: The essential guide to a nature-rich life*. Algonquin Books.

Mannion, G., & Lynch, J. (2016). The primacy of place in education in outdoor settings. In *Routledge international handbook of outdoor studies* (pp. 85–94). Routledge.

Margalit, D., & Ben-Ari, A. (2014). The effect of wilderness therapy on adolescents' cognitive autonomy and self-efficacy: Results of a non-randomized trial. *Child & Youth Care Forum, 43*, 181–194. Springer. https://doi.org/10.1007/s10566-013-9234-x

Martin, P. (2005). Human to nature relationships through outdoor education. In *Outdoor and experiential learning: Views from the top* (pp. 28–52). Otago University Print.

Mayer, F. S., Frantz, C. M., Bruehlman-Senecal, E., & Dolliver, K. (2009). Why is nature beneficial? The role of connectedness to nature. *Environment and Behavior, 41*, 607–643.

Mezirow, J. (2000). *Learning as transformation: Critical perspectives on a theory in progress* (The Jossey-Bass Higher and Adult Education Series). ERIC.

Michael, P. (2005). Helping children fall in love with the earth: Environmental education and the arts. In *Ecological literacy: Educating our children for a sustainable world* (pp. 111–125). Sierra Club Books.

Mulvahill, E. (2020). *Danish schools are heading back to school—Here's what it looks like*. Retrieved April 24, 2020, from https://t.co/TGGJ6BpMKi?amp=1

Myers, Z. (2019). *Wildness and wellbeing: Nature, neuroscience, and urban design*. Springer Nature.

O'Gorman, L. (2019). *Promoting children's wellbeing and values learning in risky learning spaces: School spaces for student wellbeing and learning*. Springer.

Palmberg, I. E., & Kuru, J. (2000). Outdoor activities as a basis for environmental responsibility. *The Journal of Environmental Education, 31*, 32–36.

Palmer, P. J. (2017). *The courage to teach: Exploring the inner landscape of a teacher's life*. John Wiley & Sons.

Parker, G. (2020). We are living in a failed state: The coronavirus didn't break America. It revealed what was already broken. *The Atlantic*. Retrieved May 24, 2020, from https://www.theatlantic.com/magazine/archive/2020/06/underlying-conditions/610261/

Passy, R., Bentsen, P., Gray, T., & Ho, S. (2019). Integrating outdoor learning into the curriculum: An exploration in four nations. *Curriculum Perspectives, 39*, 73–78.

Ransbury, M. K. (1982). Friedrich Froebel 1782–1982: A reexamination of Froebel's principles of childhood learning. *Childhood Education, 59*, 104–106.

Sahlberg, P., & Doyle, W. (2019). *Let the children play: How more play will save our schools and help children thrive*. Oxford University Press.

Selhub, E. M., & Logan, A. C. (2012). *Your brain on nature: The science of nature's influence on your health, happiness and vitality*. John Wiley & Sons.

Varty, B. (2013). TEDtalk 'What I learned from Nelson Mandela'. https://www.ted.com/talks/boyd_varty_what_i_learned_from_nelson_mandela?language=en

Varty, B. (2014). *Cathedral of the wild: An African journey home.* Random House Incorporated.

Wells, N. M., & Lekies, K. S. (2006). Nature and the life course: Pathways from childhood nature experiences to adult environmentalism. *Children Youth and Environments, 16,* 1–24.

Wilson, E. O. (1984). *Biophilia.* Harvard University Press.

Philosophy Walks: Thinking on Our Feet, from Outdoor Learning to a Philosophy of Education

Graeme Tiffany

Introduction: Background and Borrowings

This chapter is about a modest form of outdoor learning that I call 'Philosophy Walks'. Yet, in its writing, it has evolved into a wider exploration of the philosophy of education, which intimates at new ways of thinking, and maybe even a philosophy of education in its own right.

On reflection, this might have been anticipated, as Philosophy Walks are iterative processes, in which movement through a constantly unfolding environment stimulates discussion and philosophical enquiry on matters un-prescribed. Therein, Philosophy Walks include at least some of the characteristics of a way of thinking about education and democracy that values uncertainty and aims to act in an autonomy-enhancing way by positioning learners and *their* interests at the centre of that philosophy.

G. Tiffany (✉)
Independent Education Scholar, Leeds, UK

R. Cutting, R. Passy (eds.), *Contemporary Approaches to Outdoor Learning*, Palgrave Studies in Alternative Education,
https://doi.org/10.1007/978-3-030-85095-1_16

At least some of these ideas have their roots in simple observation; when we walk we are never sure of what we will come across, whom we will meet, or what might happen. And the same can be said of processes where it is up to participants to determine how those processes unfold; democratic processes, if you like.

In this sense, Philosophy Walks are an example of what I call 'uncertainty-appreciative practices' (Tiffany, 2020, p. 251). I align these with other autonomy-enhancing and empowering educational methodologies and pedagogies such as those associated with Freire (1990 [1972]), who, in a subsequent book, talked of the learner as 'creator, re-creator, and re-inventor': roles essential to the 'act of knowing' (Freire, 1978, p. 11) rather than the consumption of knowledge determined elsewhere and by others.

Today, we might say such practices are identifiable by the unpredictability of 'learning outcomes'. This represents a radical contestation of the many technical and instrumental approaches to education typified by the pre-figurative narrative: 'the learning outcomes *will be* …', typically uttered at the beginning of any encounter, as if to 'put the cart before the horse'.

Before I get ahead of myself on philosophical matters, let me conclude this introduction by locating the idea behind Philosophy Walks, simply enough, *in* interest, as philosophy and walking have long since been passions of mine. Let me consider these interests for a moment, with some memories of walking first.

Walking

Growing up, walking was amongst the many outdoor pursuits I was passionate about and that I'd experienced through my involvement in youth work. These experiences engendered in me a deep concern for environmental issues, which I hold to this day. But it also gave me the confidence to walk independently of adults (although with similar age friends), which I did often and in increasingly challenging (for me, adventurous) environments. These adolescent experiences of self-determined outdoor learning framed a desire to work in environmental, outdoor and adventure education, which I did for several years. Significantly, this was at a time when the provision of outdoor education by local authorities was coming under attack by central government, intent as it was on pushing a wider model of privatisation and contracting this work out to the non-governmental and private sector.

From my point of view, the educational aspects of outdoor education were being eroded. Practitioners with professional education in Outdoor Education were being replaced by those without. For sure, those who took their place had National Governing Body (NGB) awards in the various disciplines associated with 'Outdoor Ed.', such as kayaking and climbing. But they lacked knowledge and know-how of education, of the pedagogies associated with outdoor learning. Critical engagement with fundamental questions, such as 'What *is* education?', 'What are its aims?', and 'What is it to *be* an educator?' were left to the academics. The shift was toward practitioners as technicians, as outdoor work was constructed more in terms of leisure and recreation, often little more than a 'pastime', rather than a powerful medium for learning. In practice, we walked less with those we worked with; 'sexier', more 'adventurous' activities were considered more saleable.

But I had already got a grip on the floating concept of 'adventure' (the sense that it could mean many things to different people), and wondered whether adventure could just as well be conceived as 'adventures of the mind', the exploring of new thoughts, and reaching (if not new heights) new understandings of the world.

These were little more than theories of mine at that time, but what I did know, and what I had learnt through my experience of working in the outdoors, was that walking generated countless opportunities for conversation among those who walked together. This was not something that could be said for those other pursuits, where technical training and risk-management often squeezed out the possibility of conversation, and a focus on safety was demanded. This was another concept that troubled me; surely, uncertainty-appreciative practices contested the value of being and feeling 'safe'—if not in physical terms, in conversational and dialogical (i.e. educational) terms?

My studies in informal and community education had taught me that conversation was a form of education worthy of comparison with any other. Indeed, the democratic education I was particularly interested in seemed to necessitate conversation.

One conversation, in particular, seemed essential: that relating to the language of 'outdoors'. Working as I had for many years with young people from disadvantaged communities, many of whom felt disenfranchised from schooling, I experienced a resistance to 'outdoor education'. To many, 'The Outdoors', and especially 'The Great Outdoors', invoked an alien environment, somewhere other, and for Others. And yet, as 'detached' youth workers (educators purposefully disconnected from institutions precisely so that we could be more accessible) we so often observed these young people *outside*, albeit mostly in the urban realm of the inner-city estate in which they lived. They seemed comfortable there. We knew there was something important about working in public space, and this was as much to do with the philosophy as the physicality of these spaces. 'Outside', I imagined, was a better term, as it seemed to invoke a language (and geography) that young people might more readily engage with, not least because these were spaces over which they had more control. Perhaps here was a philosophy of 'education outside', a philosophy better understood through the study of philosophy.

Philosophy

I first studied philosophy as part of my professional training in Informal and Community Education. This *informal* context matters to me, as it's been a theme in my academic work that explores in particular what it means to be an educator in 'non-institutional' settings—an educator 'outside'. The logic of environmental philosophers appealed to me, especially as it seemed to be consistent with the philosophy of informal education:

> Scientists, economists, politicians and lawyers are not professionally qualified to address all the questions raised by environmental issues. Take the clearing of rainforest to provide open land for cattle ranching. Ecologists can explain the effects of this practice on rainforest ecosystems; economists, politicians and lawyers can assess its financial, political and legal ramifications. But various questions remain: are we *morally* obliged to protect the rainforests? If so, *why* are we so obliged? These sorts of questions cannot be answered using the methods of science or economics. They cannot be left to politicians and lawyers. It might seem that they could be addressed using the research methods of the social sciences, and it is true that one could use such methods to find out how most people would answer them. But empirical approaches are not enough. For although surveys and the like can tell us what people *believe* to be right and wrong, they cannot tell us what really is right or what really is wrong. To determine that—or at least to do so in a systematic and critical way—one needs philosophy. (James, 2015, p. 1)

I realised that these were precisely the kinds of questions that often emerged while walking with groups.

A Synthesis

This synthesis of philosophy and walking, and of learning 'outside', would not be complete without a consideration of geography. According to Smith (1994), the work of informal and community educators is identifiable by its geography, 'Their main workplace is not the classroom. Shops, launderettes, streets, pubs, cafés and people's front rooms are the settings for much of their work' (ibid., p. 1). These are, as geographers say, *spaces* and *places*, where 'place' is ascribed to spaces we give meaning to (Tuan, 1977). Geographers also concern themselves with movement, they talk of 'mobilities', and sometimes '*immobilities*', where mobilities are constrained. Beyond the language of 'social mobility', philosophers of education rarely concern themselves with ideas about movement. However, in thinking about philosophy and walking, we can see 'movement', and movement 'outside', and 'adventure', in both conceptual *and* physical terms, terms that have both a philosophical *and* practical character.

Next, we require a synthesis of the conceptual terrain of outdoor education and informal education. In 'Informal Outdoor Education' (Tiffany, 1995a, 1995b, 1995c). I considered methodological questions, including those related to the process and product of learning. I made links to experiential education, the use of activities, dialogue-based pedagogies, and approaches that emphasise the value of reflection and action. I sought to tease out an earlier practical attempt to integrate the work of Paulo Freire (a primary source of inspiration for many informal and community educators) into my outdoor work (Tiffany, 1994), particularly the integration of Freire's problem-posing dialogics (1990 [1972]).

I was especially interested in Freire's account of 'generative' processes, the idea that communities, by participating in dialogue, could 'generate' questions of their own; questions, that is, that those communities created and *owned*. This was part of wondering what it takes for the 'space' of conversation to become 'place'.

I also recognised in the dialogical and enquiry-based practices of 'P4C' (Philosophy for Children and Communities)[1] that I had become increasingly familiar with the value of *philosophising*, as distinct from the study of the 'canons'. What would it take then to put all this practice; to secure a marriage of philosophy and walking?

[1] See, for example, the work of SAPERE, The Society for the Advancement of Philosophical Enquiry and Reflection in Education, https://www.sapere.org.uk/

Early Experiments in Philosophy Walks

Lacking a template, putting all these ideas together meant the first 'Philosophy Walks' I led were tentative affairs. In fact, I dared not call them this, fearing any reference to 'philosophy' might be off-putting. Rather, they were just walks, in which I employed some Socratic questioning techniques learnt during training in P4C and adapted for Community Philosophy[2] as part of the 'everyday' conversations that took place while walking with others.

Of course, people walking together talk about all sorts of things, and a good walk leader will happily engage with whatever comes up. Indeed, in my training as a Mountain Leader it was implicit that you had knowledge of, and could talk about, many aspects of the environment you were in.

But Socrates would surely have had an eye for conversations with a philosophical bent, and would ask questions that resist a definitive answer—a reminder perhaps of what philosophy at its simplest 'is': an enquiry into questions of meaning and value. With this as a framework, the walks started to develop a philosophical orientation, with participants being encouraged to *philosophise*, to engage in the practice of philosophy:

> On a walk in the Yorkshire dales National Park, the group met and talked with a park ranger. She spoke of the park authority's commitment to conserving the natural landscape but also of the need to support local employers and businesses. I spotted the possibility of an intervention that framed this as a dilemma, which almost always makes for a good philosophical discussion. I encouraged the group to explore the concepts of conservation and preservation by using 'concept-mapping' tools,[3] and in response to a values-based question I posed about the quarrying of road stone within the park: How might these competing demands be met, if at all?

In this case, the stimulus for enquiry was a chance encounter with someone we met on our walk. Compare this with P4C, where a stimulus is usually prepared and presented by the facilitator. Here, the environment, and

---

[2] See https://communityphilosophy.co.uk

[3] Typically, participants are asked to identify and consider words they view as related to the central concept. The words can be written on cards (weighted down with a stone if windy) and placed on the ground, 'mind-map'-style, moved, and removed, as appropriate. Being outside allows a freedom to move, thereby viewing the map from different perspectives. There is a physical and tangible character to the activity, capable of engaging many senses, each stimulating critical thinking.

movement through it, acts as a stimulus for enquiry; there is no need for preparation. Indeed, the unanticipated and emergent nature of potential stimuli seems to add to a sense of the group being in control of the things they want to discuss. Following Freire, this advances the idea that participants are able, and have the right, to frame these discussions. This also protects against the challenge that the stimulus selection of someone in authority can be manipulative. The position to work toward is mutuality in stimulus selection. This means that the walk leader/facilitator also has to tune into possibility and potential and play a role in identifying what might be the subject of enquiry. Fundamentally though (with Freire and concepts of 'place' in mind), the practice promotes the belief that all participants are able, and have the right, to participate in making these decisions.

Shaping Philosophy Walks

Having developed greater confidence in the language and practice of philosophy, and seen this among participants, it became clear that calling the walks 'Philosophy Walks' need not be a barrier to participation. Indeed, some groups particularly valued the idea that they would learn something of the history of philosophical commentary on walking.

With some groups, I decided to make explicit a philosophical introduction to the walks. In this, I would speak for a short time, usually with the aid of a few quotes, about the many references made by philosophers to walking. Frédéric Gros's *A Philosophy of Walking* (2014) deserves particular mention as he provides a wonderful collection and overview. He cites the thoughts of Nietzsche, Rimbaud, Rousseau, and Thoreau, among others. Many of the quotes he chooses are extraordinarily accessible, which makes them ideal in connecting to popular cultural references to walking and for initiating conversation; for example:

> *Sit as little as possible; do not believe any idea that was not born in the open air and of free movement—in which the muscles do not also revel.* (Friedrich Nietzsche, *Ecce Homo*, 2009)

Gros's own commentary is just as effective: 'walking empties the mind' (ibid., p. 97), for example, is precisely the kind of comment many of us might make. Indeed, my mother often says 'I'm going for a walk to clear my mind', an everyday comment that pushes back at the perceived exclusivity of philosophy.

There are, though, valuable developmental moves, designed to encourage a deeper engagement with both philosophy, and the practice of philosophy—a process I earlier called 'philosophising'. Here, it becomes possible to makes links between this everyday commentary and that of acclaimed philosophers. By way of example, Gros details some of Nietzsche's writing in *The Wanderer and His Shadow* (1996 [1878]), a book literally written *en route* during some of his countless walks: [I had been] 'taken over by a new gaze that marks my privilege over the men of today' (ibid., p. 17). This quote seems to connect well with the more popular 'walking empties the mind'. I have taken some liberties with this, in suggesting a logical follow-on: 'so new thoughts can become present', which so often resonates with participants when they see something from a fresh point of view or have a moment of unexpected insight. Likewise, reflection on lived experience can be a trigger for conversation and dialogue. Intriguingly, many participants say they perceive their engagement with philosophy as a licence to verbalise what they had previously only thought. They come to value the 'examined life'.

A More Detailed Account: Considering the Process

Hallissey (2018), a participant in a Philosophy Walk and also a journalist, provides an illuminating account. This begins with details of a conversation initiated by my question as to what he and fellow participants hoped to get from the day:

> John wants to "accept things less" and ask why people believe the things they believe. Peter just wants to get away from "the noise and the clutter", and Mark talks about walking as an "escape" from everyday life.

He then recognises the strategy of 'concept capture', where the facilitator or a participant identifies a word and uses it as a potential starting point for discussion:

> And then comes our first debate. George—a teenager who has come with his mum Kay—says 'escape' is the wrong word. "I like family walks because they get me away from college life, but I like that life too," he says. "I don't want to escape from it. But maybe just a bit of distance. Separation."

And notes my response:

> Graeme is delighted by this. [He says:] "The definition of words is vital. In essence that is what philosophers do: argue about the meaning of words and the values they represent."

* * *

I think this account captures well what is going on in Philosophy Walks; care and attention are paid to the philosophical character of conversation, and a deliberate attempt made to engage with it. In this example, the value of 'escape' is problematised, and this acts as a challenge to the original author to explain their reasoning. This, in turn, leads to the whole group engaging in concept analysis, which is a hallmark of philosophical activity. See here:

> Is it *really* escape they are after, or might there be something other going on? When I ask George to say more about the value of 'separation', he points then to 'difference', which leads to Mark changing his mind; he too appreciates much of 'everyday life', and thinks now it is the stimulus of being in a different environment that he values.

Philosophers often refer to this act of changing one's mind as 'self-correction', where a person's judgement is willingly altered in the light of new reasons provided by others in conversation. Let me be bold in suggesting that, in an era of often polarised thinking, this is unusual; processes such as this may have a valuable role in progressing dialogical and democratic virtues, which hints at an aim of public philosophy.

Hallissey (2018) also relates the value of experiencing these processes. Philosophy Walks constitute both physical and philosophical journeys, often into the unknown; there is the inevitable trepidation associated with 'being lost'. This can be disconcerting, and yet, in the context of a supportive community of philosophical enquiry, easily transformed into something positive. In this case, the decision to leave the path and abandon the planned route is re-imagined as 'exploring'.

Hallissey notes:

> It might be a digression, but it's one that Graeme loves: changing plans, embracing the risk of getting lost. From his sheaf of useful quotes he finds one from fellrunner, philosopher and former Chumbawamba guitarist Boff Whalley (2015): 'Being lost doesn't make you a loser, it reinforces the

reason you're doing this—it says, in a hail of metaphors, change plans. Adapt. Try new routes. Run off the beaten path. See what's over there. Explore. Take a chance. And if you get lost often enough, you'll start to learn how to get unlost, and you'll begin to understand how to find your way to somewhere familiar, to the finish line, to home. And you'll feel all the better for the detour that you made'.

Here again, Philosophy Walks can constitute a dialogue between the conversations of the group and the thoughts of writers and academic philosophers. We might refer to Rebecca Solnit's (2006) *A Field Guide to Getting Lost*, in which Solnit writes of the art of being at home in the unknown, so that being in its midst isn't cause for panic or suffering, of being at home with being lost (ibid., p. 10). Solnit goes on to suggest that ability may not be so far astray from Keat's [negative] capability "of being in uncertainties, mysteries, doubts" (Keats, 1817), which draws upon the philosophical quality of a great deal of poetry.

Likewise, the Platonic dialogue in which Phaedrus convinces Socrates to join him for a walk in the countryside—an alien and unsettling environment for Socrates who judged everything of value was within the Athenian city walls. And yet, with Phaedrus's provocation, Socrates acknowledges the stimulus of the world beyond: 'you seem to have discovered a drug for getting me out' (*Phaedrus* 230d-e, in Verdenius, 1955).

So, literature, poetry, and the philosophical canons (and no doubt these days other media) can all have a role to play in initiating and contributing to philosophical discussion, especially when married with being, and moving, outside.

* * *

I return to Hallissey's account for a description of a typical culmination to a Philosophy Walk.

Given a process that draws on the metaphor of journeying, it's important to identify some sort of end. By design, there needs to be a physical end, ideally, a comfortable place where it's possible to relax and take some refreshment, an environment that supports reflection on the day (in this example it's the back room of a pub). Here, the group participates in a more substantive form of the Community of Enquiry methodology used during their walk. A commitment to a generative phase is maintained, with the group being asked to reflect on their experiences of the walk and identify emergent questions. These are discussed and, finally, one chosen for the enquiry:

We agree on it pretty quickly: "Why does the outdoors make us happy?" The theories fly. We crave a simpler life. We want to touch our ancestry. We think being healthier is a good thing. It gives us more control over our minds and bodies than daily life usually allows us. It's an act of rebellion: we are not in a town or city where society expects us to be, consuming things and 'being digital'.

A theme of 'contrast' surfaces, which creates the opportunity to 'test' the theory that happiness is derived from experiences identifiably different from daily life. Freire's act of 'problematising' proves useful; I ask: 'what might be *bad* about being outdoors?' Hallissey notes the effect of this move: 'Our thoughts turn to people who spend all their lives outdoors, but for whom it may not be such a dreamy paradise.' We discuss the view that many farmers endure a very difficult life, experiencing social isolation and a high prevalence of suicide. Which leads the group to re-evaluate their experience of the city; it's noted that access to art, music, cinema and culture also makes for happiness. To which a group member counters: 'I love all those things, but they can't immerse me the way walking can. In a theatre I'm a spectator. On a walk, I'm totally immersed. It's my thing, not someone else's.'

We see in this a number of traits common to the practice of Community Philosophy; a *collaborative* process of truth-seeking, undertaken in a *caring* manner (such that the focus is on reasons rather than potentially upsetting attacks on one another's personal opinions), a preparedness to test ideas—to think *critically*—in pursuit of good reasons, and a valuing of *creative* thinking, where ideas can be experimented with; or, as I say, 'half an idea' offered in order that others might contribute the remainder. These are, of course, the '4Cs', which can act as a template for encouraging conversations to embrace these multiple, complementary, dimensions.

Once again, the opportunity arises for engagement with the philosophy of walking; Gros (ibid., pp. 89–90), invokes Thoreau's 'new economics' (in Walden, 2016 [1854]) where Thoreau argues walking teaches us how to distinguish between profit and benefit: '... walking is thoroughly useless and sterile. In traditional economic terms, it is time wasted, frittered away, dead time in which no wealth is produced. Nevertheless the benefit to me, to my life ... is immense. Nature lavishes all its colours on me. In the end, walking has been more beneficial for being less profitable'.

The dialogue becomes even more nuanced, and culminates in a group member's suggestion that walking is 'slow-release happiness'. 'In a world of instant gratification, walking is a pleasure-delayer. You're always making for something: that distant stile, those woods, that summit, that stone circle, the pub. The cycle of anticipation and reward is continuously turning.'

There is unanimity here that there is something valuable in this conclusion, which invites a round of 'Last Words' to close the day. As part of this, I suggest 'this sounds like we have a working theory,' to emphasise the hermeneutical nature of our endeavours—the sense that the truth the group has arrived at may, in time, and on the basis of further enquiry, be nourished by reflection on new experiences (perhaps future walks), and this might result in the emergence of new truths.

Postscript

Thus far, the accounts given concentrate on walks that have taken place in the countryside, and yet I have led many others in urban environments, and in the urban fringe. Walking in these settings asserts the important distinction I earlier drew between 'outdoors' and 'outside', in an attempt to think critically about the challenges of inclusion, where the former can prove off-putting. This was a context to a philosophy walks themed project, 'Step-into-Dialogue', in which workers, leaders and activists from a wide range of community groups came together to walk together with the aim of engaging in dialogue that might inform mutually beneficial forms of social action, positive social change, and enhanced community cohesion.

In a notable moment, one person commented on the architecture of a private house. This generated a response from a group member of Kashmiri heritage, who explained that the style was reminiscent of building in Kashmir and this style of architecture helped first-generation immigrants in particular (many of whom were now elderly) maintain a cultural attachment to their birthplaces. Others in the group had no idea about this until then, and this led to a powerful conversation about concepts of 'home', 'culture', and 'identity'.

Here, Philosophy Walks are explicitly designed as learning experiences, in the dialogical tradition of informal and community education referred to above. Following Freire, Jeffs and Smith (1990, p. 10) remind us that this can never be 'value-free'; to the contrary,

(*continued*)

(continued)

it implies a commitment to understand and value the 'social systems and cultures through which learners operate' (ibid., p. 11). The aim is to help the community develop an enhanced appreciation of its needs, through enquiry into the political and cultural questions it considers of greatest importance (op. cit.). Working in this way can be empowering for groups like those in the Step-into-Dialogue project that represent disadvantaged communities, as they often have to engage with funding regimes that externalise their needs (these needs are prescribed by commissioning agencies and administered in terms of targets and 'outcomes' to be achieved). This inhibits internal and local democratic activity.

This is precisely why Jeffs and Smith suggest that dialogue offers 'a measure of protection against the cultural imperialism of some forms of education' (op. cit.). They conclude, 'the whole purpose of informal education is to develop forms of thinking and acting that fit the situations that people find themselves in. In the end this can only be done by the participants, which makes *their* analysis and view of the world a central reference point' (op. cit.). Philosophy walks aim to work in this tradition.

Other examples include philosophy walks used as 'away days', such as for a housing association, in which a journey was undertaken through the housing estates the organisation administered, and beyond, through the urban fringe, and into the neighbouring countryside, each environment providing a different stimulus for thinking about the association's work.

Moving On: Thoughts on Philosophy Walks as a Philosophy of Education in Its Own Right

What might help in 'moving on' and in addressing the questions 'what now', 'what next', and 'so what'? Well, I think there is value in reviewing the philosophical precedents that underpin the theory and practice of Philosophy Walks. It is here we find a rationale that might constitute a philosophy of education in its own right: a philosophy of 'outside'.

Key to this is the significance of (and value ascribed to) uncertainty, and Philosophy Walks are examples of 'uncertainty-appreciative' practices.

These are practices that invest responsibility in participants to be true to their *own interests*, and especially those of philosophical character. These are practices where group members collaborate in the generation of questions and in the mutual exploration of those questions. This brings individual interests into an explicit community context, with the assertion that 'we think better together'. This rationale regards walking and talking together as means to create *place*, in both physical and metaphorical/philosophical terms; therein, *places* that can be owned and shared in a manner that makes the experience of them mutually empowering. Philosophy Walks can also inform activism and social action; they can catalyse social change.

The Deweyan roots of this thinking are evident. In *Democracy and Education* (1957 [1916]) John Dewey provides a context: 'If there are genuine uncertainties in life, philosophies must reflect that uncertainty' (ibid., p. 382). What appears to be a rhetorical device (asking: *is* life uncertain?) leads to a provocation, to shape and employ philosophies—in life, in education, and so on—that take account of these uncertainties. Dewey follows with: 'If there are different diagnoses of the cause of the difficulty, and different proposals for dealing with it; that is, the conflict of interests is more or less embodied in different sets of persons, there must be divergent competing philosophies' (op. cit.). And, 'With respect to what has happened, sufficient evidence is all that is needed to bring agreement and certainty. The thing itself is sure. But with reference to what it is wise to do in a complicated situation, discussion is inevitable precisely because the thing itself is still indeterminate' (op. cit.).

Pulling these threads together, what's imagined is a philosophy of education that values uncertainty, especially the uncertainty that is implicit in democratic processes; it is antithetical to think that we can know the outcome of participative decision-making processes *before they begin*. In turn, uncertainty-appreciative methodologies and pedagogies are needed. These centre on questioning (and where communities generate these/their own questions and value particularly those without definitive answers); they are dialogical and they are enquiry-oriented. Likewise, conclusions and recommendations for social action cannot be pre-scripted, they have to be iterative, the product of experiments in thought and deed, freed from narrow and constraining definitions of pragmatism. As Dewey says: 'It is for the sciences to say what generalizations are tenable about the world and what they specifically are. But when we ask what *sort* of permanent disposition of action toward the world the scientific disclosures exact of us we are raising a philosophic question' (ibid., p. 379).

We see also the power of 'outside'. On the one hand, this offers a celebration of the stimuli offered by learning outdoors. This is an unashamedly Romantic proposition, with echoes of Rousseau's Emile, where going for a walk requires no pre-prepared provocation; the outside is stimulus enough, capable of eliciting new thoughts. And on the other hand, there is also the sense of being *outside* institutional systems, particularly those that demand subservience to curricula and instrumentalised 'learning outcomes'.

What emerges is an education appropriate to the development of democratic communities, where, as Dewey suggests, 'intentionally progressive' social groups 'aim at a greater variety of mutually shared interests'. None of this sounds radical until that is we recognise the distinction between this and those communities and systems that aim at 'the preservation of established customs' (ibid., pp. 375–6). Indeed, for Dewey, 'It is the greater freedom allowed their constituent members, and the conscious need of securing in these individuals a consciously socialized interest, that establishes the democratic quality of these communities.' Again, we might recognise radical intent; Dewey pushes back at the tendency to trust mainly to 'the force of customs operating under the control of a superior (sic.) class'.

The Philosophy Walk is, then, a powerful acclamation of the value of association, born of accompaniment and the solidarity of walking side-by-side. It values freedom of interaction, it values participation, and it values uncertainty. Walking demands (and tangibly demonstrates) agency, self-determination, and autonomy; after all, as Thoreau states, no one can walk *for you*. Through their own actions, learners develop shared interests, through the sharing of experience, and dialogue about that experience. The conversations that take place cannot be prescribed or assumed to develop in predictable ways. This is a philosophy of education that demands 'uncertainty-appreciative practices', without which true democratic education cannot occur.

References

Dewey, J. (1957 [1916]). *Democracy and education*. Macmillan.
Freire, P. (1978). *Pedagogy in process. The letters to Guinea Bissau*. Writers and Readers.
Freire, P. (1990 [1972]). *Pedagogy of the oppressed*, Penguin.
Gros, F. (2014). *A philosophy of walking*. Verso.

Hallissey, N. (2018, August). Solvitur Ambulando. *Country Walking Magazine*. https://communityphilosophy.co.uk (Philosophy Walks).

James, S. P. (2015). *Environmental philosophy: An introduction* (p. 1). Polity Press.

Jeffs, T., & Smith, M. (Eds.). (1990). *Using informal education*. Open University Press.

Keats, J. (1817 [1958]). *The letters of John Keats*, 2 vols. (H. E. Rollins, Ed.). Cambridge University Press, i, pp. 193–4.

Nietzsche, F. (1996 [1878]). *The wanderer and his shadow. Part II of Human, all too human: A book for free spirits* (R. J. Hollingdale, Trans.). Cambridge University Press.

Nietzsche, F. (2009). *Ecce Homo* (D. Large, Trans.). Oxford World Classics.

Smith, M. K. (1994). *Local education: Community, conversation, praxis*. Open University Press.

Solnit, R. (2006). *A field guide to getting lost*. Canongate.

Thoreau, H. D. (2016 [1854]). *Walden*. Penguin Random House.

Tiffany, G. (1994). Youthwork as an educational process: Freire for young adults. *Adults Learning (England)*, *6*(2), 64–66.

Tiffany, G. A. (1995a). Informal outdoor education: Part 1: Introduction, methodology, and character of informal outdoor education. *Journal of Adventure Education and Outdoor Leadership*, *12*(2), 11–14.

Tiffany, G. A. (1995b). Informal outdoor education: Part 2: Curriculum, process and product, experiential learning, use of activities, importance of dialogue, reflection and action. *Journal of Adventure Education and Outdoor Leadership*, *12*(3), 7–9.

Tiffany, G. A. (1995c). Informal outdoor education: Part 3: Issues and conclusions. *Journal of Adventure Education and Outdoor Leadership*, *12*(4), 26–28.

Tiffany, G. (2020). Thoughts on moving philosophy, 'outside'. In A. Fulford, G. Lockrobin, & R. Smith (Eds.), *Philosophy and community: Theories, practices and possibilities* (p. 251). Bloomsbury.

Tuan, Y. F. (1977). *Space and place: The perspective of experience*. University of Minnesota Press.

Verdenius, W. J. (1955). Notes on Plato's *Phaedrus*. *Mnemosyne, Fourth Series*, *8*(4), 265–289.

Whalley, B. (2015, Spring). Get lost. *The Fellrunner Magazine*. http://www.pudseybramley.com/get-lost/

Conclusion: Love in a Time of Pandemics

Roger Cutting and Rowena Passy

In the beginning of Kenneth Grahame's Wind in the Willows, after the long winter, Mole is spring cleaning his home. However, even under ground the sense of Spring moving above permeates through the soil and causes him to abandon his labours and to dig upwards. Struggling through the darkness, he suddenly arrives on the surface in the warm sunlight and cool breeze of a glorious spring day. He goes on to wander through the meadow (ignoring the demands of a recalcitrant older rabbit) and eventually finds his way, in a state of almost complete happiness, to the river bank where he becomes enthralled by its beauty.

It may be a tenuous metaphor, but in 2020, the terrible tragedy of the Covid-19 global pandemic not only seemingly brought an economic 'pause' to the world, but also the closures of schools and universities, theatres and galleries facilitated a cultural hiatus that have almost been akin to a winter hibernation. The world slowed and as a result, pressure on the natural environment also seemed to ease with significant reductions in carbon emissions and, in some of the most polluted cities, marked

R. Cutting (✉) • R. Passy
Institute of Education, University of Plymouth, Plymouth, UK
e-mail: roger.cutting@plymouth.ac.uk; R.Passy@plymouth.ac.uk

R. Cutting, R. Passy (eds.), *Contemporary Approaches to Outdoor Learning*, Palgrave Studies in Alternative Education,
https://doi.org/10.1007/978-3-030-85095-1_17

reductions in air pollution. Certainly, the significant planetary problems we face remain but there is some evidence that there is an opportunity to emerge from this pandemic winter and, like Mole, put aside our tasks and addictions and to strike out for the promise of something new, something beyond the mundane, something better and ultimately, like the river that Mole discovers, something beautiful.

Political leaders in the United States, the OECD and the EU are seemingly committed to rebuilding global economies that will be cleaner, greener and sustainable. The comment of EU President Ursula von der Leyen that 'There is no vaccine for Climate Change' (Davis & Green, 2020) seems to be typical of a sentiment expressed by many, namely, that we need to recognise the danger and human cost of the global climate crisis in the same way we have approached the danger and human cost of the global pandemic. Politicians and policy makers seem, at last, to be using the same language at least of the environmental activists. Everyone now has seemingly recognised the size and significance of the problems we face.

Of course, stating the intention is the easy part. Instigating and realising the change is significantly more problematic. With Covid-19, a necessary part of the approach had to take place at community level. Cities and towns went into lockdown, people were asked not to travel to work or study. People needed to take action at individual and community levels to reduce its transmission. There may have been top-down, imposed regulations but, nevertheless, many took individual responsibility. As we begin to move out of the pandemic, that sense of individual responsibility needs to be maintained if we are to move forward into the much heralded Green rebuild.

Education is innately about the future, so it is somewhat downhearting to be writing about the importance of education in the development of a sustainable future in the full knowledge that it was 27 years ago that David Orr wrote the seminal work, Earth in Mind, highlighting the essential role that education needed to play in the development of a sustainable world (Orr, 1994). Since that time the aims of education and the objectives of many curricula have undoubtedly adopted sustainability themes and approaches. However, if we were to analyse our effective influence as educators through the application of the simple metric of greenhouse gas emissions and the rate of decline of both terrestrial and marine biomes, the results, at best, would be underwhelming.

However, perhaps now, after the pause caused by the pandemic, there is an opportunity to really move forward many of the recent research findings around the importance of different pedagogic approaches in realising behavioural change around environmental curation. It is an opportunity to reset our aims and use approaches predicated by research and tempered by practice. It is an opportunity to genuinely re-engage with the great problems that education faces in helping to build a sustainable world. This volume has provided an intriguing set of views and research findings around practices and outcomes relating to Outdoor Learning. While ideas around sustainability may not be explicitly stated, the implicit contributions that such approaches can make, to our relationships with others and the world around us, are very clear. Indeed, many of the outcomes from the practical examples described in this book are much are very much at the centre of any further development of, or around, Environmental Education and Education for Sustainability.

Of course, when talking about re-aligning or resetting education, an intriguing aspect of Outdoor Learning is that it is not new. Its history, in a UK context, is written up extensively by Ogilvie (2013) who traces attitudes around learning from the outdoors to the writings of Ruskin, Wordsworth and Rousseau, before looking in detail at its history across the twentieth Century. It seems curious therefore to talk about Outdoor Learning being a developing area of education. Perhaps, a more precise description is that '*The study of outdoor education pedagogies is a developing field*' Evans and Acton (2021, p. 1). It is these studies that are needed to provide a critical mass of research literature, the force of which, should necessarily drive any required attitudinal change to the effectiveness of Outdoor Learning. A number of chapters in this book (Kelly, Sherwin, McCree, Morgan and Hepburn and Gray and Bailey) have highlighted just such research findings and observations as to how the outdoors not only engages students but also how it can change them. If we were to identify the types of learners that we need to face the future the promotion of confidence, engagement, and social and emotional learning would be key. In these chapters we bear witness to their development.

In this volume we have also presented a number of chapters that address the importance of relationships. They emphasise the importance of relating to those around us, of caring and of trying to understand how our actions influence and affect others. This may be developed through activities that challenge stereotypes (Blackwell), challenge our pre-conceptions (Winks) or by those that are promoted from simply thoughtful reflection in the environment (Tiffany). It is these ideas that are already beginning to provide alternative strategies and innovative perspectives to Outdoor Learning, which it in itself perceived by some as alternative provision. We are already beginning to develop alternatives to the alternatives.

Of course, our relationship to the world around us is important in determining the actions we would take to protect it. A great deal of the practical literature relating to teaching in the outdoors involves developing an appreciation of the natural environment. While this is highly laudable and necessary, a cursory glance through such practical outdoor activities rarely seem to explore our relationships with the living and sentient component of the natural world. The promotion of learning though and from animals seems curiously overlooked. This also extends into the current research literature. It seems that Outdoor Learning journals reflect research and subsequent articles on such aspects as engagement, and emotional and social learning, but very rarely is there a paper concerning research around learning and animals. It seems odd that we take children and young people into woodlands, to beaches and out onto meadows, and yet a pedagogy based around learning from animals seems underrepresented. Yet, how much more enhanced is learning when it concerns another, sentient, creature. Chapters presented in this book (Cooke; Passy, Gulliver & Gompertz; Hart; Cutting; Warren) all stress the potential value of such teaching. If the promotion of care, compassion and responsibility our paramount to an education that promotes a sustainable future, then what better way can there be than animal-based pedagogies? One of the problems, perhaps at the heart of the environmental crisis that we face, is the perception that we are somehow separate from the living world around us and that human need outweighs the needs of other sentient creatures. It is in challenging such perceptions and promoting a sense of interconnectedness that potential of such an animal-based pedagogy resides.

After all, animal-based therapies are increasingly used with troubled children who display anti-social behaviour, who do not wish to participate in the wider school community, or for those who are disruptive and display self-destructive tendencies. We are left to wonder how appropriate this description is as metaphor for the behaviour of High Income Countries relative to the wider global community? It seems that many of the hoped for outcomes of animal therapies and indeed, alternative provision, seem appropriate for the sort of education we need to meet the significant global problems that we face.

While such approaches could well make a considerable contribution to the furtherance of a sustainable world, there is already some signs that it faces significant obstacles. The chapters in this volume that deal with Alternative Provision (such as Care Farms, Forest Schools and Outdoor Learning Interventions) appear to demonstrate that such delivery, at present at least, is provided for those excluded from the so-called mainstream. The research cited in these chapters clearly suggests the evident benefits of such experiences to those children. This is seen in both participation, relationships, even some degree of cognitive acceleration (McCree). Of course the question is, what of those who remain in the schools? For those children and young people for whom their behaviours and cognitive abilities are deemed 'appropriate' what does their education look like? Increasingly, in the UK at least, they are condemned to a National Curriculum that traditionally places greatest emphasis on mathematics, literature, sciences. The focus is on simple and, somewhat perfunctory, academic success. Personal relationships, emotional learning, risk-taking, collegiate and supportive approaches to problem solving, all key components of Outdoor Learning, are side-lined.

This may ultimately leads to a dichotomy of provision. One the one hand, there are those who stay within school and follow an 'academic' route and, on the other, those who are excluded and move to a different sort of environment with a different, allied, pedagogical approach. It would be tempting to suggest that one would be more effective at promoting a deeper engagement with the natural environment and, therefore, would be the more effective route to take in the new post-Covid world. However, this would require changing the common political mindset that 'academic' learning and assessment is somehow the 'gold-standard' form of education. It is a misconception, but one that is particularly persistent as it is pernicious. Through examinations it is easy to measure and to quantify and they have a degree of familiarity, not only to education policy makers and politicians, but also to teachers and lecturers, many of whom have come though such a system. It therefore provides degrees of familiarity, confidence and security. This innate conservatism provides mainstream schools and academic curricula with a certain momentum that, despite an obvious need given the state of the planet, has proved exceptionally hard to challenge.

However, let us end this volume on a brighter note. In Outdoor Learning we genuinely appear to have an alternative approach that the education 'establishment' understands, that teachers appear to appreciate, that research supports as effective, that children seem, for the most part, to enjoy, and that forms the basis for a deeper attachment to the living and natural environments. In a time when a pandemic tests our humanity through our relationships with each other and, at the same time, when climate change continues to test our relationship with the environment, we need education to explore and enhance both. Obviously, Outdoor Learning is not a panacea for the problems that we face, but its contribution to the promotion of care and curation is the type of approach that we so urgently require.

References

Davis, P., & Green, M. (2020). *The EU recovery fund: 'Building back better' in a post-COVID-19 world: Do European Commission ambitions signal a new, more sustainable direction of travel for the EU and globally?* Retrieved May 29, 2020, from https://www.globalelr.com/2020/05/the-eu-recovery-fund-building-back-better-in-a-post-covid-19-world/

Evans, N., & Acton, R. (2021). Narratives of teaching in outdoor and environmental education: What can we learn from a case study of outdoor education pedagogy? *Journal of Adventure Education and Outdoor Learning.* https://doi.org/10.1080/14729679.2021.1902828

Ogilvie, K. C. (2013). *Roots and wings. A history of outdoor education and outdoor learning in the UK.* Russell House Publishing.

Orr, D. W. (1994). *Earth in mind: On education, environment, and the human prospect.* Island Press.

Index[1]

A

Alternative Provision (AP), 8, 9, 12, 131–144, 255
Animal butchery, 169–183
Animal-human relationships, 69
Animal welfare, 24, 25, 29, 72, 73, 75, 78, 79
Anthropomorphism, 44, 66, 77, 81, 90
Attainment, 117–129

B

Barriers to outdoor learning, 27, 191
Behaviour, 4, 11, 17–20, 25–27, 29, 31, 32, 40, 56–60, 62–66, 78, 84–87, 91–97, 101, 102, 104, 105, 108, 110, 111, 118, 121, 122, 125–127, 132–136, 138–144, 157, 169, 172, 179, 183, 194, 196, 217, 254, 255

Benefits of outdoor learning, 32, 133
Building confidence, 4

C

Care Farm, 4, 7–21, 46, 255
Caring relationships, 97
Case studies, 4, 123, 148, 152–158, 190–192, 197
Collaboration, 79, 111, 144, 194–195
Community Philosophy, 240, 245
Compassion, 5, 21, 40, 41, 50, 51, 77, 80, 254
Connection to nature, 44, 95
Covid-19, 3, 4, 70–72, 148, 158, 228, 229, 251, 252
Critical thinking, 79, 134, 220, 240n3
Curriculum, 10, 41, 72, 80, 132, 133, 136, 141, 143, 144, 164, 187–192, 194, 197, 218, 228, 229

[1] Note: Page numbers followed by 'n' refer to notes.

D
Dads groups, 5, 101, 106, 108–111
Discomfort, 5, 65, 169–172, 174,
    176–178, 180–183, 221

E
(Eco)identity, 201, 203–210
Ecological identity work, 201–211
Emotional resilience, 127
Enjoyment, 88–90, 103, 164
Environment, 4, 16, 18, 23–32, 39,
    41–51, 55, 56, 58, 61, 62, 70,
    74, 75, 83–97, 106, 122,
    126–129, 132, 134–141, 144,
    148–152, 163, 165, 169, 172,
    175, 179, 187–189, 192, 194,
    195, 204, 208, 215–229, 235,
    236, 238, 240, 243, 244, 246,
    247, 251, 254–256
Environmental curation, 40,
    41, 51, 253
Ethical tensions, 169–183
Ethics, 42, 72, 137, 181, 183, 188,
    203, 204, 206, 210
Exclusion, 3, 11, 13, 131–134, 137,
    142, 144

F
Forest School, 7, 9, 14, 17, 23, 46,
    48, 106, 109, 118, 125,
    128, 255

H
Hegemonic masculinity, 101,
    104, 108
Holistic development, 218, 226,
    227, 229
Human-marine connectedness, 148
Human wellbeing, 25, 75

L
Learning, 4, 5, 7, 8, 10, 14–16,
    18–20, 23–32, 39–51, 55–66, 70,
    72, 76, 77, 80, 81, 92, 101–112,
    117–120, 122–129, 131–144,
    147–165, 169–183, 187–198,
    201–206, 215–229,
    235–249, 253–255
Learning experiences, 29, 32,
    101–112, 132, 135, 143, 183,
    188, 195, 226, 246

M
Marine outdoor environmental
    learning (MOEL), 147–165
Marine science, 148, 151, 155, 158
Maritime activities, 148, 154
Masculinity, 101, 102, 104–109, 111

N
Natural environment, 23, 41, 43–46,
    48, 49, 126, 128, 134–136, 138,
    141, 144, 208, 216, 219, 222,
    223, 226, 227, 251, 254–256
Natural world, 4, 10, 14, 25, 29, 31,
    43, 45–48, 50, 56, 71, 75–77,
    79, 80, 84–86, 95–97, 135, 148,
    169, 172, 182, 183, 216, 219,
    223, 224, 226, 227, 254
Nature-based learning, 7, 18, 19, 223
Non-human animals, 40, 45, 65, 97

O
Ocean, 147, 149, 158, 160, 163, 227
Ocean Discoverability (OD), 148,
    151–158, 164, 165
Ocean literacy, 5, 147–165
One Health, 74–77, 80
One Welfare, 75–77, 80

Open Space for Dialogue (OSD), 208
Outdoor learning experiences, 32, 101–112, 132, 143, 226
Outdoor learning (OL), 4, 5, 8, 23–32, 40–42, 45–49, 70, 71, 101, 105, 111, 112, 117, 118, 125, 126, 128, 133, 134, 136, 143, 144, 148, 187–198, 209, 210, 215–229, 235–249, 253–256
Outdoor play, 125–129

P
Pedagogical approaches, 45, 47, 72, 131, 132, 143, 144, 170, 176, 255
Peer relationships, 19, 132, 140
Personal growth, 5, 55–66, 151, 216, 218
Philosophy of education, 235–249
Philosophy walks, 5, 235–249
Place-based learning, 46, 187, 189, 197, 219
Positive relationships, 23, 95, 123, 134, 135, 141, 164

R
Relationship development, 132, 133
Resilience, 11, 45, 50, 121–122, 124, 127, 218, 221, 229
Re-wilding education, 5, 215–229

S
Self-regulation, 121–122, 127, 128
Sense of belonging, 218, 221
Social and emotional development, 4, 142
Social and emotional engagement, 253
Social justice, 79, 170, 206
Solidarity, 205, 249
Special needs, 148, 152
Student teacher identity, 187–198
Student-teacher relationships, 133, 143, 144
Survival, 40, 41, 58, 59, 92, 216

T
Transformative learning, 170, 171, 179, 182, 201, 207, 227

U
Uncomfortable learning, 169–183

V
Visual storytelling, 209, 210

Z
Zoos, 48, 73, 83, 84, 88–89, 92, 95, 97